Digital Transformation Game Plan

34 Tenets for Masterfully Merging Technology and Business

Gary O'Brien, Guo Xiao, and Mike Mason

Beijing · Boston · Farnham · Sebastopol · Tokyo

Digital Transformation Game Plan

by Xiao Guo, Gary O'Brien, and Mike Mason

Published by O'Reilly Media, Inc., 1005 Gravenstein Highway North, Sebastopol, CA 95472.

O'Reilly books may be purchased for educational, business, or sales promotional use. Online editions are also available for most titles (*http://oreilly.com*). For more information, contact our corporate/institutional sales department: 800-998-9938 or *corporate@oreilly.com*.

Development Editor: Alicia Young	**Indexer:** Ellen Troutman
Acquisitions Editor: Melissa Duffield	**Interior Designer:** Monica Kamsvaag
Production Editor: Katherine Tozer	**Cover Designer:** Randy Comer
Copyeditor: Octal Publishing, LLC	**Illustrator:** Rebecca Demarest
Proofreader: Tracy Brown Hamilton	

November 2019:   First Edition

Revision History for the First Edition

2019-10-24:   First Release

See *http://oreilly.com/catalog/errata.csp?isbn=9781492054399* for release details.

978-1-492-05439-9

[LSI]

Contents

Foreword

Change, change, change. For as many years as I've been working in the industry (which is sliding past 50 now), pundits have talked about change and the need to respond appropriately. Is the next decade different or more of the same? My vote is for different. Klaus Schwab, author of *The Fourth Industrial Revolution*, seems to agree:

> The speed of current breakthroughs has no historical precedent. When compared with previous industrial revolutions, the Fourth is evolving at an exponential rather than a linear pace. Moreover, it is disrupting almost every industry in every country. And the breadth and depth of these changes herald the transformation of entire systems of production, management, and governance.[1]

According to Schwab, there have been four stages so far in this industrial revolution:

- The age of mechanical production
- The age of science and mass production
- The digital revolution
- The age of technology transformation

---

1 Schwab, Klaus. "The Fourth Industrial Revolution: What It Means, How to Respond." *World Economic Forum*, January 14, 2016.

Each of these ages caused major disruptions to businesses, government, and other institutions. What can we learn from these disruptions? First, big changes are inevitable, and they usually happen fast. Many institutions don't survive the change. Surviving and thriving requires the ability to adapt, and often a bit of luck. As the authors of this book point out, "around half of the current S&P 500 members will be replaced over the next 10 years." So let's make a broad-brush assumption that 50% of today's organizations don't thrive (and might not survive) in the next decade. How will you manage to put your enterprise into the 50% category that succeeds?

Leaders need to truly *think* through the extent of changes facing their enterprise in the next 5 to 10 years and *think* about their response. In this period of disruptive change, success won't come from small adaptations here and there. Success will come from massive adaptations in every aspect of corporate and organizational life. Gary O'Brien, Xiao Guo, and Mike Mason have thought about this, and they have given us the benefit of their thoughts and experiences in *The Digital Transformation Game Plan*.

The authors point to three areas that enterprises need to embrace in this new world and provide you with strategies and tools to do so. First, you need to move rapidly to the position of being driven by customer value. Second, you need to create Agile, responsive organizations that can deliver that customer value. Third, you need to integrate technology into a core competency of everyone in your enterprise.

Businesses today usually drive to increase shareholder value at the expense of customer value. One company that bucked this trend is Amazon. Jeff Bezos has been unconventional from day one: don't worry about competitors, the short term, or Wall Street. Focus on customer service and the long term. Even though customer focus has been a business mantra for some time, traditional financial measures such as ROI and shareholder value have dominated management attention; using customer value, and determining how to calculate it, has often been left to the marketing department. Business processes, practices, structures, financial matters, and much more have developed over decades to support internal functionality versus an external customer view of the world. Creating a responsive, Agile organization that can deliver customer value sustainably over time requires that you examine your traditional functional and hierarchical organization and align your business to the flow of customer value. The complexity and interconnected nature of today's economic system means that you must simplify business models and streamline your organization. The authors of *The*

Digital Transformation Game Plan provide principles, guidelines, and actions about how to accomplish these things, but they wisely refrain from advocating specific organizational structures. As they say, every industry and enterprise is different, and therefore the extent of fluency in various responsive building blocks will be unique to your organization. To find that uniqueness, they propose a thin-slice approach to learning and adapting to your specific needs. Don't try to clone anyone else's approach—even Amazon's. It doesn't work. They advise creating your own unique approach to digital transformation using fundamental building blocks.

The third component of your digital transformation is technology, which is both the source of disruption and also what provides your enterprise with the capability to adapt to that disruption. For many years, technology was primarily used to support business functions, from manufacturing to finance. Today, technology, particularly software, is core to your product. As such, everyone in your organization, not just technologists, need to integrate technology knowledge into their core capability. This book provides practical strategies on how to accomplish this monumental undertaking—again, in thin slices—providing a foundation for sustainable, continuous growth and change.

We are living at an inflection point in economic history, from the predigital to the digital age. How will you respond—with bandages here and there or with a sustained revamping of your organization's measures of success, organizational structure, and approach to technology? Will you respond to change and create change for your competition? If you need a good road map to the future, look to *The Digital Transformation Game Plan* by Gary O'Brien, Xiao Guo, and Mike Mason as a great place to start your journey.

—Jim Highsmith
Executive Consultant, ThoughtWorks
Coauthor of EDGE: Value-Driven Digital Transformation
Author of Agile Project Management

Introduction

We can see the Digital Age unfolding everywhere we look. After getting out of bed, you might find yourself checking your watch for the quality of your sleep and asking Alexa for the weather; before walking out the door, you could order your favorite Starbucks coffee on their mobile app, get a ride to work with Uber, and start listening to your favorite music on Spotify. This doesn't even include the time you might spend checking emails, Twitter, and Facebook, among all the other digital social activities.

Here is another story: on September 17, 2018, a small grocery store opened in an office building in downtown Chicago. It sells mostly prepared grab-and-go food and staples. You need to scan a QR code from your mobile phone at a turnstile when you walk into the store. When you finish your shopping, you can walk right out without seeing a cashier to pay. In fact, there is no cashier in the store at all. Your account is automatically charged for the items you take.

How does the store know which items you take from the shelf? The moment you walk into the store, a network of cameras and sensors begin to capture your shopping actions. These are not the simple security cameras we usually see in stores; they are computer vision, weight sensors, motion sensors, radio-frequency identification (RFID) tags, and more. When you take a sandwich from the shelf and put it in your bag, a variety of digital footprints related to this action will be collected and sent to a system. Artificial intelligence (AI) and deep learning crunch this data, identify the sandwich, and add it to your virtual cart. When you change your mind and put the sandwich back onto the shelf, the system is smart enough to recognize this and remove it from your virtual cart.

This store is Amazon Go, the next generation cashless grocery store. Amazon announced that it is going to open three thousand such stores by 2021. No more waiting in check-out lines.

The Digital Age is not just affecting our daily life; it is having a broad and profound impact on industries and companies. In 2007, the world's largest companies by market capitalization were (in order) Exxon Mobil, General Electric, Microsoft, ICBC, Citigroup, AT&T, Royal Dutch Shell, Bank of America, Petro China, and China Mobile. In 2017, they were Apple, Alphabet, Microsoft, Facebook, Amazon, Berkshire Hathaway, Alibaba, Tencent, Johnson & Johnson, and Exxon Mobil. All but three are technology companies. It's not just the largest companies. USA Information Technology's share of MSCI Market Capitalization increased from 15% in 2007 to 25% in 2017.

According to a 2016 study, in 1965 the average tenure of companies on the S&P 500 was 33 years; by 1990, it was 20 years; by 2026, it's forecast to be just 14 years. To put that in context, it means around half of the current S&P 500 will be replaced over the next 10 years. Empirical evidence is now also supporting the profound financial impact of digital. The Digital Strength Index "Topline Report," published in July 2018 by Isobar and alpha-DNA, noted that companies in the top decile of the DSI have "next-year revenue of +14.5%, whereas the bottom decile has –7.8%. Companies in the top decile also beat quarterly estimates 65% of the time over the past five years; the bottom decile just 52.7% of the time." It went on to state that "the long-term impact of being a digital laggard is devastating, with a 14.9% loss in shareholder value over a three-year period, a decline that increases with time."

There is more pressure on leadership teams to come up with new approaches to corporate strategy now than at any time in recent memory because of this volatility in our industries and society.

This change in technology has been so fast and so disruptive that it became a main theme at the 2016 World Economic Forum (WEF) flagship annual meeting in Davos, "Mastering the Fourth Industrial Revolution." The founder of WEF, Professor Klaus Schwab, published a book on this topic, *The Fourth Industrial Revolution* (Currency). He argues that there is no longer any question that the early twenty-first century is witnessing a set of economic changes of historical importance characterized by a much more ubiquitous and mobile internet, smaller and more powerful sensors that have become cheaper, and AI and machine learning.

But we have seen technological changes before. What is so special about this round of digital technology change that it is being compared with the previous industrial revolutions? A key difference, at a fundamental level, is the speed of the change.

Digital technology is driving the disruptions, and digital technology itself is progressing at an exponential speed. Moore's Law has been proven for several decades; it famously predicted that the transistor count on an integrated circuit would double every two years. This simple exponential growth trajectory is an immensely powerful concept. As the reward for winning a chess game against the king, a legendary Indian sage asked for just a few grains of rice in the following manner: the king was to put a single grain of rice on the first chess square and double the number of grains on every subsequent square. It turns out that by the 64th square, the king would have had to put more than 18,000,000,000,000,000,000 grains of rice. That is about 210 billion tons and is enough to cover the entire land mass of India with rice to a depth of three feet.

That's kind of what happened to the number of transistors on each chip. It grew from a few thousands per chip in the 1970s to a few billions per chip in the 2000s. Some argued that there is a limit to exponential growth (otherwise we are going to fill the universe with transistors in another 50 years) and we might now be seeing the tail end of it. They may be right, but the exponential growth curve is not just limited to transistors per chip, it can be seen in other technology improvements, too, some of which are just getting started. For example, we are observing network bandwidth improvements and cost decreases in a similar, if not exactly the same, exponential trajectory; cloud computing costs decrease, the computing power of sensors continues to increase, and manufacturing costs are decreasing in a similar manner. These are the fundamental engineering improvements driving explosive or even "magical" phenomena like big data, the Internet of Things (IoT), AI, and mixed reality (augmented reality and virtual reality). These exponential curves build on top of one another and form combinatorial growth curves.

Digital technology isn't slowing down to a linear trajectory. It continues to accelerate in an exponential manner. The number of things that can now be done "at the speed of thought" continues to increase and the speed of the intellectual enterprise is becoming a critical success factor. This means that the digital disruptions we are observing across the financial services, retail, travel, and media industries are not going to slow down. Disruption will go deeper into those industries, and will continue to spread to health-care, manufacturing, automotive, and all other industries. For example, in health-care you can now describe scientific experiments using code and have a machine replicate or verify the science on the other side of the world.

The exponential growth of technology has led to three main challenges for companies:

- Heightened customer expectations
- Speed and ambiguity, which forces companies to come up with new competitive advantages more frequently
- A plethora of emergent technology that could create a competitive advantage in the future and requires investment and understanding today

Digital transformation is about dealing with these challenges. It is not just a technology revamp to do things the same way faster or sell the same product for less. It is a business transformation and should transform the entire organization to work, think, and collaborate in a different way. Instead of automating existing processes or embedding digital technology into existing offerings, we should be ready to obliterate them and start over. We should be ready to rethink our businesses: what new kinds of value can be delivered to our customers and can we deliver them with the power of digital technology? Even though the answer might not be clear at the beginning, leaders should clear the path to potentially take advantage of the power of modern digital technology to radically redesign their business to unleash dramatic improvements or innovations.

Digital transformation is not just about reaching an end state where more things are digital; it's a shift in how you think and operate, how you learn to listen, respond, and constantly change. It is about the sum of the parts—you can't "apply digital" in one area and expect it to survive surrounded by the current state of the organization. Indeed, there is no end state to digital transformation. Perhaps the phrase should be *digital evolution*, not digital transformation.

For enterprises, speed and responsiveness *are* the new battleground, and while everyone is trying to solve the same things, not everyone has the same constraints holding them back. Therefore there is no silver bullet or recipe that you can turn to. It will come down to your ability to learn how to listen for weaker signals and solve for your unique constraints.

This book attempts to provide an authentic look at the difficult things companies need to face in order to deal with this fourth industrial age. Based on our experience working closely with a variety of organizations going through their digital transformations, we grouped our learnings into three main areas:

- How to realign the business and operating architecture to focus more on customer value in this age of heightened customer expectations
- How to build a more responsive and Agile organization to deal with speed and ambiguity
- How to build next generation technology capability as a core differentiator

Across these three areas, we provide 34 actions to take that will help you move your company successfully along the path toward digital transformation. Each chapter has a Key Points section with two associated actions, and the full list is included in Conclusion: Getting Started.

Digital technology will transform how our companies and industries collaborate and compete, and how our entire society lives and works together in this still-young century. For leaders in the middle of this global and societal change, digital transformation is not a brisk change program. It's a long, drawn-out campaign with many battles and stages. The journey will be full of progress and setbacks, wins and losses, momentum and inertia, and breakthroughs and detours. We hope these observations will be useful references and meaningful food for thought for any business or technology executive who is about to start or is in the middle of this difficult but important journey.

O'Reilly Online Learning

O'REILLY® For more than 40 years, *O'Reilly Media* has provided technology and business training, knowledge, and insight to help companies succeed.

Our unique network of experts and innovators share their knowledge and expertise through books, articles, conferences, and our online learning platform. O'Reilly's online learning platform gives you on-demand access to live training courses, in-depth learning paths, interactive coding environments, and a vast collection of text and video from O'Reilly and 200+ other publishers. For more information, please visit *http://oreilly.com*.

How to Contact Us

Please address comments and questions concerning this book to the publisher:

> O'Reilly Media, Inc.
> 1005 Gravenstein Highway North
> Sebastopol, CA 95472
> 800-998-9938 (in the United States or Canada)
> 707-829-0515 (international or local)
> 707-829-0104 (fax)

We have a web page for this book, where we list errata, examples, and any additional information. You can access this page at *https://oreil.ly/digi-trsfmn-game-plan.*

Email *bookquestions@oreilly.com* to comment or ask technical questions about this book.

For more information about our books, courses, conferences, and news, see our website at *http://www.oreilly.com.*

Find us on Facebook: *http://facebook.com/oreilly*

Follow us on Twitter: *http://twitter.com/oreillymedia*

Watch us on YouTube: *http://www.youtube.com/oreillymedia*

Acknowledgments

We would like to begin by thanking our colleagues at ThoughtWorks for reading the early drafts and providing their valuable feedback: Brandon Byars, Ange Ferguson, Martin Fowler, Rachel Laycock, Jonny Leroy, Chris Murphy, Jonathan Pangrazio, Rebecca Parsons, David Robinson, Jonny Schneider, and Sue Visic. Their incredibly broad and diverse experience with real-world digital transformations gave us many more perspectives to think about than we originally had in mind. Their stories, reflections, and insights added a lot more color and depth to the book.

Special thanks to Martin Fowler for your advice on writing as a craft beyond the content itself. Thank you for helping us to get started on this journey.

We sincerely thank our peers in the industry for the careful review of the final draft, especially Rick Freedman, Jim Highsmith, Dave McKeown,and Xavier Paz. Your valuable comments, critiques, and suggestions allowed us to reflect on the flow of the content, the focus of our messages, and the relevance to different types of perspectives. Thank you, Jim, for the thorough review and the wonderful foreword.

We'd like to thank everyone at O'Reilly for green lighting the project and having confidence that our book was differentiated enough to stand out from other books about digital transformation. Many thanks to Kristen Brown, Melissa Duffield, Bob Russell, Katherine Tozer, and, in particular, our long-suffering developmental editor Alicia Young, who provided great insight and suggestions that have helped to shape the book.

From Gary O'Brien:

I'd like to thank those who helped me on this therapeutic journey of expunging thoughts from my head. Xiao, thanks for pushing me to do something I didn't think I was capable of, and, Mike, for being the voice of reason through the process. To my wife, Nicki, and my children, Jayden, Taylor, and Emilie, for their support, patience, and enthusiasm that kept me at it. I'd also like to thank the executives I have had the pleasure of working alongside for their candor, trust, confidence, passion, and patience —friendships built and pains shared. Lastly, to my colleagues who stepped onto the transformation roller coaster with me and enjoyed the ride, especially to Sue Visic, who tolerated it more than most.

From Guo Xiao:

To my wife, Hao Dan, thank you for your indispensable patience and encouragement when I needed them most. I wouldn't have completed the daunting project without your support. Gary and Mike, thank you for your willingness to compromise and co-create on top of your brilliance and intelligence. I couldn't think of a more pleasant experience collaborating on such mentally challenging tasks.

From Mike Mason:

I'd like to thank my coauthors for their boundless energy and enthusiasm. Undertaking any kind of writing project is daunting—especially a book on a difficult subject such as digital transformation—but their dedication and prolific efforts created an incredible backbone for the whole work. Thank you, Gary and Xiao, for bringing me along for the ride!

PART I

Heightened Customer Expectations and Alignment to Customer Outcomes

> *To dramatically increase the quality of the customer experience using digitization...requires fairly radical organizational surgery.*
> —Peter Weill, chairman of MIT-CISR

Digital transformation is not just about a technology trend or a business trend, it is a redefinition of both. Not blurring the lines between IT and the business, but completely removing them until you emerge with technology at the core of your business. In this state, you operate comfortably when surrounded by ambiguity and use technology to redefine the value you deliver to customers and how you deliver it. To really thrive in the digital era, businesses need to commit to continuous evolution and strategic innovation, responding rapidly to market changes and opportunities. But not many organizations are actually built to do this.

Success will be determined by your courage to act. Can you simplify your business model—how work flows through the organization—in a way that allows you to identify and measure the value you are delivering to customers? Your organization needs to align itself to this value so that you can increase feedback loops and become more responsive and adaptable to change. Can you create the thin slice through your organization as a way to begin to execute the new model, to expose the antibodies that exist in the current operations that might constrain a sustainable digital transformation? The test will come when you are able to create the transparency and visibility required to capture these weaker leading indicators of change that you need in order to keep up, learning to validate ideas quickly, scaling what works, and stopping what doesn't.

Start by simplifying the business model; putting the customer value at the center of your business model and strategy.

The Simplified Business Model

Before diving into simplifying your business model toward customer value and how digital technology is reshaping it, you must first consider the broader backdrop of the corporate management landscape to understand why customer value should be at the center of tomorrow's business strategy, instead of other factors like revenue and profitability. In this chapter, we discuss why creating value for customers should be at the center of your business strategy and how focusing on the delivery of value to customers can create a single coherent focus for simplifying your business model.

Shareholder Value Versus Customer Value

The most influential management theory of the past three decades has been shareholder value maximization; that is, companies should aim to maximize returns to shareholders above everything else. Although this should in theory better align the management team's interests with those of the shareholders, it has also resulted in some bizarre and detrimental behaviors. For example, by linking pay to share prices, some corporate executives focus more on manipulating those prices than running a healthy business; as many as 80% of managers are willing to cut R&D spending to hit their numbers. There seems to be a close association between shareholder value maximization and the pursuit of short-term profit.

The Downside of Shareholder Value

Once when we were working with a major financial institution on adopting more technology solutions, we ran into the following situation: the bank was investing in an initiative to build more ATMs in certain branches. When we asked why, a manager explained that the traffic at these branches' bank teller counters was too high compared with others. Investing in more counter space or adding more people would drive up the operating cost per branch. Operating cost per branch is a main factor behind the profitability of the bank and a critical performance metric for the manager. Building ATMs should drive more traffic to the machines than the tellers and therefore benefit the bank's bottom line.

We wanted to test this hypothesis, so we conducted some user journey experiments and user research in a few target branches. We found out that despite increased availability of ATMs and more prominent signs for the ATMs, some consumers still preferred to talk to a bank teller in person. It became clear to us that, for this customer segment, the trust and comfort that comes from talking to a real person is more important than the convenience and speed of simple transactions. After taking some time to digest these findings (and probably talk to supervisors), the manager came back with an interesting suggestion: "We should figure out how to design the space better so that they *have* to walk by the ATMs before getting to the tellers. Maybe this will get them to use the ATM."

"But why? We already found out that it's not what the customers want," we pointed out.

"It's good for the business; we need to reduce the branch operational cost," the manager replied.

Interestingly enough, it was the most prominent corporate hero during the age of shareholder value maximization—Jack Welch, CEO of GE from 1981 to 2001—who gave the most stringent rebuttal of the idea. In an interview with the *Financial Times* in 2009, Welch said, "On the face of it, shareholder value is the dumbest idea in the world." Welch's comment is widely quoted in various criticisms of shareholder value. In a question-and-answer session with a journalist (his wife, Suzy Welch), Jack Welch elaborated:

In a wide-ranging interview about the future of capitalism, I was asked what I thought of "shareholder value as a strategy." My response was that the question on its face was a dumb idea. Shareholder value is an outcome—not a strategy...Shareholder value is a result, not a strategy...Your main constituencies are your employees, your customers, and your products.

We believe the shareholder value maximization principle rose to prominence in the early '80s because of the need to deal with growing business model and organizational complexity. There is always a strong need to create a purpose, a unifying focus for an organization. As a business grows bigger and more complex, especially in a time of rapid change, it can be very difficult to make sense of ever-expanding product offerings, geographic boundaries, and partnership models. Shareholder value filled the gap of the purpose of a business, often overshadowing the purpose that should have remained at the center: customer value creation, the very reason an organization exists in the first place. As Peter Drucker said as early as 1973, "The purpose of a business is to create a customer."

Focusing on delivering value to customers could be the rallying point for a business—the playbook to simplify its business model. Here are a few reasons to shift focus:

- It gives a better and more fulfilling sense of purpose for employees.

- It makes the organization more resilient than an internal-focused and self-centered mindset.

- It results in higher client satisfaction, stronger growth, higher productivity, and higher employee satisfaction.

The digital technology trend is not the fundamental driving force behind this revamp—society and consumers are. Digital technology is simply exacerbating the problems with the current strategy of optimizing around organizational hierarchy and financial models. Digital technology is also accelerating the transition to the new customer-centric business model by providing the necessary tools and capabilities to make it happen. Digital innovation is the perfect storm for the business strategy revamp. Just like the main issues that plagued the industry in the '80s, facing the fast-changing digital world, many businesses found themselves too complicated and bureaucratic to respond quickly enough, let alone to ride the trends and get ahead through innovation.

If we have to name the single most important lesson learned from what we have seen in various digital transformation efforts, we would say that it's never just about the technology; it's first and foremost about the business strategy. To speed up and become more responsive and innovative, it won't be enough to just add more technology to automate the existing process or create a new channel to engage with consumers. It requires a deeper look into the business strategy and model, and how to simplify it by shifting the purpose and the unifying focus from internal goals to customer value.

Creating customer value should be at the center of a business strategy and shape the business model. Profitability, short term or long term, is a result of this strategy. The level of profitability required can also be viewed as guardrails or constraints that investors and creditors put on the business, but it should not be the purpose of the business. Amazon invests most of its profits back into the business to create value for customers and grow sales. Despite a radically different profitability level, it still became the second company to reach a trillion-dollar market capitalization in 2018, just a few months after Apple.

Jeff Bezos, in his founding letter to shareholders in 1997, wrote:

We believe that a fundamental measure of our success will be a direct result of our ability to extend and solidify our current market leadership position. The stronger our market leadership, the more powerful our economic model. Market leadership can translate directly to higher revenue, higher profitability, greater capital velocity, and correspondingly stronger returns on invested capital.

He went on to say that Amazon places the customer first, ahead of "short-term profitability considerations or short-term Wall Street reactions."

Identifying Your Simplified Model

Although the prospect of simplified business models is enticing, facing simplified business modeling can be challenging for traditional enterprises built on decades of optimizing around organizational hierarchy and financial models. There are a number of main obstacles:

- Customer value can be difficult to define and capture while digital technology continues to reshape it.

- Large transformation programs are inherently difficult to execute. A broad transformation effort on both business strategy and technology can be too expensive and complicated to pull off.

- An intervention is required on the engine and norms of how value runs through the organization and to the customer—existing structures, budgets, and thinking often get in the way.

- Teams are structured around functions and systems, not aligned to customer outcomes.

- There is a lack of visibility and transparency to facilitate and encourage real meaningful changes.

- It takes courage from leaders in the face of ambiguity to stay the course and make the shifts necessary for sustainable change.

Following are five areas of patterns and ideas for realigning and simplifying the business model to be more customer focused and attempt to address these obstacles. We cover them in brief here and provide you with more in-depth strategies for putting them into practice in Part I.

1. UNDERSTAND CUSTOMER VALUE

The journey to simplification begins with connecting the reason your business exists and the value customers pull from you to your strategy. For a bank, it could be as simple as helping people succeed financially. Translating this purpose into a set of medium-term outcomes that form the guardrails to the organization's operations helps you focus everyone's efforts—it's the wood behind the arrowhead. These outcomes are not many in number; the last few large corporations we have worked with ended up with around 20 high-level customer outcomes in total.

The key is to not just focus on the goods and services the business provides to customers, but also the consequences of these goods and services in customers' minds—their goals and purposes. Although digital technology gives you more tools to understand the customers' mindset and what they value most, it is playing an even more critical role in reshaping how customers perceive value. So as technology changes what is possible, so too will customer value change. We are entering a new era of *transient value*. Peace of mind, the feeling of control, and ultimate personalization are becoming the new dimensions to gauge customer value, which we look at in Chapter 2.

2. USE A THIN-SLICE APPROACH

Instead of designing a transformation program with a prescriptive road map to change the entire organization in a Big-Bang approach, we strongly suggest an incremental approach to move the needle on outcomes. For each outcome, have those with expertise come together to brainstorm ideas that might make the needle move. This can include the employees doing the work, domain experts, customers, and partners. Some lightweight test-and-learn techniques will help you to refine the ideas into those most likely to succeed.

As you begin to execute these ideas, you will rub up against organizational constraints like investment cycles and structural lines. Going thin but deep exposes these change resistors more readily and allows you to consciously plan to minimize their impact.

The first few thin slices tend to take longer because there's more learning involved. After three or four thin slices, there should be a good momentum built from small wins and outcomes delivered. Constraints will be visible, with some being addressed, revealing an emerging business and operating architecture that will make it a lot easier to scale the transformation to the rest of the organization.

Chapter 3 explores this concept in more depth and shows you why the thin-slice approach tends to accelerate with each new slice as well as why this method is a great starting point to deep-dive into an organization.

3. HAVE THE CORRECT MEASURES OF SUCCESS

What you measure defines what you care about, and even who you are. If you mainly measure revenue and profit, if not exclusively, it sends a message to the entire organization that this is what you care most about. It will be very difficult to push a customer-centric agenda if you don't change how you measure success. To simplify, value is what customers get from your organization; it's the reason they have come to you. Benefits are what you get in return. Revenue and profit are important benefits to the business, but value to the customer should lead to the benefit, not the other way around.

Output measures like the amount of work and activities accomplished can be easily tracked and reported; however, the impact work has on a customer's outcome and value is much more difficult to measure. But "difficult to measure" should not be an excuse to focus purely on organizational benefits and quantifiable vanity measures.

Chapter 4 provides you with strategies for putting the appropriate value measurements in place for measuring customer outcomes and organizational improvements It also shows you how to avoid the pitfalls of more traditional, individual-focused measurements like key performance indicators (KPIs).

4. ALIGN EVERYTHING TO THE WORK

Aligning teams, structures, architecture, decision making, and funding with customer outcomes is easier said than done. It makes perfect sense when designing a small organization from a clean slate. But for a large organization, some of the existing structures and lines of management will actively work against it. Chapter 5 shows you how the cascade model can help break high-level customer outcomes into a backlog of smaller chunks of testable hypotheses that can be implemented by smaller teams.

It also explores how a lightweight governance and prioritization model like EDGE[1] can help connect and align all of the working streams to ensure that you are working on the highest-value items to achieve the outcome while allowing the teams to test, innovate, and deliver in fast cycles.

5. CREATE VISIBILITY AND TRANSPARENCY

Visual elements and indicators make it easy to roll information up and down the system and keep everyone informed. For executives and leaders, a map of all the ongoing work's clear visible alignment to specific outcomes helps to create a focused mindset for making strategic business decisions. For teams, visual representations of progress, output, and their alignment to business outcomes give the ability to test, learn, and pivot with a clear direction and sense of accomplishment. Chapter 6 examines how visibility and transparency can help create a safe environment in which work is depersonalized, conversation is centered around facts, and decisions are not influenced by personal bias.

These five principles form the most important areas to work on in order to realign and simplify the business strategy to be centered around customer value and customer outcomes. It's not meant to be a step-by-step road map for a transformation journey. It's a logical sequence designed to help you understand the connections and dependencies between those areas. We have seen companies

---

1 Jim Highsmith et al., *EDGE: Value-Driven Digital Transformation* (Addison-Wesley, 2019).

focus on these areas in various sequences with their own pros and cons due to the specific challenges and opportunities faced by each business.

In the rest of Part I, we dive deeper into each of these five topics with more examples and details.

Key Points

Following are the key points that we hope you take away from this chapter as well as two actions for you to take to begin implementing what we've discussed:

- Simplifying the business strategy to be centered around customer value instead of internal benefits will help improve decision making through greater transparency and visibility.

- Focus on the following interconnected five areas to gradually realign the business architecture and organization to be more customer centric:

  — Define success as customer outcomes

  — Use a thin-slice approach

  — Have a clear view on what to measure and why

  — Align work and teams with customer outcomes

  — Create visibility and transparency

Here are two actions to take:

- Form your team to design your simplified business model—your "road map": Discuss the five areas of a "simplified business model" in Chapter 1 and what these might look like for your organization.

- Advocate for customer value: Build your business strategy around customer value and using customer language.

Understanding Customer Value

Customer value forms the basis for your digital transformation; it is the beginning point. Understanding what value means to your customers is the input to the work you need to do and therefore informs how you need to redesign your organization. However, the definition of customer value is a little more elusive than most would assume.

We once were privileged to listen in on a few call-center calls at a large telecommunications company. A customer asked whether their service had been connected. The operator looked up on the system to see a connection at the exchange and answered in the affirmative. After a pause, the customer repeated themselves in a way that made the value aspect really obvious: "So I am about to drive for four hours to that location. If I cannot connect to the internet when I get there I will need to turn around and drive all the way back and still do my full day's work. So, is my service connected?" In this case, what the customer valued was not whether a system thinks a connection at the exchange is on: this person valued whether they could access the internet from a particular location given that an eight-hour drive was at stake. The point is to always see value through the eyes of the customer.

There are two different lenses on customer value: the value a business believes they are delivering to the customers (in this case, the ability to know whether an internet connection is established to a premises); the "consequence" the customer desires and perceives, their outcome. Your organization's ability to orient around these customer outcomes as the definition of value will go a long way toward determining the success of your digital transformation. Value defined this way is a constantly moving target. Digital technologies are playing a prominent role as both a way to better explore and understand value through the customer's eyes and also in changing how customers perceive value. This chapter shows you how to hit those targets by focusing on customer outcomes.

Focusing on Customer Outcomes

To build the strategy of an entire organization on the concept of a simplified business model based on customer outcomes is never easy. In the Industrial Age, many successful businesses focused on the goods and services—offering more features, better quality, and lower cost.

The need to review, assess, and develop the organization and your strategy around customer value has always been there, with or without the digital technology improvement. Digital changes didn't create this approach as a new concept, but it is driving the sense of urgency to adopt this approach.

Recently, an online real estate portal announced its acquisition of a mortgage broker. Consumers have become accustomed to online real estate portals to search for homes, sometimes as their primary touch point to the home market, rather than agencies. For some dominant portals in various regions of the world, their registered users and unique visits per month place them among the highest ranked websites. Given the knowledge the portals have gained through the home searching process, it's easy to see why it makes perfect sense to guide the consumers to the next step of the home ownership journey: getting a mortgage.

It doesn't need to stop at a mortgage. Home ownership is a long journey that involves many previously separated product and service providers—insurance, gas, electricity, waste management, moving, and so on. Digital technologies make the discovery, contracting, and even integration of these services a lot easier than ever before. With today's digital capability, a business is more likely to discover new ways of adding value for its customers when it focuses on its higher-level purposes and goals.

These are not just marketing tricks or product promotion techniques. These are real shifts of business models and operational priorities. Sometimes, shifting focus to customer value is driven by internal investment and improvement. Jet engine manufacturer Rolls-Royce and razor producer Gillette have one thing in common: they are both in the parts and maintenance business. Gillette sells its razor at a lower margin—if not sometimes even giving it away for free—and gains most of its business from selling replacement razor blades in a recurring model. Similarly, Rolls-Royce sells jet engines at a much lower margin and recoups the benefit of value creation through maintenance and services contracts.

An engine is very expensive and requires very complex domain expertise to maintain. It's so expensive and complicated that not many banks are willing to finance jet engine purchases. Although Rolls-Royce was not the first to focus on selling parts and services instead of engines as its core business model, it was the first to push it to another level. What airplane owners or airline companies care most about—besides fundamental safety—is that engines are working smoothly and predictably. Any unexpected down time could cause delays, keep hundreds of passengers waiting, and incur high rerouting or rebooking cost. They don't want more maintenance time and services; they want less maintenance and services. In fact, as little as possible. They want more hours of smooth operation from the jet engines. So why not align the business model with this value and sell "hours of operation" instead of parts and services? This model is well aligned with the airline company's interest: predictable fees that are tied to its revenue generation (flying airplanes).

What really made the transition to this business model possible was the emergence of new digital technologies. When it comes to sensors, a jet engine is like a fully decorated Christmas tree. Some of today's engines have more than 5,000 sensors and generate more than 10 GB of data per second. Improvements in storage and computing power, analytical tools, and algorithms allow Rolls-Royce to analyze this data frequently, predict engine maintenance needs, and schedule them at the proper time. In-flight connectivity and real-time analytical tools even give them the ability to diagnose and detect potential problems in flight so that maintenance crews can prepare a fix even before the aircraft lands, reducing delay and increasing aircraft availability.

Rolls-Royce's global operations room in Derby, England is full of big-screen monitors displaying dozens of graphs and dashboards, televisions tuned to 24-hour news channels, and swarms of software engineers and technicians. This digital hub is becoming the new center of competitive advantage for Roll-Royce, driving its value creation for customers. Today, 80% of Rolls-Royce jet engines are supplied using this hourly fee model.

For some industries, shifting focus to customer value is driven by more radical external trends. The iconic Ford Motor Company has been one of the most successful companies in modern industry. Instead of seeing automobiles as expensive toys, Henry Ford and others viewed them as a tool for mass transportation in a nation of great distances. Cheaper and higher-quality vehicles made car ownership a real possibility for the majority of the population. "Sell more cars" has since then been at the center of business strategy for Ford and most other car companies. Most successful business strategies are built around vertical integration and producing affordable cars for individual customers.

The rise of Tesla, an electric vehicle producer, started a countdown to retirement for the internal combustion engine. But the business model and value creation of the entire automobile industry will not be fundamentally challenged by the electric vehicle. Apart from the engineering innovation on batteries and chassis design, there is a more notable difference in Tesla's approach from traditional car companies. Tesla treats the car not just as a piece of hardware with some software embedded, but rather as if it is a piece of software that happens to have a hardware component. In the modern Digital Age, software upgrades are done frequently and remotely; you shouldn't need to bring your computer to a shop to get an upgrade on the work-process tool you are using. It's done through the internet. Tesla took that approach and was the first to upgrade the "operating systems of the car" (the firmware) over the air. This allows the company to release updates much more frequently than a traditional recall approach. Given the digital mindset, Tesla was also the first to offer semi-autonomous driving technology to a commercial vehicle.

Tesla is only one of the companies trying to build the ultimate self-driving car. Apple, Google, Uber, and many other startups have joined the race to the fully autonomous vehicle. This is giving traditional car manufacturers a lot of concerns. One must ask the question: with fully autonomous vehicles, why would consumers still want to own cars? Given the fast-evolving car hailing capability provided by Uber, Didi, Lyft, and other *e-hailing* companies, the entire transportation value chain is being reshaped. Where do car manufacturers fit in this new digital world? They might be reduced to hardware subcontractors by the digital innovators who own the primary customer interactions and customer relationship.

This is both a challenge and an opportunity for car manufacturers. Major automobile manufacturers have embraced this challenge and adjusted their business strategy. Most are focusing on a higher level of customer goals and purposes than just owning cars. Fundamentally, people use cars to get around. On Daimler's public website, in the "Our Strategy" section, it says:

> Our goal as one of the leading vehicle manufacturers is to become a leading provider of mobility services.

Daimler wants to be in the business of moving people around instead of just building cars. To enact the strategy, Daimler began to build more business units in the mobility sector instead of just focusing their core automobile manufacturing business. Daimler acquired mytaxi, an e-hailing app similar to Uber and Lyft. It invested in car2go, a cars-by-the-minute share service company similar to Zipcar. Daimler also founded Moovel, which provides mobility services to the urban market, suggesting the most optimal transportation option by combining ticket availability, pricing, traffic, and other information the moment users request it. These investments provide new opportunities to deliver value to Daimler's customers and to grow into new markets. The emergence of new digital technology and platforms are creating these new opportunities, and perhaps also making it the right time for car manufacturers to shift their focus.

Many major car companies are on a similar journey. General Motors started Maven to compete in the car-sharing services sector and also invested in Lyft to get into the e-hailing business. Ford Motors added more acquisitions to its mobility group and realigned the organization to accelerate and expand its activities in 2018 to deliver a broader suite of mobility products and services to its customers —current personal vehicle owners.

Given the root of Ford Motor, the original vision of "seeing cars as a tool for mass transportation in a nation of great distance," it is perhaps less surprising to see Bill Ford, Jr. embracing the new paradigm with more excitement than gloom and doom.

It's not just the banking industry and automobile industry. Digital technology is forcing companies in every industry to reexamine this very basic question of customer value. More often than not, the answer is more obvious than you think. The health-care industry in many countries is known to be either overly expensive or less effective, or sometimes both. Digital players are rushing into this market because they know that what people really want is good health, not pills and bills to cure disease. A healthy lifestyle can effectively prevent certain diseases and greatly reduce the need for drugs and hospital visits. This is forcing health-care providers to focus more on the value of staying healthy through preventative products and services than just curative ones.

Digital technology doesn't just create disruptions; it is also helping companies to better understand how customers appreciate the value they think they are delivering to them. Your holistic strategy needs to orient itself around a good understanding of customer outcomes as the way to measure the value you are delivering. Digital technologies are increasing organizations' ability to better understand what the outcomes are, and thus they are creating new ways to achieve the outcomes. Toward the end of this chapter, we offer some suggestions on how to ask questions about your own industry and business in order to design and target the best customer outcomes.

The Impact of Technology on Value and Expectations

Traditionally, businesses mostly focused on the value they believed they were delivering to their customers: product/service features, attributes, and performance. What tends to be overlooked is the consequences arising from the use of these products and services in achieving the customer's outcome; hence, the perception of the value from the customer's perspective. The latter is more situational and circumstantial than the former. It's also more personal and difficult to articulate.

Before digital technology became so prevalent in our daily lives, marketing teams relied on focus groups, interviews, and surveys as their primary tools to gather insight on a customer's needs. Digital concepts like connectivity, mobility, user interfaces, cloud computing, algorithms, and other technology improvements are giving businesses a greater understanding, leading them to broaden the scope of goods and services they provide to consumers in physical and digital channels. New technology-driven startups continue to discover unmet needs and new ways to satisfy the outcomes; existing companies continue to take advantage of technology to expand into adjacent markets or industries, driven by a greater understanding of the consequences of what they are providing to customers.

Digital technology gives us some new ways to gather data and generate insights about the customers and their aspirations:

It's possible to build a single, complete customer view.
Organizations have always had a lot of data about their customers—personal details, transaction details, communications, and interactions with the organization. But the data could be locked in various legacy systems, duplicated, fragmented, and inconsistent. In the past 20 years, many companies have invested in building customer relationship management (CRM) systems to create a single repository of data that provides a complete view of every customer. Having access to this data, as well as the intelligence derived from it, gives product teams, sales agents, and service teams more chances to understand the behavior and needs of a customer.

It's possible to access more external data sources.
More than a billion people are active on Facebook; Twitter has about 330 million active users per month; and Snapchat has about 200 million. An

enormous amount of data is being generated by social media every hour, every minute. There are ongoing debates around the ownership of this data and corresponding privacy concerns; a highly important topic, indeed. That discussion is beyond the scope of this text and has been well articulated in the book *Mining the Social Web* (O'Reilly). We would highly recommend anyone interested in this topic to give that book a read. But social media has become a key new source of customer data. It shines a different light on the behaviors, goals, and aspirations of customers unknown to most business before.

It's possible to learn more from the data.
Cheaper computing power and new algorithms give rise to an entire new family of modern data mining and data analytical tools, some of which are powered by the latest machine learning technology. Machines are much better at finding needles in a haystack than humans. By studying purchasing patterns of customers, a retailer can discern a young woman's pregnancy more easily than her parents, as one did in Minneapolis (the sudden purchase of unscented lotion and vitamins indicated pregnancy).

It's possible to access more real-time data.
Cheaper and more powerful sensors that consume less power are now being embedded in all kinds of wearable devices, from bracelets to shoes and clothes. Together with the mobile phone, these devices provide a plethora of sensing data including location, voice, movement, temperature, and so on. Combined with other customer data like calendar and social media, good machine learning algorithms can crunch it at real time and infer meaningful context; for example, the activity the person is engaging in, the environment, and the person's mood and stress levels. This could give us new insights into what consumers want in real time. New services and products are being designed to take advantage of these insights.

We used the phrase "it's possible" because progress is unevenly distributed across industries and companies. Nevertheless, most companies are building tools and capabilities to learn more about their customers.

Digital technology is also heightening customer expectations and shifting how customers perceive value. The following sections give some examples.

THE VALUE OF PEACE OF MIND

Fred Smith, the founder of FedEx, once remarked, "Early on, we knew the information about a package is as important as the package itself."[1] In the 1970s, FedEx was the first to put a computer-readable serial number on every package in order to track them and improve their internal package handling. It worked very well. That's how the tracking number practice was born in the package shipping industry.

What FedEx realized was that the tracking information was not only important to FedEx; it might also be important to the people sending the package, and so it decided to build a system to offer that information to its customers. During those preinternet days, you could call FedEx to ask them where your packages were. It provided visibility and assurance, reducing uncertainty and anxiety in customer's minds. The customer was less stressed and much happier knowing the progress of their package. That experience, the *emotional* experience, is of value to the customer. Today, real-time tracking is a standard practice in the package-shipping industry. Consumers would not expect any less from any provider, not just FedEx.

Peace of mind is also important to a customer expecting a college admission decision letter. Is it also important during the 15-minute period when you are waiting for a pizza delivery? Customers said yes. As mobile phones, mobile data, and GPS technology became widely available in developed markets, it became possible for pizza companies to build the digital capability to provide real-time pizza tracking on a customer's phone with a reasonable amount of investment. Turns out that customers like the tracking app as much as they like their hot and tasty pizza.

In the airline industry, the anxiety and stress of flight connections, delays, cancellations, and missing baggage are familiar ones. Digitization and automation can reduce the time required to rebook a flight to the point that a rebooking resulting from a delay can be complete before the delayed plane lands. Even better, that information can be pushed to a customer's mobile app so that as soon as the flight is on the ground, the new connection details are available from the moment they turn on their phone. More airlines are now offering travelers the ability to know where their checked bags are in real time, every step of the way from the check-in counter to the baggage claim carousel. All of this is aimed at

---

1 Fred Smith, "Continuous innovation fuels FedEx success" (*https://oreil.ly/AxL6X*), FedEx, September 8, 2015.

putting the customer's mind at ease and creating a much better travel experience. With digital technology, airlines can achieve that with more than just increased leg room and hot towels.

When customers experience peace of mind waiting for a package from FedEx, they have something with which to compare the wait for other kinds of deliveries. After their expectation is raised, the value of a better delivery experience becomes higher than just the receipt (and consumption) of the product itself. Every industry that ships or delivers products becomes affected.

THE VALUE OF FEELING IN CONTROL

Digging deeper from peace of mind to a potential root cause, psychological research has long argued that a basic human instinct is to exert control over their environment to obtain desired results. The perception of having control is not only desired, it's a psychological necessity. Giving consumers choices, and therefore control, has always been a focus for product and experience designers, especially in the consumer goods and retail sector.

Digital technologies have escalated giving customers control to the next level. Before buying a product, consumers can now go online to do extensive research on the features, performance, prices, post sales support—essentially everything they need to know—and compare the different brands against one another. They can buy a product online or in the shop; they could also buy online and pick up in the shop, or buy in the shop and have the product sent home. They can find instruction from online videos, discuss questions or issues with a support team through online chats, or use self-servicing diagnostic tools. If they are really not happy with the performance, they can return the products through websites that print you a free shipping label.

The abundance of information, choices, and the ability to make our own decisions make most of us happy consumers. That heightened expectation, the appreciation of feeling in control, is being compared against and extended into other industries.

One industry that is being significantly affected is the health-care industry. Most of us were used to being told what to do in the health-care system until digital technology demonstrated the possibilities in other industries. Many health-care providers, insurers, doctors, and hospitals have started to use digital technology to give patients more information, more choices, and more control. Every patient touch point is being redesigned and reimagined through the technology lens, from making appointments, accessing information, preparing for visits or treatment, to digital self-monitoring tools, remote diagnosis, and virtual doctors. Wearable technology is going to further empower people to manage their own health so that they don't even "need to" engage the health-care system at all.

The CIO of a US hospital told us that they had to change their mindset to think about patients almost as consumers. Patients' experience with the visits, the treatments, the doctors, and the hospital is as important as the actual results. Just having the best doctors and medical equipment is not enough. In the digital world we live in today, people, whether they are acting as consumers or patients at a particular moment, know what *good* feels like, and are making their choices accordingly. Digital technology is both the reason for and the solution to that shift.

THE VALUE OF PERSONALIZATION

If you grew up in the '80s, you might still remember the "old way" of watching TV: getting in front of the TV at the exact time the most popular show was about to start, or flipping through dozens of channels to discover some interesting program when you had extra time to kill. That was the most common way to discover and select content. This one-size-fits-all approach is no longer the case today.

Taking advantage of the internet's unprecedented ability to organize and search for information across multiple consumers, on-demand streaming services created a bigger disruption to the content discovery and selection process than the delivery of content itself. Netflix and others realized that it was not just the ability to stream content over internet that pleased their customers. More important was the ability to discover the content they liked most—it was not always the most popular shows. This shouldn't come as a surprise. Even though we are social animals and would like to be able to discuss the latest most popular show with friends, we are also very different individuals after all. It turns out that we have a great variety of subtly different tastes when it comes to content. The ability to discover and select the content we truly enjoy is as important as, if not more than, being able to watch the most popular shows media companies, experts, and reviewers collectively decide for us.

The rest of the media and entertainment industry quickly caught up. Channel discovery and selection become more user friendly, and is increasingly driven by voice or gestures as these technologies mature. But online streaming service providers like Netflix have built yet another advantage. Content recommendation is generally based on broad genres and self-indicated preferences. Netflix has far more nuanced data about customers' viewing habits: what people watch, what they watch afterward, what they watched before, what they watched a year ago, what they've watched recently, and at what time of day. Netflix can use machine learning algorithms to crunch all of this metadata and find surprising insights about people's preferences, sometimes contrary to the customers' own notions. According to Netflix,[2] one in eight people who watch one of Marvel's movies is new to this kind of comic book–based superhero content. More than 80% of the TV shows people watch on Netflix are discovered through its recommendation system.

Content can be personalized more than ever before, thanks to progress on data analytics and machine learning. Because it believes it knows so much about people's taste and preferences at a very nuanced and detailed level, Netflix went on from finding the content people want to watch to creating the content people want to watch. Netflix's original content strategy has produced popular TV series like *House of Cards* and *Orange Is the New Black*. It's even producing award-winning movies now. According to Netflix during an earnings call, 5 of the 10 shows people searched for most in 2017 were Netflix originals.

Today's consumers expect a much higher level of personalization than the previous generation. Stitch Fix is a new type of retailer using machine learning to create a personalized styling experience for the mass market. Instead of having customers shop for the clothes they want, Stitch Fix thinks it can learn more about a customer's personal taste and preferences from crunching data. Stitch Fix sends customers clothes and accessories periodically without the usual "ordering" or "shopping" process. Of course, you can return the items you don't like after you receive a batch. But Stitch Fix's success is built on its ability to predict and cater to an individual's taste and need in a mass market.

THE VALUE OF LOWER TRANSACTION COSTS

The increased accessibility of goods and services online and through multiple channels changes the economics of purchasing costs for customers. Digital platform businesses, in particular, have excelled with dramatic reductions in the cost per transaction, whether on the demand side—hailing a ride with Uber or renting a room with Airbnb—or the supply side—selling an app to customers through iTunes, allowing you to capture the long tail of innovation. Platform businesses have existed for decades (credit cards, shopping malls), and maybe

---

2 "Decoding the Defenders: Netflix Unveils the Gateway Shows That Lead to a Heroic Binge" (*https://oreil.ly/a4jiw*), Netflix, August 22, 2017.

even centuries (town marketplaces), but digital advances have lowered the friction of doing business with machine learning filters to effectively connect demand to supply. Customers now regularly expect affordable, quality services at the click of a button on their mobile devices.

The individual, as opposed to the target group, is what defines user experience (UX) in the age of machine learning. Personalization, perception of control, and peace of mind are just a few notable examples. The emotional reward and experience from consuming a product or service is being perceived as more and more valuable from the customer's perspective. When companies try to make investments or build products based on creating value for the customers, they need to make sure that they focus on the values that matter to the customers.

What do customers value most? As we have shown through some of the examples, there is not a single static answer to it in the Digital Age:

Value is perceived through different lenses; it could change over time.

How do we build the business strategy around the multifaceted and ever-evolving customer value?

EVOLVING TO CUSTOMER OUTCOMES

At ThoughtWorks' Paradigm Shift event in 2015, Glenn Morgan, head of digital business transformation at International Airlines Group, talked about the paradox faced by incumbents in the digital era. He talked about both the challenge and the opportunity for corporations, constrained by pace but enabled by scale, and concluded that the best way to move forward was to "think big, act small, learn fast, scale quickly."

To really thrive in the digital era, traditional businesses need to commit to the attributes of "small" that let them continually develop themselves to keep up with rapid changes of customer expectations. But not many organizations are actually built to do this for the following reasons:

"Think big" tends to result in big plans. For many business leaders, it's important to think big, be bold, and have a long-term vision. Although that generates ambition and builds confidence, it could also lead developing fully fleshed-out strategic and operational plans that map the vision to several strategic initiatives, with clear road maps to build up the capabilities, platforms, and investment required to support the new initiatives. When a multiyear megaplan is broken down into thousands of small disjointed pieces, there is no simple feedback mechanism. It could be difficult to see the connection between the tasks and customer expectations. Many parts of the organization end up spending too much time internally navel-gazing without a true understanding of how to connect their actions and outcomes to customer value. More important, after this train of big initiatives has left the station, it becomes challenging to change or stop even when new learnings from customers and the market say you should change your plans.

To be able to "learn fast," a lot more changes need to happen, the magnitude of which is commonly underestimated. Planning and strategy are just the beginning. Organizational structures need to change. Technology delivery practices need to change. Portfolio management needs to change. Measures of success need to change. This can be overwhelming for even fast-moving organizations. That's why "act small" is so important. You don't need to do everything at once.

A senior executive at a bank once asked in frustration, "What is the first step we need to take to transform?" Our reply was to first truly understand what customers want. He gladly replied that they had just spent a whole lot of money on this very topic and the answer from the research was clear, "70% of our customers want a mortgage!" A mortgage!? We don't think we have met any customer who actually wants a mortgage because it's such an exciting product or an enjoyable experience. What they really want is a home.

In a "sell more mortgages" traditional banking mindset, you would expect to see measures around how many mortgages are being sold and the dollar value of the mortgage. When you extrapolate, you could imagine the work being something around product bundling, digital mortgage advisors, and so on; you can see the functional allocation of work into teams that build features and complete products.

Now flip that around to customer outcomes and value measures. The customer value is "put people into a home." See how straight away there is an emotive reaction to the aim? Your employees will feel that too. But what is key here is what happens around it; the increment of the work would not be features, but services like helping customers to know what they can afford and where they could live. The skills you need to bring together in teams would be cross-functional, and of course what you measure as success would change. Imagine employees going home counting how many people they put into a home that day.

IT TAKES COURAGE TO ACT

The important thing is to know what value means to a customer. Using that, you can then find ways of capturing the weaker signals of change that will help you to maximize the volume and frequency of the value you deliver. Technology is the key enabler for this, whether it's the use of machine learning and AI to create new ways to deliver value, or having a platform architecture using microservices to allow for adaptability and frequent experimentation and change. We are not just talking about doing the same things faster, but rethinking the value you deliver and how you deliver it. The new strategic approach should focus on responsiveness, the ability to act small, learn fast, and scale quickly.

Of course, knowing it and doing it are two different things. Knowing isn't the difficult part; measuring can be, listening can be, and having the courage certainly is. It takes *courage* to act on what you learn. Responding might mean stopping something else. It might mean moving people around, reallocating money, or deprioritizing that favorite project. This is where this is where you are really tested—can your executives act as one for the benefit of the customer and the business or are you locked into constant functional showdowns and adversarial behaviors? You need to find that core strength in the company culture to create the impetus for change. We hope it's not just the threat of extinction driving the transformation; maybe it's compassion, aspiration to be the best, pursuit of excellence, or commitment to a higher purpose.

It's really that simple: understand the purpose of your business, align to customer value, and have the courage to act on what the data tells you to do to optimize value delivery. The leap-of-faith assumption is that the more value you deliver and the more aligned every aspect of your business is, the more benefits and profits the business will generate and retain in the long run—and more shareholder value will result from this, too. The University of Michigan conducted a study of companies with high scores on the American Customer Satisfaction Index that shows that between 2000 and 2012 their stock went up 390%, whereas the S&P 500 dropped by 7%. This is just one of many examples that proves the direct link between creating customer loyalty through a focus on value and the long-term benefits for the business itself.

HOW TO GET STARTED

We know that changing the language or taxonomy of your organization is not a trivial task; it takes practice and constant reinforcement. Our experience is that leaders find this a very difficult mental shift to make. It's not that the information is unavailable or the knowledge absent from the organization, it's the connection that this information needs to have with strategy rather than simply the facade of customer centricity. Too often, organizations become caught up in using customer data as a marketing tool or for demand generation. Meanwhile, the businesses run their day-to-day based on strategies that focus on productivity and profitability and "coincidently" the work in flight matches the lines of business of the company, just with the addition of new buzzwords from technology trends like "cloud," "SaaS," or "platforms."

Have a look at this list of multiyear plan items we have collected along the way:

- Drive growth and customer acquisition.

- Extend position in X market.

- Deliver superior customer experience.

- Increase margins by X%.

- Enhance technology capability in X.

- Increase sales in product X.

- Hit revenue objective of X.

- Increase share price by X.

- Achieve Net Promoter Score of X.

These are just a few, but hopefully the point comes through. This could be any company—these goals are not unique and are very internally focused. They describe company benefits, not outcomes for the customer. They are highly likely to be based on each of the lines of business in the organization rather than on what customers actually want and are certainly not reflective of how a customer sees value from you. A senior member of a large organization once complained to us that if the organization's strategy was accidently left in a McDonald's restaurant, no one would care because it had nothing unique in it. This has to be your litmus test: if your competitor saw your strategic outcomes would it matter, would they be worried?

There are many approaches to designing the precise outcomes and it is largely dependent on the knowledge and expertise of the leaders to navigate the ship in the correct direction. Here are a few examples of how to help make the mental shift so that you can better represent the customer in the outcomes of the organization:

Jobs to be done, a theory from Strategyn

We once witnessed a client use a "jobs to be done" canvas as a really effective tool to help leaders reset their language toward what the customer would see as value. By knowing how customers measure value, organizations are able to articulate outcomes in the customer's terms. Strategyn uses a great example on its website describing the use of herbicide: at first the value is thought to be to "kill weeds," later it's identified as "prevent weed growth in crops," which can then be broadened out to a value-add of "growing the best crops." You can see the varied lens that occurs as you look at these three scenarios and how different the work might be depending on the lens.

Personas

This is an effective tool that has been around for a long time and uses fictional representations of common patterns of customers. The objective is to learn more about the needs, behaviors, and goals of customers as a way to create and orient outcomes.

Segments

These are an organizing construct based on segmentation such as by life cycle stages and designing outcomes based on each stage, outcomes are the entry and exit points of a stage. Other segment examples could be customer type, demographics, or location.

Design thinking

The use of evidence instead of instinct along with design techniques to study customer behaviors. The idea is that you frame the problem in terms of why the customer would need the product (e.g., to improve health) rather than in terms of the benefit to the organization (sell more healthy food).

Scenario planning

Scenario planning is a structured way of getting executives to think differently about the future. It is effective at bridging the gap between the world of facts and the world of perceptions. By exploring the facts and information available today, the process aims to change the perceptions of decision makers. The purpose is to gather and transform information of strategic significance into fresh perceptions.

Using these types of techniques, the multiyear plan begins to take a different shape, perhaps becoming more like this:

- Help me plan for my future with a predictable income.
- Help me grow wealth, protect it, and pass it on later.
- Help me control my money.
- Help me retire comfortably.
- Help me buy a home.
- Make it easy for me to assess my current situation to make better life decisions.
- Make starting and running a business easy.
- Make it easy for me to make a claim so that I can recover quicker.
- Help me improve my health.

A favorite simple example is of a national mail service that redesigned its divisions around how customers interact with the service. The end states of "send mail" and "receive mail" just feel logical and makes it easy to design outcomes that align to the value the customer expects.

The key is to have intimate knowledge of what value customers are coming to you to get, find ways to grow that value, make it easier to get, and look for ways to diversify into value-add areas. These are the outcomes that help the organization be what the market needs and that ultimately lead to profitability.

Now that you have the outcomes your business wants through the lens of customer value, or at least a fresh set of hypotheses about what outcomes your customers want, you need to define how to measure them and align the organization's work to achieve them or validate and develop them. Before getting to measurement and work alignment, you need to pause for a minute and talk about the approach to manage change and transition. This is the time when changes begin to really happen—organizational structure, budget allocation, governance model, and so on. How should you go about making these changes? Is there an upfront design you can follow? Is there a proven model you can follow from another business? Chapter 3 addresses these questions.

Key Points

Following are the key points that we hope you take away from this chapter as well as two actions for you to take to begin implementing what we've discussed:

- Customer outcomes need to be understood and placed at the center of your organization's strategy and digital transformation.
- Digital technology is a double-edged sword. It improves an organization's capability to understand customer outcomes and find new ways to meet the needs of these outcomes. However, it is also shifting how customers perceive value, making it even more difficult to maintain alignment between your organization's strategy and the delivery of value to customers.
- The change required to make this alignment is being underestimated. It requires a new set of capabilities and organizational design to be able to listen and respond to constant change and the courage to act on the data regardless of the implications.

Here are two actions to take:

- Learn what value means for your customers: Using some of the example techniques in this chapter, describe what value means to your customers.
- Let customer value define your outcomes: Rewrite your strategy as outcomes in customer language. Apply a clear single measure of achieving the outcome.

The Thin-Slice Approach to Transformation

The thin-slice approach to digital transformation is an iterative and incremental approach to develop the business to organize and operate around the principle of maximizing customer value delivery with digital technologies. We build cars *incrementally*: build the chassis, add the engine, add the tires, and so on, and at the end of it we can drive from point A to point B. We *iteratively* find better ways of moving from point A to point B; for example: walking, riding a skateboard, and driving. You need both forms of thinking at scale.

It's not different from the prescriptive, Big-Bang, all-in approach when it comes to the need to build a strong sense of urgency, a clear vision, a powerful coalition, and effective communication. It's different when it comes to designing the road map of what needs to be changed and how to change it. The thin-slice approach does not assume that the executives or the change team already have the answers, or that you can just copy from a successful company or peer. It recognizes that the pace of business today requires rapid learning and leading through ambiguity. You need to come up with some hypotheses about the changes you need to make, test them, learn from them, and rinse and repeat to advance the organization incrementally based on what you find works for you. This chapter shows you how.

To better understand the need for this approach, let's first look back at why current approaches fail.

Why Big Transformation Programs Fail

There are not many big digital transformation programs that can claim roaring success. Some even fail miserably. Most of them are somewhere in between. They achieve some positive results, make the appropriate directional impacts here and there, but slowly run out of energy. Their fate is either to fade away or to be reshuffled and subsumed into yet another new transformation program. We have seen this play out in many organizations, large and small, in mature and developing markets.

It's worth calling out that running large change programs is inherently difficult, whether in the digital world or in previous times. In the 1995 book *Leading Change* (HBR), Harvard professor John Kotter laid out the classic eight-step change model. It is not surprising that so many organizations and executives struggled with some of these aspects:

- Create a sense of urgency.

- Form a powerful coalition.

- Create a vision for change.

- Communicate the vision.

- Remove obstacles.

- Create short-term wins.

- Build on the change.

- Anchor the changes in corporate culture.

People just don't like change. Many transformation programs have change leads or consultants equipped with various change management theories and guidelines. But it's easier said than done. While executives generally see a good reason to change—declining revenue, missing opportunity in new markets, or strong competition—it's not often a life-and-death issue for the main business. Executives are humans too, and are subject to the loss aversion cognitive bias in which things we will lose weigh three times heavier in our mind than the things we will gain, even when their value is exactly the same. It's not a trivial task to get executives to overcome their own loss aversion and mentally commit to stepping into the unknown.

Digital transformation is not so different. If you act only when it has become a life-and-death matter for the business, it might already be too late. Acting early, when the main business is still doing well, requires a lot of intellectual and emotional skills to create this sense of urgency. There will be a lot of good reasons not to do it—existing revenue could be cannibalized, additional cost could reduce the near-term profitability, morale of long-term employees could drop, technologies are not mature enough, and so forth. The existing comfort zone is a good place compared with the risky digital world.

Even when you create a sense of urgency and have executive teams aligned and committed, communicating to the entire organization still requires relentless determination and energy, which is often significantly underestimated. Executives are always busy with more higher-priority tasks than there is time for. Communication effort is often perceived as having diminishing returns after the first one or two rounds of all-hands meetings. It's also not so exciting the 25th time you have to repeat the same message and present the same idea.

When the changes begin, there will be real obstacles: corporate constraints to stretch, existing commitments to delay or cancel, personal aspirations and egos to dampen, and current reporting lines to break. A sense of urgency and vision alone are not enough to remove these obstacles. It takes courage and real effort to clear the path for transformation, sometimes more than the leadership is offering. When too many compromises are made, obstacles become permanent roadblocks, morale of change agents drops, and transformation stalls. Eventually, the transformation program reaches a point at which the current situation looks new but has little difference from the way things were other than a few organizational structure changes and new strategy words. The "transformed" engine of work finds its way back to the old norm.

For a recent client, we built a visualization in a room of the entire portfolio of work for the organization and its relationship to the expected outcomes in the company strategy. Although initially this seemed like an effective exercise, it appeared almost too neat, too aligned. Through further investigation, we found that more than 80% of the work in progress had its origins more than three years earlier. It turned out that most of the work in progress predated the current strategy by years! The ongoing work was simply being "repositioned" each year to make it look like it matched the new direction. This allowed existing projects to get into the funding buckets, justified continued efforts, and validated the current organizational structures. The core engine was just using the facade of change to justify the status quo.

There is no evil intent here. Traditional organizations can't just stop everything and start again. Broad transformation approaches force people to comply rather than give them the capability to adapt or even stop what they are doing. This turns the transformation into more bluster and words than true sustainable change as teams or middle management fight to keep their pet projects afloat, happy to support the words and look to others to change, just not themselves. In the end, the mere magnitude of broad transformations and the lack of capability or empowerment to stop or adapt the current train of work makes the thought of digital transformation overwhelming and leads to many companies looking to copy the answer from others.

Digital businesses organize and operate around the principle of delivering more value to customers. They listen and observe and are prepared to do anything necessary to respond to customer outcomes. They are born this way; they don't carry the legacy of systems, processes, and thinking. For them everything is on the table for change and adaptation. It's a way of working, not just words— and the knowledge about change comes from those who do the work. More traditional organizations can't ignore these things when tackling digital transformation. They must resist the lure of a silver bullet answer, because there isn't one.

We see this in one of the greatest fads of today. To copy the "Spotify model," organizations are all implementing their "squads" and "tribes," "guilds" and "chapters" and are all ready for great cross-functional change. Yet Spotify itself screams, "Don't copy us" because it is the lessons it learned along the way, the culture it created, and its constant evolution that goes missing when organizations try to copy. A transformation is a journey to learn your own lessons, build your own culture, and improve your own organization. It's a journey of learning and evolution. There is, unfortunately, no shortcut, and no silver bullet.

The problem word here is "implement." Digital transformation is something you do, a culture you create, the new norms or ways of working. It isn't something you just implement as if it were a program of work. "Implement" suggests that there is a master plan with all the answers already defined. "Copy Spotify" suggests that, too. A traditional transformation mindset tends to be comforted by this kind of Big-Bang approach with predefined implementation road maps, tracking, and "all in" scope; hence, it sees it as the preferred approach.

This prescriptive, Waterfall implementation approach with a detailed road map comes with some big challenges in digital transformation. Here, we highlight the three main ones:

- Broad transformation approach

- Biased decision making

- Copying others rather than learning for yourself

BROAD TRANSFORMATION APPROACH

It almost sounds like a contradiction, but broad transformations are rarely holistic. The intention of a broad, upfront, designed transformation is to change everything and everyone at the same time, from organizational design, process, and role definition to budgeting, KPIs, and performance reviews. Each department has a road map to transform itself accordingly.

But each department almost always has some areas that can claim: "We are too big, too important, in the middle of something, not changeable, bound by compliance," and so on. Despite the strong sense of urgency and the powerful coalition, the organization begins to apply exemptions everywhere and tries to cordon off areas to remain untouched by the changes.

Too many workarounds are created in order to limit the impact of changes across departmental boundaries. Over time, each of the departmental change programs begin to run at a different pace, get disconnected, and lose synchronization. Organizations by definition are cross-boundary, complex organisms not defined by the structural lines: cross-boundary impact is unavoidable. Change inevitably creeps beyond the artificial hierarchical boundaries and will affect everyone. It's not realistic to think that you can change the pace and responsiveness of a single operation when it is affected by all other functions.

Although a big department- or division-oriented change road map looks holistic on paper, it is rarely holistic in reality because every department still has different purposes and priorities. There are too many battles to fight early on, and many of the battle plans become outdated as soon as the real change begins. There is simply not enough time and room to learn, adapt, and stay coordinated all at the same time. A well-designed execution plan quickly dissolves into a collection of isolated fire-fighting activities.

For these same reasons, you can't have multiple, separate transformation programs going on at once. Transformation decisions are not line-of-business decisions. They need to be made taking the whole into account. With the explosion of theories for scaling Agile and other methodologies, it's not unusual to see several in use at one company. This is OK if they are just loosely applied "best of breed" practices, but there are often conflicts.

A good example is something like the "Spotify model" being applied to the business while IT is implementing IT-as-a-Service. One asks for cross-functional teams where IT would be thin, the other makes IT heavy, and the disciplines remain in IT. One optimizes for customer outcome, the other optimizes for cost. Neither is right or wrong, but clearly the two are in conflict. Or, it could be the opposite. IT begins to drive the adoption of Agile methodology without the alignment and commitment from the business to do the same. It ends up with an Agile sandwich where a part increases in speed, but as a whole you are delivering value no quicker to the customer.

BIASED DECISION MAKING

One financial organization we worked with took the time to ask its customers to describe what value means to them. The company came up with a list of more than three hundred things. It decided to focus on the top 20 most referenced items. The company then asked each of its executives what they thought the top things that customers wanted were; of all the things the executives named, only four were in the top 20 of the customer list.

In this example, you see the current work and opinions as to what is important really being challenged. Resistance to change is at its peak when this occurs because what you thought or wanted to be true come under scrutiny.

Frequently, decisions are made to justify the status quo rather than challenge it, to suit the existing power structure rather than change it. What seemingly matters to people up and down the hierarchical chain are their personal objectives; for example, completing the work they started, being seen to deliver, meeting the numbers, and meeting prior commitments. Many fight against the transformation, seeing it as a fad that will disappear when the consultants leave; they prefer skewing information toward doing work that is in their domain of interest and doing work that suits the skills of the staff that report to them.

This kind of decision bias creates an almost never-ending list of obstacles to be removed. In theory, it's possible to break away from the existing anchor by throwing the entire organization into a new structure, with new role definitions, new reporting lines, new KPIs, new rewards, new budgets, and so on. But these issues are not just to do with the business outcomes to be achieved and customer value to be delivered. They have a lot to do with the human beings involved. Personal aspirations, skill sets, strengths, weaknesses, and relationships cannot be ignored when designing the new organization. The "right" way of getting things done is often learned and developed rather than implemented according to a nonpersonal design.

At this point, we focus on the general approach: why an iterative and incremental approach is better at addressing these issues. In Part II of this book, we discuss these decision biases and organizational constraints in more detail as well as ways to tackle them during the transition.

COPYING OTHERS RATHER THAN LEARNING FOR YOURSELF

It's tempting, and almost logical, to think that simply doing what successful companies did or what the digital leader in your industry is doing will get you similar results. There is an element of truth to that. Some of the smaller pieces they have implemented will be of great value to you and contribute to your success. The key there is the parts, not the whole—there is no blueprint or road map to follow, no magical endpoint that you will all reach. It is 100% about the journey and the way you approach digital transformation as a set of small wins, not a single win; as experiments that are scaled when proven to succeed. It is about creating the environment in which capturing learnings gives you the data to make the right choices—choices that will optimize how your organization maximizes the volume and frequency of value it delivers to customers.

Copying is a fast way to get the plan together. It makes it easy to explain what you are doing and will set you a cracking pace early on; it gets to "start" quicker. It will require the scramble of all scrambles when you very quickly begin to see cracks as the copy rubs up against your organization's norms and culture, and you see the misalignment of certain pieces against your uniqueness. It will challenge your courage—how willing are you to say, "We got that bit wrong; let's do something different," when the inevitable becomes obvious?

Copying organizational structure is especially difficult to roll back because it traps organizations into "embedding" the change too early. A client we worked for made early organizational structure change following the successes of a peer organization. It was a massive roll out that caused many people to lose their positions and change roles. Although this was a great demonstration of courage, it was also quite disruptive to the organization. But the "copy" didn't work very well for the organization due to a combination of factors. Suboptimal teams were formed, accountability gaps emerged, and collaboration issues arose. It needed to be fixed, but the situation was nearly impossible to reverse. The company couldn't just do another massive reorganization and revert to the previous structure and have people go back to the old teams and report to the old bosses. Organization structure change causes more change fatigue than anything else. You can only do it once in a while to be effective. After the copy approach, the suboptimal teams and accountability gaps became the new starting point.

The large transformation decisions, when it comes to scaling, need to be delayed to the last possible moment that a decision can be responsibly made so that we maximize knowledge of which way to do it. Holding off on these allows you to maximize data collection and learning to help improve the accuracy of your transformation. Through incremental validation of what works, the bits that truly improve your outcomes emerge as the ones to scale out. Decide too early, and you could lock yourself in to a suboptimal change.

Implementing a Thin Slice

By definition, a thin-slice approach is first and foremost narrow and targeted, and thin and deep (see Figure 3-1). Determining a thin slice is a bit of an art, akin to principles of design thinking. We have seen success with organizations that orient their thin slice to customer outcomes. As Chapter 2 discusses, even a very large organization should have only 10 to 20 major outcomes defined by customer value. One such outcome, for example, "Be there for me during unexpected life events and market turbulence," could be the focal point around which to build a thin slice.

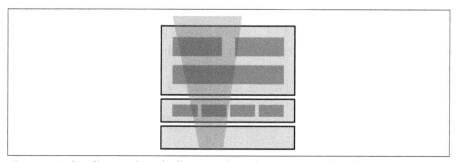

Figure 3-1. A thin slice cuts through all aspects of your business so you identify impediments to change

Some companies choose to focus on customer journey episodes such as "Researching my options." There are others who use customer segmentation as the main framework to build the thin slices. There is no prescribed best way to do this, and it is influenced by the specific business and operational model of your business and your industry. But there is a definite antipattern: the thin slice within a functional unit (and this is certainly not just the IT function). Too many times we have seen "building a new data analytics tool" or "reducing call-center staff numbers through a chat bot" used as a thin slice to start the digital transformation journey. Customers just don't view or interact with your business that way, so there is no way that optimizing by functional unit will maximize value delivery.

A thin slice should absolutely be considered a holistic approach. One of the common misconceptions is that it means a small piece of the pie, and, in fact, most organizations see a division or line of business as a thin slice. To the contrary, a thin slice means a vertical cut through the entire company, integrating all elements of the business involved in a value delivery piece; the slice is a complete piece of value. A thin slice is both thin and deep; it's similar to the Agile concept, just at a much higher altitude.

MEASURE THE SLICE

After a specific outcome is defined, you need to work out the proper measure, and how to capture weaker signals and leading indicators that tell you earlier whether you are heading toward the outcome. Next, cascade it down to a series of work that can improve the measures—accepting that it's only a hypothesis and that such work will improve the measures. The backlog of work itself is dynamic and should have lightweight governance applied to it to constantly review the learning and then decide when to double down, stop, or pivot to a new hypothesis. We go into a lot more depth on this in Chapter 4.

GET EVERYONE IN ON THE SLICE

A thin slice needs to be an end-to-end, executive-to-developer slice of customer value, as defined by customers. It needs the involvement of all organizational functions to truly identify and test the constraints of the organization's processes, culture, and thinking. It should include representation from most of the functional units, some of which will have people dedicated to this full time (e.g., business and IT); some of which will provide expertise in a part-time capacity to help resolve related functional constraints (e.g., finance or HR). It should expose a lot, if not all, of the systemic antibodies that could resist the changes. This is where the sense of urgency, the vision, the powerful coalition, and the communication will be needed to help build alignment, remove obstacles, and push against the decision bias anchored in the status quo.

ARRANGE TEAMS AROUND—AND ACROSS—THE SLICE

Cross-functional teams need to be assembled around the focus areas to deliver the work. This is where the traditional line-of-business or departmental boundaries will be stretched and tested. Along the way, role definition, reporting structure, KPIs, performance views, and other traditional HR issues will be exposed as well. As we have argued repeatedly, digital transformation is fundamentally driven by the accelerating pace of technology improvements, so it's important to keep your technology in mind throughout this entire process. At the same time, because the technology improvement outcomes should be delivering more value to customers, the business domain and operational perspective are also critical in defining the proper outcomes and performing the work to deliver them. It is thus essential to assemble a cross-functional team around each piece of work. Later in the book, we dive into each topic in detail: measurements, aligning work and team, visibility, dealing with operational and functional constraints, technology implications you need to understand, and leadership.

Because this is only a thin slice, the coalition doesn't need to spread its precious energy and resources too widely across the organization; it should focus only on pushing this single business outcome driven through a smaller group of people as opposed to the entire organization. No matter how committed the executives are to creating a sense of urgency, build the vision, and communicate it, there is a finite amount of bandwidth and energy to be prioritized across a broad and complex organization.

Ambitious plans and grand visions don't need to begin with a Big Bang and a massive shock wave that disrupts everyone from day one. A thin slice is designed to capture the maximum amount of learning in the least disruptive way. It also gives the teams time to test, learn, and improve.

It's important to create small wins quickly and celebrate them to build momentum for the overall transformation mindset. It's even more important to fail early and fast if the hypothesis and designs are wrong. Smaller changes are easier to revise or reverse. A thin slice gives the team opportunities to test these hypotheses early on. It could be anything from new product ideas or customer engagement improvements to team organization, working environment, or location. If the experiments based on the hypothesis work well, they should move the needle to better customer outcomes and faster value delivery as the measurements indicate. If they don't, it's an opportunity to examine the real cause, adjust the execution, or change the hypothesis. These smaller-scale experiments give the team the room to test, succeed or fail, and learn.

SLICE PATIENTLY

The first thin slice is often the most difficult one. It's not just about finding solutions to the problems popping up along the way. It's also about building a new muscle. The new muscle is the institutional ability to test and learn, understanding how to discover the robustness of an idea and then capture learnings to inform decision making. The transformation itself must stand up to these same principles. You need to accept that you cannot predesign the outcome, because you don't have enough knowledge going in as to what will work for you and your unique culture.

After you have made enough progress in the first thin slice—in terms of identifying problems, coming up with solutions, and building the test and learn capability—you can then turn to the second thin slice.

Again, this will require identifying the right business outcome defined by customer value, working out the measurements, cascading it down to a backlog of work, and then building teams around the work and measurements. The main focus of the second thin slice is to validate the learnings and solutions. It will most likely involve a similar deep, end-to-end cut across the functional boundaries, but in a different position, with a different group of people. These differences will stretch and test the solutions and learnings and almost certainly break some of them. Again, this is the opportunity to learn from intentionally designed small experiments and come up with new solutions. It's alright to have two different solutions to a seemingly similar problem in two different thin slices. The important step here is to understand the root cause of the difference and come up with a hypothesis at a higher level of abstraction.

Consistency of solution *principles* are more important than consistency of the solution *details*. Is it a compromise due to functional constraints, or is it a legitimate difference due to the different nature of the business outcome or the process/technology involved? For example, you might have two slices each needing to solve a customer activation solution. At first, a natural instinct is to see this as duplicated effort, but don't jump to this conclusion too quickly. Let both teams experiment, and you might get to a more innovative solution or find that both are required due to a uniqueness between the two areas.

Typically, after two thin slices, there will be enough learning and test-and-learn muscles to consider potential faster scaling. The third thin slice could begin with a much better-defined and more-detailed plan, still with a healthy dose of trial-and-error mindset. There will certainly be plenty of learning to improve the model and the solutions, but there is a good chance that they will be small, incremental improvements as opposed to radical departure from the current design evolved from the learning. It's certainly not the time to declare victory yet, but the third thin slice should give the executives and change teams a great level of confidence that the correct model of operation and organization has emerged.

MIXING THIN SLICES AND BROADER TRANSFORMATION INITIATIVES

For most organizations, three thin slices will touch a quarter to a third of the organization due to the connected nature of most modern businesses' functions. By the time the fourth or fifth thin slice is rolled out, the rest of the organization should have heard and seen changes around them. With continued communication efforts on the vision and sense of urgency, most parts of the organization should be ready to fold in around the next thin slice with a greater willingness to participate and a more validated scaling pattern that will fit your organization.

In reality it is unlikely that the rest of the organization will be content with sitting still while the thin-slice teams get to evolve at pace. To satisfy the urge to change we suggest that you use a "T-model," considering a mix of thin-slice work and other broader transformation initiatives. Some examples of broad activity include the following:

- Learning and education
- Adopting hypotheses and experiments everyone can participate in
- Changing the language and taxonomy used into customer terms
- Conducting visibility activities such as team and program wall spaces
- Implementing value-driven portfolio management concepts

This will also be great input for you to identify low-hanging fruit for change and the likely next slice teams. During our interview with a senior vice president we worked with, they highlighted the importance of being exceedingly transparent and inclusive:

> *You may think you've assembled a good coalition of change agents, keeping everyone informed of and involved in both the principles of the change and the progress, but chances are you're missing critical influencers within the organization—or you've yet to fully engage teams that are already working this way behind the scenes. At best you're missing an*

opportunity to engage additional minds and hearts; at worst you risk alienating a set of people that feel they are (already) modeling the solution.

Seek out and welcome transformation team members or co-leads that will connect to and engage with different parts of the organization (especially those where your own influence may be limited) so that the entire organization can feel connected to and excited about the mission.

The test-and-learn traits of a thin slice will help you to truly identify what will work and what won't. They stop you from making the charade of wordsmithing the current to look like the future and avoids putting everyone into a mass change state that builds resistance and forces people to falsify success. You will learn your unique new business architecture, your North Star, where business and technology work in harmony to maximize the delivery of customer value.

The Non-"End State"

The most important thing to keep in mind is that the transformation does not stop after the new business architecture has emerged. Transformation has to change how you do things, not just the organizational structure and process, but also how you look at future changes and how you respond to them. This continuous learning, and iterative and constant change mindset must become part of the new corporate culture.

Often clients ask us about what the end state is, what success looks like. We believe that part of the reason behind the use of the word "end state" is a desire to declare victory, move on, and get back to business as usual. Transformation is difficult work. Pushing against the system inertia and learning new things requires additional effort and creates fatigue. It's generally outside of most people's comfort zone in today's business. As a reflection of that, "change fatigue" is often called out as a reason to finish a transformation program—to reach an end state at which there is no change any more. Digital transformation basically means implementing the faster learning that is required in the Digital Age and taking advantage of new ways to capitalize on learning from the growth of technology.

In the digital world an "end state" does not exist outside of the organization, so it cannot exist in it. A traditional competitive advantage, built around a unique product, intellectual property, or barrier to entry, will last a lot shorter in today's world than it used to. It now takes months, not years, for competitors to catch up.

New services and products or new competitors, powered by digital technology, will make significant inroads into an incumbent's market in months, not years.

MANAGING CHANGE FATIGUE

Even though change fatigue is not unusual in today's traditional organizations, you might need to find better ways to manage it. A different kind of change fatigue is now ever present and driven by market changes, customer expectations, and the external competitive landscape. A business cannot simply call "stop" on that external trend in order to catch a breath. Disruption is inherently not comfortable. Most human beings, if given a choice, would probably prefer not to be disrupted, but we have collectively created this new era of accelerating technology change and the continuous, never-ending disruptions that come with that. To survive and thrive in this new, constantly changing market, we have no choice but to embrace the new paradigm.

A successful digital transformation program should build stronger muscles to handle changes more effectively and with less fatigue. Changes will not go away, but fatigue should reduce. There will be no "end state" with fewer or no changes, there is only a "future state" in which changes continue, driven by customer expectations, whereas the business knows how to handle it quickly and do so with much less "fatigue" than it feels today.

As mentioned in the introduction, *digital evolution* might be a better term to describe this process than *digital transformation*. Transformation tends to imply a start and a finish, a transformed state—in reality the transformation is to a state of constant learning and adaptation. A thin-slice approach gives you the ability to achieve this much better than a Big-Bang, prescriptive transformation program. The future will be an almost never-ending cycle of thin slices as opposed to the kickoff of the next big transformation program.

This will be part of the new way of "how we do things around here." This is a more fundamental culture shift for many businesses than they would expect or be ready for. As we have seen in our experience with Agile transformation in software teams, successful digital transformation should eventually be anchored in corporate culture change.

Building the new business architecture based on the current state of digital technology development is important, but building the expectation to continue to test, learn, and change is another dimension of the digital transformation. The thin-slice approach sets this expectation with the organization better than one big transformation program. It tends to be a longer journey than 18-month or two-year transformation programs. The accuracy of the business architecture and the institutional muscles to change are the trade-offs that justify it.

With this in mind, leaders need to become better at accepting ambiguity and change as the constant rather than a plan or an implementation. Instead of asking what the end state and the big win look like, you should focus on how to recognize the small wins and small learnings and celebrate them more.

Now that we have walked through the thin-slice approach to the transformation journey, let's get into the steps to tackle the first thin slice. After you pick the business outcome defined by customer value to focus on, before designing a backlog of work to achieve that and building teams around it, you first need to understand what measurements you can rely on to know whether you are making real progress towards delivering more value to customers.

Key Points

Following are the key points that we hope you take away from this chapter as well as two actions for you to take to begin implementing what we've discussed:

- The all-in big transformation program approach often fails to meet high aspirations and achieve results. It will struggle even more in digital transformation.

- A thin-slice approach is better at exposing functional constraints and antibodies with less disruption and allowing you to evolve the organization into a more fit-for-purpose business architecture.

- Continuous change will be the new norm in the digital future. A thin-slice approach is better at building the test-and-learn muscles needed for continuing to evolve the business operating model driven by the changes in the external markets and customer expectations.

Here are two actions to take:

- Nominate an outcome to be your first thin slice: Make it a substantial enough one that will expose the core constraints of the organization.

- Form your outcome team: Make visible the hypothesis you have about your digital transformation, and use these to identify the cross-functional team needed to capture maximum learning.

Measures and Decision Making

What you choose to measure has an impact on both the timeliness of decisions and, as a consequence, how weak a signal you can detect. The weaker the signal you get, the more value you can deliver to customers. Digital transformation in part is about capturing weak but important signals so that you can make more time-critical decisions in the moment.

The thin-slice approach gives you the opportunity to test and learn in an end-to-end environment. As early as possible, you need to rely on some kind of signals to know whether you are moving closer to the outcome or further away from it. Measuring the correct signal will allow you to make better decisions earlier to maximize the value you deliver to your customers.

Of course, the challenge is not the lack of signals, but often the opposite: there are too many signals and the system is fairly noisy. The challenge lies in capturing those signals aligned with measuring customer value. The strong, easy-to-measure signals are not always the appropriate ones to measure; in fact, the strength of the signal has almost no correlation to the relevance of the signal for progressing the outcome.

In the early days of Taylorism, the Industrial Age was optimizing for labor productivity and economic efficiency based on logic, rationalism, and empiricism that could be assessed with standardized "certainty" of process and tasks. In the Digital Age that certainty and standardized practice has diminished, yet we still try to apply many of the theories from that time. Take for example software development—we have known for a long time that the value of a piece of software is not proportional to the number of lines of code it contains. Still, we continue to see again and again examples in the industry in which "lines of code" or "Velocity" are incorrectly used as a key signal associated with a programmer's productivity. It's as if the most difficult part of software programming is typing. Perhaps the same can be said for how finances are managed for which the exact spending of the budget, not over and not under, is celebrated in lieu of any customer value that is delivered as a result.

Value measures are often confused with the need for our work to appear valuable, or for ourselves to be valued as individuals. Herein lies an epiphany: true value is rarely a quantitative measure, but rather a yes/no question (was the value received?) and, as such, needs to be asked each time and be dependent on the transaction at hand. That's the real issue: customer value can be difficult to measure; that is, the proper measure is not always easy to get, so organizations tend to favor simpler, less-relevant, unaligned alternatives. This is especially true when you want to focus more on customer outcomes—often due to the time lag between the transaction and the realization of the value. There are no obvious metrics that can gauge the value of peace of mind, the value of personalization, the value of convenience, or the value of feeling in control. You must live with ambiguity and sometimes use approximations.

One example, Net Promoter Score (NPS), has been widely adopted as an indicator of customer satisfaction and loyalty to a company's products and services. There are many factors that could affect a customer's overall satisfaction and loyalty over an extended period of time. Although NPS is a great tool to gauge the longer term trends of customer satisfaction, it's not always useful for getting real-time or early feedback on the products you develop, improvements you make, and the more granular-level tasks you do. We have seen situations in which a customer has left comments that they are completely satisfied and scored a 7 (on a scale of 0 to 10, with only 9s and 10s counting as "promoters"). If an unhappy customer also left a 7, reporting would show them as equal when clearly they are not. Worse would be the linking of these type of trend-based analyses to an individual's performance given that the state of the customer and the relating score is very often nothing to do with the employee; the customer is rating their feeling toward the company not necessarily the person. It is not difficult to understand why you hear an agent state, "Please remember the survey is about your interaction with me," or why unhappy calls are cut off prior to the survey being asked.

An all-too-common scenario for traditional organizations is that their structures, policies, and behaviors make it too difficult to truly measure customer value (on top of the fact it's difficult to measure to begin with). So it gets replaced by a combination of different types of measurements that appear as proxies to show progress, such as benefits to the business like revenue and profits, individual KPIs for performance, or activities like tasks, work completed, and budget spent.

To be clear, we are not advocating that traditional measures are bad and new ones are good; you need to apply the appropriate measure for the time and need. Good measures are often temporary and directly linked to the outcome—after it's done or it's good enough, the measurement could become meaningless. That will be the right time to throw them away and focus on the other (or next) important measure for the other or new goals. The key is to review measurements regularly to make sure that they still serve a good purpose and not just blindly use traditional long-lived measures for a purpose they were not intended. The critical step is to separate measures back into their original intent—the horses for courses approach; for example:

- Customer value should be the determining measure of what work we do next to meet the outcome. It's how we decide what projects, programs, initiatives, and experiments to invest in.

- Financial measures are for company health, leading to fiscal responsibility.

- Individual KPIs are to help people improve.

- Improvement measures show whether the company is getting better, more efficient, and effective over activity measures.

Of course, these all need to stay aligned to the outcome dial; that is, the work we are doing is moving the needle to tell us we are achieving our strategy. Let's now dive into some details of some of the different types of measures such as customer value, financial and individual KPIs, and improvement. We then examine the impact they have on the purpose of delivering more value to customers.

Customer Value Measures

Value is what customers pull from your business; benefits are what you receive in return, such as revenue, profit, and so on. Value to customers should lead to benefits to business. The leap of faith you need to take is that the more value you deliver to customers more often, the more profitable and successful your business will be (i.e., the more benefits you will get).

As described earlier, a major shift in corporate governance took place in the last three decades of the twentieth century focusing on maximizing short-term returns to shareholders. The *shareholder-value-maximization* theory dominated management principles and defined the ultimate success for a company as profit maximization. As a result, most companies focused on measuring revenue and profit-related metrics, sometimes at the cost of customer, employee, and society-oriented metrics.

However, revenue and profit metrics lag far behind the immediate impact of a company's actions to customers' value delivery; in fact, the short-term correlation is often the opposite. Building a new feature that improves customers' experience will cost money and reduce profit instantly, and the future revenue as a result of increased customer satisfaction and loyalty might not be reflected in the near-term revenue.

Leading Indicators over Lagging Indicators

An understanding of value measures is intrinsically linked to timeliness. Lagging indicators, although not bad, are measures you count over time and indicate performance at that time based on all the activities of the past. It is difficult to identify which of the activities had what impact on these types of measures. The measures themselves often take months of analysis to create, and they are "aged" by the time they are in a readable format. A quarterly financial report is normally representative of data from at least a month ago.

Lagging measures reduce the organization's ability to capture weaker signals, causing you to miss the opportunity to respond to changes:

- You end up measuring milestones or completion of tasks over achieving the outcomes.

- Work becomes fragmented and distributed broadly across the organization losing its intricate alignment and rarely being pieced back together.

- Decisions become difficult to make in the moment because the data takes too long to provide feedback.

- Prioritization calls are difficult because it's too difficult to find a common way to compare diverse pieces of work and customer value is invisible.

- Employees don't have line of sight of the outcome to which their work is supposed to contribute, rendering them unable to explore better ways to achieve it.

Leading indicators are signals to you of a likely future result. The more you study actuals, the better you get at predicting these and the more valuable leading indicators become. Some of the best examples of leading indicators are seen in so called "start-up metrics" or pirate metrics (see Figure 4-1)—Acquisition, Activation, Revenue, Retention, Referral, or "AARRR." Organizations can use these measures to make decisions about growing their business. Perhaps you start by measuring the eyeballs on your site as the leading indicator, and then track the conversion of eyeballs through the pirate-metrics funnel; for example, X% of the total volume of Acquisition converts to Activation, and Y% of those convert to Revenue, and so on. Using this type of leading indicators you can set a strategy to fill more in the top of the funnel, so you end up with more volume at the same conversions, or you can focus in on improving the conversion rate of one or more elements. It can also provide signals of where there may be issues.

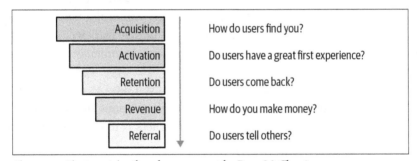

Figure 4-1. Pirate metrics (based on a concept by Dave McClure)

We recently observed the use of leading indicators in an airline company. The company was trying to increase customers booking flights directly through its online channel. However, after many feature releases, search engine optimization, and other marketing efforts, conversion rate and revenue from the online digital channel remained flat. After doing some analytics, the company found out that there were definitely more visitors to the website, more people searching for flights, more people booking flights, and even more people selecting seats. However, 75% of people dropped out of the payment step—much worse than the industry average of 25%. It turned out that as the team added more features to the payment function, they also introduced small defects and delays. Even though the defect rate and delays were not higher than average compared with other user journey segments, somehow customers lost patience (or became frustrated) more easily at this step and dropped out at a faster pace. Minor defects and issues from one team ended up offsetting the great work done by half a dozen other teams. If this were caught earlier by measuring the leading indicators rather than just the revenue, the customer booking success during this period could have increased by 300%!

Pirate metrics, as explained in the preceding sidebar, are a great example of leading indicators, but we need to reiterate the need for them to be linked to customer value measures. The talent you need to build is to use these types of cascading leading measures using the strong link to customer value, used in isolation they are benefit measures and might not reflect value to the customer.

When you focus too much, or exclusively, on revenue and profit measurements, the balance will often tilt toward benefits to the business as opposed to delivering value to customers. What you choose to measure decides what you optimize. Optimizing the benefits to the business in the short term could significantly undermine customer value and long-term health of the business. This is why we are seeing corporate behaviors like "80% of managers willing to cut discretionary spending like R&D, advertising, and maintenance to hit the numbers."[1]

But business benefit is, of course, something you need to watch so that you don't provide customer value at unsustainable cost. Without any constraints, the easiest way to maximize value delivered to customers is to give everything away for free!

In 2014, McDonald's tested a new menu called "Create Your Taste" in a few countries, allowing customers to build their own burger from 30 premium ingredients ordered from in-store kiosks. The strategy outcome was offering a value add to higher-end customers. The company started the rollout to China, Europe, and the US in more than two thousand restaurants in 2015. Over the course of the rollout, it became clear that besides the higher cost to produce the burger

---

1 John Graham, et al., "The Economic Implications of Corporate Financial Reporting" *Journal of Accounting and Economics* (September 15, 2005).

(about twice as much as a Big Mac), store owners also had to invest about $125,000 per restaurant to just install the kiosks, and it slowed down kitchen operations significantly. So although customer value was there, the cost to offer it made it prohibitive. McDonald's decided to hold back on the rollout plan and eventually dropped the "Create Your Taste" menu altogether, replacing it with "Signature Crafted Recipes," high-end options on a predetermined menu.

Finding the right connection between business benefit and customer value is at times very obvious and easy to synchronize; other times there is no obvious connection. In these situations, the ability to find the leading indicators becomes crucial. You need to be able to hypothesize that a change in one measure will eventually lead to a change in the greater measure, and ultimately in business benefits like profit. This hypothesis should be tested and then validated or proven wrong quickly, allowing further hypotheses to be formed and tested. Testing and identifying the appropriate leading indicators early on can help to find the correct approach to deliver customer value and generate more business benefits at the same time. Some of the potential leading indicators in the "Create Your Taste" example could be as follows:

- Percent of customers who are aware of the new menu item in a restaurant

- Percent of customers who stopped by at the kiosk

- Percent of customers who used the kiosk to customize the burger but stopped at the payment step

- Percent of customers who ordered a customized burger and then ordered a regular burger in the following visit:

  — Percent of customers who attributed it to wait time

  — Percent of customers who attributed it to price

Some of these potential leading indicators could be difficult to measure, but digital technology is making it possible and easier to capture these weak signals. Some of them could have helped to discover that "Signature Crafted Recipes" was a better offer than "Create Your Taste" before the high investment was made.

We recognize that this test and learn style comes up regularly through this book. It would be much easier if there were just a set of answers already sitting there, but that's the fast-changing digital world we live in today. It requires smaller bets with clearer measurement and the ability to validate that the connection is true. It takes time and patience to establish an undeniable link from customer value to business benefit, but after you have this, the return on investments is much shorter and far greater.

Financial Measures

It can be very easy to blame the bean counters for all the woes that stop agility. The pressure to "make the numbers" becomes the dominant conversation especially as the end of the financial year approaches.

The impact of these conversations is often that work is slowed or delayed, money is quickly spent to use up budgets, and organizations generally make poor decisions on low-value work for which budget balancing is more important than for high-value work. In the case of a major telecommunications company, we witnessed some common patterns of fiscal behavior:

- Operating expense (OPEX) and capital expense (CAPEX) budgets being decided by different teams with no correlation; in other words, no link between the capital work you want to do and the operational cost of doing it. So you are forever struggling to pay for the staff needed for work you committed to do in business cases.

- Overspending in the first half of the fiscal year, causing budgets to be cut in the middle of the fiscal year. This generally leads to scope pressure on the in-flight work and delays to new work, reducing value delivered for the year.

- The predictable January hiring freeze (first month of the second half of the fiscal year). This causes functional units to feel pressure based on the luck of the draw with outstanding vacancies, not based on the value of the work.

- The Q4 EBITDA target rise. This causes the inevitable scramble and readjustment of goals and priorities for spending

- The end of fiscal year work slowdown due to the need to reduce spending and meet the targets, resulting in the giant hockey stick of work in month one of the following years, which in turn takes you back to the first bullet point.

That said, financial measures are important; they describe the health of the business and in large part are what you are held to account to as an indicator of the business performance. It's just that they are not the only measure and should not be used to prioritize or decide work. The timing of them is usually such that they are too lagging; that is, they occur too long after the work is done to accurately attribute that work to the movement in the financial measures. Financial measures are lagging measures that ultimately should improve as a result of the value you deliver to customers.

Managers and teams need to be clearly aware of the ongoing fiscal measurements to understand the collective fiscal accountability. They should also have a clear understanding that these are constraints that limit some of their options for delivering more value to clients, not targets by which to align everything in order to maximize them. Financial measures should be reviewed periodically to ensure fiscal responsibility.

It should also be clear that financial measurements are largely lagging indicators. The key is to find leading indicators and establish the connection to the financial measurements so that the team can focus on using the former to provide feedback on the day-to-day work.

In reality, you could make this a very powerful and insightful category by making the environment "safe to fail." Finding incentives for transparency and visibility is probably one of the more productive cultural changes a company can go through. This would allow the business to understand the relationship between the outcome desired, money spent, and value delivered along the way.

Take Figure 4-2, which shows money spent versus value delivered. This is what we all should aspire to being able to use as the key communications and reporting construct for the business. At its heart lies the concept that money spent is linear, so you are funding known capacity rather than project by project, and that you can incrementally track value delivered at points in time. The two measurements are percentages, allowing you to compare apples and oranges, and when added together at any point, lead you to a conversation about the value trajectory. It also allows you to roll the graphs up and down; one graph can be the accumulation of percentages of multiple graphs below it, an outcome graph made up of the sum of the work being done to achieve it, right up to a single view across the business.

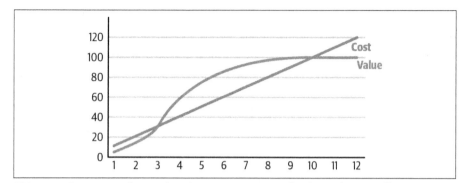

Figure 4-2. Cost versus value graph: using percentages to track value and money allows comparisons across work to make sure you are investing in the most valuable things

If value is tracking below spend, you need to ask whether what you are doing is not having the value impact you expected and whether you should stop or pivot. If it is tracking well above, perhaps you should be looking to add further investment to accelerate and increase the value impact. Or, if as per Figure 4-2 you are starting to see a plateau of the value line, you want to be able to ask whether enough is enough. For example, if you look at the 90/70 coordinates, you want to know whether it is worth spending the last 30% of the money for only a further 10% of the value. Sometimes it is, but the question should at least be explored.

Of course, Agile is a dependency for this kind of view because it is based on the incremental delivery of consumable value through appropriate design slicing. Work needs to be done in small autonomous chunks of value for which relative value percentage can be reasonably predicted and understood. Where many digital-native companies have succeeded is in scaling Agile in ways that allow them to continue to achieve beneficial value with continued spend. Most organizations reach points of diminishing returns as coordination costs overwhelm value beyond a certain point, but digital-native companies can use such measures to realize when it's worth investing in shared self-service tooling, for example.

In this context, meeting commitments is more about providing a safe environment in which you can be transparent enough to track the progress toward a realized outcome, building in a way that allows you to change course when needed. (We refer to this more when we discuss finance constraints in Chapter 8.) Then, with a lightweight governance process in place, you should be able to review and realign customer value delivery and fiscal responsibility every two months or quarterly—certainly more frequently than once or twice a year. It will help mitigate, if not remove, some of the fiscal-year behavior patterns mentioned earlier.

Individual KPIs

The need for a business to introduce measurements to gauge people's performance can make value measurements complicated. Individual KPIs are often associated closely with recognition, financial reward, career progress, power, and status. KPIs need to be designed to measure and reflect the value of an individual's activity isolated from the rest of the team, division, and company. This need to isolate and break out an individual's contribution tends to make the KPIs too granular and sometimes disconnected from team and company goals: deliver more customer value. They also tend to be more designed to measure the person's contribution to the business, not value to the customer. For example, in a global transportation service provider business, there was a clear theoretical understanding of the importance of customer experience because one of the company's four strategic goals was to increase customer satisfaction. But when we looked into the division's team and individual KPIs that were being measured regularly, they were mostly revenue, margin, and efficiency improvement targets. Most of the people talked about value-based, customer-centric outcomes and goals, but it was not being reflected sufficiently in the metrics.

KPIs were invented in a time when the pace was slow and much could be planned and scoped. They measure the success, output, quantity, or quality of an ongoing process or activity. KPIs measure processes or activities already in place.

Google, LinkedIn, Twitter, and a few other companies have been using a simple and adaptive framework—objectives and key results (OKR). OKR is a goal system used to create alignment and engagement around measurable goals. The main difference from the traditional planning process is that OKRs are frequently set, tracked, and reevaluated—usually quarterly. OKR is a simple, fast-cadence process that engages each team's perspective and creativity.

When designing a performance review process and KPIs, you need to shift the focus away from managing performance to fueling performance. Indications are now that individual performance measures are suboptimal when compared to team-based performance measures. Performance comes from shared success, from the ability of people to use their talents, and from alignment to the purpose of the company. Individuals need to be able to see the value in their performance and their work as the relationship to the value they are delivering to customers.

Performance reviews should be designed around a more regular review of a person's ability to help teams achieve their contribution toward the outcome instead of their ability to optimize a fixed set of processes and activities throughout an entire year. If the outcome is achieved, the team and the individuals should succeed; KPIs should not be possible to achieve if the outcome is not. How often do we see bonuses being paid to individuals when the organization has performed poorly, or an individual achieves their target but customers are suffering? All too often there is conflict between doing the right thing by customers and achieving a bonus. People are forced to choose between the right reaction and disadvantaging themselves.

We witnessed an interesting experience of a top performing call center operator. He took a call from a woman claiming to have a great offer from a competitor. She wanted to know if this company could reward her loyalty with a better deal. Without hesitation, the operator replied yes and offered to have someone call her to discuss it further—in four days' time. She abruptly chuffed and hung up. The operator was angry, threw his headset, and stormed off. You see, the operator was paid on sales leads generated, and his performance was measured by average handling time. Even with the ability to help the customer immediately, he would have been penalized for having her on the phone too long and lost his "lead bonus." Sales leads and efficiency are measurements of benefits to the business, not value to customers, and these can put agents into ridiculous situations that hurt the customer, the organization, and the agents' performance.

Individual KPIs are quite possibly the greatest constraint to being able to measure value, especially given their attachment to pay raises or performance ratings. You need to find better ways to measure individual performance and align it better to the goals and purposes of customers so that it doesn't get into the way of doing real meaningful work serving the customers. Based on what we have seen, the best form of performance review is teaching people how to give feedback in the moment to peers, which enables teams to help each other improve as they work rather than at point-in-time reviews. And the best bonus structure is to attach targets to team goals at one level up so that individuals are accountable for the collective impact of the entire team. This tends to make it easier to connect to customer outcomes.

Improvement Measures

Improvement versus achievement is a constant tension that should exist in the organization. Achievement is about whether you are progressing toward the outcomes, whereas improvement metrics inform you as to whether you are getting better at doing that. They make you better.

How much you have done different from how much value you have delivered. In the absence of value measurement, because value is difficult to measure and sometimes nonquantitative, activities or work being done become the replacement measure.

The *Waterfall* software development approach is a classic example of measuring work completed rather than value delivered. It breaks a product cycle into multiple steps: requirements gathering, feature and architecture design, coding and implementation, testing, and, finally, going live. This is a perfect model if there is no ambiguity about the requirements, no change of strategy or market conditions during development, no surprises in technology platforms and integration points, and no difference between production and development environments. We learned a long time ago that this would never actually be the case, and that's partially how the Agile software development methodology was started: addressing Waterfall's lack of flexibility and adaptability.

The other interesting symptom of the Waterfall approach is that projects almost always appear to be on track until they are about to finish. Requirement gathering, design, coding—none of these phases deliver any value to customers because customers simply cannot use the system yet. However, from the work completed perspective, the project team is humming along smoothly, celebrating one milestone after another—neat documents and dashboards are produced and presented perfectly along the way. Alarms generally start to go off in the late stages of coding and testing. Suddenly, instead of 80% finished, only 20% of the features are production ready—if the software is ready to go live at all. Project status turns from green to deep red overnight. The schedule is delayed; the budget is increased. According to an Harvard Business Review analysis (*https://oreil.ly/zani1*), the average project cost overrun was 27%, with one in six projects overrunning cost by 200%, and schedule by almost 70%.

Using classic Agile and Lean continuous-improvement thought patterns—understanding current state, setting target states, and iterating toward them—is a foundational mindset for digital transformation. It supports the capture of weaker signals, helps you to identify constraints much earlier, encourages test and learn activities, and breeds experimental mindsets.

Improvement metrics have the added benefit of being more translatable to the traditional quantitative measures those who are not familiar with this way of working would be used to, while still giving you qualitative insights.

Some useful examples of improvement metrics include:

Quality

Defect reduction, automated test coverage, reduction in calls, work stopped because you learned new information.

Productivity

Cumulative flow diagrams for identifying areas for improvement in wait time or handoffs, the amount of work that needs to leave a team to be completed, capabilities you have versus those you need.

Throughput

The amount of value delivered in a period; the time it takes to validate ideas.

Predictability

Much like the cone of uncertainty, you should see predictability increase with time whether that be in capacity planning, skills planning, financial planning, or the amount of ideas you are able to exploit.

Financials

Money spent versus value delivered, cost per unit of value, portfolio balance between exploring and sustaining the business, return on investment (ROI) in outcomes, the impact each piece of work delivers against the customer value outcome.

Agile software delivery and continuous delivery (CD) methodologies emphasize the importance of taking a thin slice of the work, finishing it end to end, and delivering value before moving on to the next thin slice. That is also the root of the thin-slice approach we are advocating in the digital transformation journey (see Chapter 3). Using such an iterative, incremental approach creates the foundation and possibility of measuring end-to-end value instead of activities and work completed. But it does not guarantee that. In fact, we have seen too many Agile software projects measured and reported on using activities done and work completed in a similar, if not exactly the same way, as Waterfall projects.

There seems to be a stronger institutional desire to keep track of how much work is done and how much effort is put in. This is where we have seen some gaming behaviors. Because you tie it to the bidding war for budget purposes, you end up with fictional commitments and spend a large part of the time managing the message to demonstrate progress or justify the lack of progress toward them.

Improvement measures are a key muscle that organizations need to build in order to optimize for customer value and remove the constraints to its delivery. They tell you whether your digital transformation is driving the intended change and improvements. In Chapter 12, we discuss the importance of building a continuous learning and continuous improvement culture. Recognizing and implementing improvement metrics will help to reinforce that culture.

Putting It All Together

When the lights go out across the city, the power companies are at their best because the measure is clear to everyone: get the lights back on. A clear measure and a clear purpose make cross-functional teams bound into action. Talent and skills come to the fore, irrespective of roles and individual KPIs, and everyone just gets it done.

Random or unrelated measures lead to random and unaligned work. The focus becomes being busy instead of effective, complete instead of valuable. The key is to provide a set of measures that helps teams make in-the-moment decisions to ensure they do work that helps achieve the outcome, not just complete their work or become better at delivering the outcome. A useful measure aligns directly to outcome achievement—both the effectiveness and efficiency aspects. It is represented by value to the customer and is leading enough that it can be measured in a timely fashion to know that the work is achieving its intent.

The measurements should be leading indicators on customers getting the value they want. There could be many potential leading indicators—some stronger, some weaker—to consider. You need to make sure that you test the connection with business benefit indicators (often lagging), and find the ones that can link them together. You also need to be aware that work completed is not equivalent to value delivered. There is a lot to learn from Agile software development methodology in terms of both the ability to measure value delivered and the environment to encourage visibility and transparency to mitigate gaming behavior.

Achieving your outcomes and improving how you achieve them should not be mutually exclusive. Improvement measures will complement achievement measures as well as reinforce the continuous improvement culture. In addition, you need to be aware of the impact of personal KPIs and, if possible, redesign them to be more team based, customer focused, and adjustable through regular reviews.

Here is our final thought on measure: a great way to recognize whether a measure is correct is to apply the reverse and see if it holds true, much like the scientific method. So if you didn't do it, would the measure still hold? If you did nothing, could the measure still change? If you did the opposite, would the measure reduce? These are all helpful checkpoints to ensure you are applying a suitable measure.

Key Points

Following are the key points that we hope you take away from this chapter as well as two actions for you to take to begin implementing what we've discussed:

- Optimize your business to measures of customer value.

- Many traditional measures, in the current way they are applied, undermines teams' ability to deliver customer value.

- The importance of applying the appropriate type of measures for the decision being made.

Here are two actions to take:

- Create measures to tell you what work to do and whether you are improving: Redesign your organization's current measures into their categories of "intent" and by the leading/lagging nature of them, separating them from the measures that determine what work to do.

- Learn how to measure your return on value delivered: Practice the cost versus value delivered graphs by trying to build some for your current key programs.

Aligning Work to Measures

Aligning work is perhaps both the most logical and the most difficult step in a digital transformation. You now have your outcomes described in terms of customer value; you've defined the measures to ensure you are achieving the outcome; and you understand the importance of using a thin slice as the starting point. In this chapter, we describe the next step in which you *cascade the measure into the work* so that all of the work you do is for the improvement of the measure. We then look at how to adapt current work in-flight into this way of thinking so that you can prioritize work across your entire portfolio. The flow can be difficult to get your head around at the beginning, especially when surrounded by organizational constraints (we deal with those in Part II), but after you do, it becomes very simple and logical.

John Seddon perhaps explained this mental shift best when he described his Systems Thinking approach ofpurpose/measure/method as the alternative to the more traditional thinking of purpose/method/measure, where measures are the afterthought and largely describe completion rather than outcome achievement.[1] This way you are designing the work to succeed. It's almost cheating!

So often today we see the opposite; most work is already in flight inside of functional units when the organizational level strategy is written. So you either need to restructure to get work done or find ways to squeeze it into the strategy "buckets" as a way of continuing to fund functional activity. Both options result in suboptimal distribution of work across the current functional boundaries

---

1 John Seddon, *Freedom from Command and Control: Rethinking Management for Lean Service* (Productivity Press, 2005).

ending up in unaligned activity. Figure 5-1 illustrates a Sankey diagram of work alignment, or lack thereof.

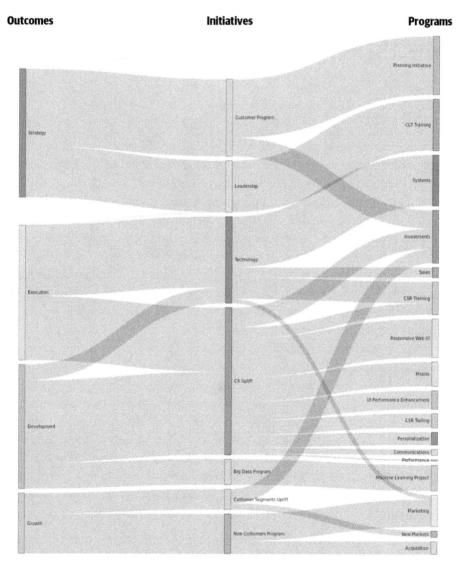

Figure 5-1. A Sankey diagram showing how work can become disconnected from strategy

On the left you can see how the work forms in line with the strategy and tries to line up with the focus areas of the organization. At this stage the leaders would feel comfortable and content that the work adheres to their strategy, and they would likely turn away and leave the rest to middle managers to execute. But you can see what happens next to the right where the work gets carved up along functional lines and loses connection to the strategy.

This "new way of working" begins with how to break the outcome down into the smaller components done by smaller teams while still maintaining connections and the ability to coordinate. For perspective, the last two major corporations we worked with had around 50,000 employees, and they began with around 20 to 25 outcomes in total, so we are talking about the large strategic outcomes. You want to take these and continue to chunk them down into smaller and smaller chunks, level by level, measure by measure until you reach as size suitable for a single team to deliver. This process of breaking down an outcome is what we call *cascades*.

Cascade Approach

Cascades provide a consistent way to describe the work and the method of breaking the work into smaller autonomous pieces while keeping everything interconnected. By following cascades, your organization has far greater visibility of the interconnectedness of your portfolio and the impact that individual pieces of work have toward outcome completion. Cascades allow you to manage smaller pieces of work and commit a smaller amount of time, people, and money upfront. In turn, this allows you to stop work that is not contributing the way you expected and scale up work that moves the needle the most.

Think about the following scenario: you decide that you want to improve your health. It's a little subjective, but a key indicator could be "number of days feeling well and energetic per month." Based on your lifestyle and habits, you could decide that improving the following few areas could improve the number of days feeling well and energetic and achieve better health outcomes: exercise more, sleep more, drink less alcohol. They are all measurable by themselves and are relatively independent areas to work on.

Next, take "drink less alcohol" as one step you decide to take, with the measure of number of drinks per week you can come up with a few initiatives that can help to achieve that. The first initiative is to go out less often, because you tend to drink more in a social environment due to social pressure. If you set a limit per week, it would be easy to measure. The second initiative is to alternate alcoholic drinks with water. Not only should this help pacing yourself better, it could also mask the fact of less drinking in a social environment. The measure for that would be the number of alcoholic drinks per meal. The third initiative is to move the alcohol at home to the higher shelves. Making alcohol more difficult to access could help to reduce the number of drinks at home. The measure would be alcoholic drinks per week at home.

As you can tell, each of the initiatives is a smaller chunk of work, relatively self-contained, and can be achieved separately. At the initiative level, they all have their own measures so that you will quickly know whether the action will improve the measure—hence whether you should continue to do that or switch to a different initiative. Maybe alternating drinks with water is easier said than done; maybe you should try a different approach: keeping the water glass closer to you and the wine glass further away so that you will reach out to the water glass more often. Maybe putting alcohol on high shelves has no impact on the result of number of drinks per week at home. Unless you are committed enough to keep all alcohol out of your home, you should give up on the attempt of making access more difficult at home.

Although they are all done separately and are self-contained work and actions, the results should roll up and contribute to the overall measurement: less drinks consumed per week. Combining this with the improvement from the other two bets—sleep more and exercise more—you should be able to see improvement on the overall measure, which is the number of days feeling well and energetic per month. Ultimately, this should help you to achieve the goal to improve your health.

Many of these are hypotheses to start with. Although they are all good general advice, you don't know whether they will be guaranteed to help move the needle on days you feel well and energetic. These are smaller experiments that you can do and learn from the results quickly to see what works for you and what doesn't. You can easily track the progress of each initiative and their impact on the overall goal. Depending on the progress and impact, you can decide to double down or stop initiatives, come up with new initiatives, or decide to completely give up on one and focus on others—maybe it turns out that drinking is not the real issue for you, eating healthy might be the one. This approach gives you the visibility and flexibility to explore the unknown and maximize the value of the work.

This is not a new concept, cascades can be found in many flavors such as a lean value tree like goal, bet, initiative, or other work breakdown language. There are other similar simple frameworks in use:

- Objectives, themes, hypothesis

- Outcomes, initiatives, minimum viable products (MVP)

- Boulders, rocks, pebbles

- Feature, epic, story

- Level 1, level 2, level 3

The intent is the same: to take a piece of work and break it into smaller, more manageable chunks. A well-constructed cascade begins with an organizational-level outcome (a thin slice) and its measure. It then uses the measure to design work that will move the needle. This next level of work repeats a similar process: for each outcome a measure is created and used to design the work of the level below. This flow of work, measure, work, measure, and so on is how the interconnectedness becomes so powerful. Each level is clearly aligned to achieving the measure of the one above and the work born from the level above.

It also brings simplicity to measurement because all of the work is associated with obvious measures and data sources. It is easy to track the progress of measures from one level of work and add up to progress against the achievement of the level above, satisfying the more traditional needs of progress metrics as well as outcome achievement. In Chapter 4, we introduced the "cost versus value delivered" graph. The cascade makes it easier to plot value.

The further down the cascade you go, the smaller the work becomes and the more leading the measures need to be. The number of times you reach out and grab the wine glass during a meal is probably a more telling and leading indicator than the end result of overall alcohol consumption per meal.

In the earlier homes-versus-mortgages example in Chapter 2, a cascade of outcomes should remain focused on helping customers to achieve homeownership instead of just selling more mortgages. The home ownership outcome also gives more freedom for teams to innovate by taking advantage of emerging technology to come up with new solutions and remove friction in how value is delivered. It keeps everyone aligned and focused on how their work moves the organization toward the outcome.

Let's look at a few examples.

CASCADE APPROACHES IN ACTION

A bank has an outcome to provide the most compelling home lending experience to customers. You can argue the quality of the outcome, but let's flow with it and see how it comes together:

- The first step is to determine the measure. In this case, the measure must be linked to the word "compelling"—that is to say, you are achieving the outcome when you know you are being compelling to customers. So you would need to do some work around what customers would find compelling. Through interviews, surveys, focus groups, and other marketing techniques, you learn that the time it takes to apply online for a home line affects the "compelling" measure. You can check that it is a good measure by considering the opposite, as discussed in Chapter 4. If you increase the time it takes to apply online, would it be less compelling? Yes, it would be. Now you have the first hypothesis in the first level of the cascade: provide a more compelling experience through a reduction in time to apply online.

- You then design work that you believe will reduce that time. This backlog of work is made up of opportunities with varying degrees of certainty as to whether they will save time. Focusing on the ones with the greatest likelihood, you have the second level of the cascade. These are at a project level of altitude for comparison, each has a subset of the "time" measure as their leading indicator.

- Last, a team uses Agile principles and practices to break this work into small chunks of autonomous work that it can complete in its sprints or iterations to build solutions aimed at reducing the online application time. Each of these project-level work streams use even more leading, hypothesis-type indicators following the format, "If you do X then time to apply will reduce."

It's important to continue validating and evaluating the overall goal—making the home lending experience compelling to customers. At this level, reducing online application time is not the end itself, it's the means to achieve the overall goal, and it's also a hypothesis. If you are not seeing customer feedback improving or you start to see diminishing returns, it would be time to evaluate further investment on this initiative.

Here is another example: an organization tries to help women investors to be more engaged as an outcome. Two specific measures here are the count of new women investor accounts and the total revenue from women investors:

- In your first level of the cascade, you can design work that you believe will increase new women investor accounts or increase investment from existing women investors. You then discover through user research that confidence in investing and the terms of investing are a key to women investing.

- You can now use education as the next level of the cascade and a leading indicator. Thus, the hypothesis becomes, "Education in these areas will increase the confidence women have in terms of investing, and in turn lead to the increase in the number of women investing."

- The next level down is now easily identified as work that will increase education, and the leading measure is things that indicate consumption of these education materials is happening. This cascade results in creating a landing page specifically aimed at women investors; a range of features are piloted and tested on the site. Each feature is measured by the amount of time that a user spent on the site or certain downloads they do.

The work looks like a zig-zag from work to measure to work through to more leading measures. At this point, it is worth thinking about how to represent this within the organization to provide a mental model that people can relate to and that reflects a real-life example within your organization. Don't get hung up on headings and perfecting a cascade, because varying groups with the organization might need varied levels of a cascade—for some, three levels will get to an autonomous piece of work small enough to fit one team; for others this might be five levels. In fact, each outcome can have different levels, so it's important not to standardize on the layers and headings. Otherwise, it will very likely lead to more layers than necessary for everyone due to the many definitions groups will put on their work (epics, themes, features, stories, programs, projects, initiatives, outcomes, and so on). Going down the predefined path might feel better because it is more structured and implementable—and perhaps more teachable in a playbook—but it is the thinking that is important, not the headings.

The other important thing to keep in mind is to maintain a lean backlog. We all have great ideas and more often than not backlogs can become dumping grounds for all "good ideas." You must put the backlog on a diet. Being vigilant about understanding the value your objectives will create is one way to weed out ideas that sound cool but are simply not valuable.

The cascade approach will help to break the thin slice into smaller autonomous pieces of work that can be performed by a team. When a piece of work is small enough and autonomous enough, you can now build an aligned team to work on it with the skill sets required, which could come from different functional departments in the current enterprise structure.

Cross-Functional Teams

An important principle to call out here is the concept of *cross-functional teams*. A cross-functional team consists of people with different functional expertise assigned to a specific task. That's not how companies work most of the time. Tasks and measurements are divided into components along the lines of function and accomplished by functional teams. Functional teams are optimized to bring skills and outcomes specific to a function and that function's goals. They can include "the developers," "the project managers," "the retail team," and "the digital team." The milestones and the handovers are designed to accommodate the functional divide in the organization. But the value stream of your organization requires input from all of these functions.

The rapid test-and-learn cycle cannot work with too many handovers. If you want to learn, for example, what kind of educational materials will interest women investors, you will need to pick different content, present it in different formats and sequences, launch content into your live platforms, observe how users interact with it, make changes, and rinse and repeat. These cycles should span the range of days or even hours—not weeks or months. The investment expert, marketing expert, product manager, UX designer, and technologist need to work in the same room, around the same table to quickly move through the various tasks with minimum friction and little handover.

Cross-functional teams tend to be more innovative than traditionally structured teams. Much research has shown that a group of people with different backgrounds and skill sets generates a wider range of original and useful ideas than otherwise. People with different formal training and skill sets often look at a problem in different ways. Having people with multiple skill sets on the same team working together full time—not just a one-hour brainstorming session—can often lead to innovation in unexpected ways. Group thinking—an irrational decision-making behavior driven by conformity—becomes less likely in a cross-functional team.

Cross-functional teams are well aligned given the clear goal and measure for success. Working together closely also gives them the opportunity to learn about the work, priority, and motivations of others in the organization. It helps them to understand the bigger picture and get a feel for how their own efforts affect everyone else. Conflicts and disagreements tend to be more around problem solving, not the results of preference or bias on approach based on formal training. Given the clarity of the goal and the measures, a team is more motivated to resolve the conflict through acting and testing the results than debating the academic merits of an approach.

These teams take many forms, but they are most often set up as working groups that are designed to make decisions at a lower level than is customary in a given company. They can be either a company's primary form of organizational structure, or they can exist in addition to the company's main hierarchical structure.

Even with the overwhelming evidence of benefits, building cross-functional teams is still difficult in reality. For most businesses, the existing organizational structure is built around functions—sales, marketing, engineering, service, finance, HR, and so on. Further down, reporting structure within functions is built around skill sets. Functional heads have their own targets, budgets, and priorities. Employees have their own reporting line and KPIs. Dealing with these organizational constraints takes different types of effort and potentially different routes in different organizations. We discuss this in more detail in Chapter 7.

RETROFIT CURRENT WORK

Although a cascade is well and good for starting new work, what about all of the work that is already in flight? Unfortunately, this is usually the starting point of a digital transformation journey. With all of the outcomes defined in customer value and outcome, and first thin slice picked, you are ready to cascade it down to smaller, manageable, measurable chunks of work, only to find that there is already a lot of ongoing work that is supposed to achieve similar results, overlaps, or has dependencies with the cascaded backlog. Left unchecked you will be swamped in this current work and unable to act on the changes that you have identified need to happen.

It is unlikely that this current work was born from a customer outcome; it's more likely what your organization thinks or wants is what customers too want. So it will jar against what you now know you need to do. This work will have a history tied to one of the following:

- The organizational structure and budgets

- Functional lines of business with specialized skills that need to be kept busy

- Sunk cost of long-standing programs of work that are adding little value and have lost the original intent, but can't be stopped because no capitalization can occur until they are finished

- Pet projects of influential parties

Additionally, remnants of an outcome will be inconsistently dispersed across the organization, rarely able to be tied back together, making it impossible to measure each component's contribution to the outcomes. Handoffs between teams increase due to interdependencies from work being broken up by functions. Wait times increase as teams all work off different backlogs that are prioritized to maximize the local output but might not be aligned to the end-to-end output across the business. The focus is on finishing the work, not on achieving the customer outcome. Work is just decided on, funded, and done, and then everyone moves on to the next thing.

So if you ignore it, it will get in the way as it continues to consume a lot of time and money and people that you really need to be working in the new way. You can choose to include it all but the same cycle happens: Everyone will be tied up in the in-flight, and, worse, you are not starting the new work you want to. So you need to find balance, understand the outcomes and the measure, and then identify the current work that moves that measure and bring the work into the new way of working.

The critical thing is not to build your cascade to reflect the work you already have; use a retrofit technique to ensure that you don't add a bias for the current work into your flow. One example is to come up with criteria that enable the current work to become a part of the cascaded work, a baseline for how the current work must look in order to "move across." We suggest using these four questions:

- Is the work described in customer terms?
- Does it have a leading customer value measure?
- Is it broken down into its smallest possible autonomous chunk?
- Does the outcome owner agree that it will progress their outcome needle?

This should not be just a grooming process; it can be a pruning process as well. Some existing in-flight work could be designed to achieve similar goals and initiatives based on someone's great ideas. But after asking these four questions, it might become clear that it's going to deliver little value to achieve the real customer outcome, or it's a large investment that cannot be tested early. This would be an opportunity to pause or stop the work to free up people and resources to focus on the better-aligned work that can deliver more value or to break down the large programs into smaller, aligned pieces of value.

Besides getting the outcome and measure definition clear, you also need to pay attention to the team and process when "moving across" in-flight work to the cascaded backlog. If the digital transformation hasn't been driving across the broad organization at scale, it's possible that the work is being done by siloed functional teams with handovers, dependencies, and other frictions in place. This is also an opportunity to develop the team structure to be more cross-functional and to adopt a more iterative process like Agile software development methodology. It shouldn't be just a lift-and-shift—it's time to reshape the work.

During our interview with a senior vice president, they shared their experience of changing the organization to align work to customer outcomes:

As the leader of the transformation, you need to push, but not so hard that people tune you out.

In this role you'll need to relentlessly remind teams and leaders to connect the work to a customer outcome—like a toddler, constantly questioning "why" teams are doing pieces of work, what will the customer get/feel as a result of that work, and how quickly can we get something in front of the customer to learn if it delivers that value.

This can be really annoying to people—in our organization we had teams buried under piles of important and prioritized work, so they weren't working on meaningless items, but we couldn't "find" the customer in the work—we worked hard to identify a small number of high-level customer outcomes and then showed how the work could tie to those outcomes (even backend/API work), but this large step turned out to be too big of a step—not only did this push against existing organizational boundaries (hello, Conway's Law), it also had some legitimate flaws that needed to be worked out.

As the leader of the transformation, you need to figure out how to make the principle of aligning work to customer outcomes "stick" at all levels of the organization, and then experiment with incremental ways to make this resonate bit by bit (no different than the small, incremental releases you're asking the org to deliver). P.S.: It turns out just repeatedly saying that the work has to realign to a customer outcome doesn't make it happen!

Sometimes, there is an expensive replatforming or big package implementation program in-flight. It could be the migration to a new core banking system, a new airline reservation system, or a new CRM system. These are typically multi-year programs with a predefined road map and milestones for feature and function availability. These kinds of basic systems touch many customer outcomes and goals that you might pick to work on. The cascaded tasks will inevitably have dependencies on these large programs.

There is no easy way to get around this, because there is generally a large amount of sunk cost and institutional commitment on the road map. The not-so-bad news is that modern versions of these large software packages have begun to adopt the cloud-based, iterative, and continuous delivery approach in their roll-out plan rather than the traditional Big-Bang approach. It's possible to influence the package implementation program to deliver more frequently, with adjustable road map and priorities. In that case, it's more important to involve some of the big package implementation people into the cross-functional teams, part time or as shared resource across teams, to ensure that communication, alignment, and context sharing can help to reduce friction as much as possible.

A key point here is to balance cascading to optimize value delivery with effective approaches to architecture quality and sustainability. Someone always needs to maintain ownership and responsibility of architecture components as teams make changes to deliver value.

Prioritization and Governance

Given that you really don't have all the answers at the beginning, the second level and third level of the cascade are mainly hypotheses. Picking which initiatives to start with is not strictly scientific. The customer outcome definition and measure of success at the level up is the best point to begin prioritizing the work in the next level down. You want to pick the one(s) that has the best chance of moving the measure of success. Is "going out less" going to be more effective than "putting alcohol on a higher shelf at home" to reduce one's drinking? Perhaps. But the former might be more difficult if you want to go out and socialize with family and friends. Doing that is going to take away a lot of pleasure in life: a big "cost."

Even though there are a plethora of techniques that you can use, it's important that you choose the one for your organization that creates the most transparent, nonadversarial, and flexible result possible. Perhaps the critical component of a good prioritization method is that the decision is not long lived. Today's annual cycles put too many unrealistic expectations on people to predict the future; the impact of being wrong is too great because they stand for too long and struggle to support "refactoring" decisions as more knowledge is gained. Having a method that encourages constant review and reflection means that we can easily add new items or move resources to the work that is generating the most value.

The primary component of good prioritization is *the use of data over opinion* when analyzing options, this will also help speed up the decision process. When things are undeniable and evidence-based, the question changes from "what" to "how" and the trade-offs that are needed.

Other core components include the following:

- Creating open conversations about customer value and investing in the things that move the needle on the outcomes. This does not mean not investing in infrastructure elements or noncustomer value items; it just means doing this consciously and transparently.

- Providing an accurate perspective of each piece of work from which everyone can contribute to the decision on what is the most important to begin first. Having transparency and safety for honest conversation is critical to eliminating the gaming and politics that so often impede getting to the best result for the entire organization and the customer.

- Allowing the ability to change your mind, and therefore the investment, whenever you learn new information.

- Creating consistency in who is contributing to the decision making. This allows for context to be shared and maintained longer term, delegating the decisions or swapping who is involved dilutes the previous conversations and decisions that led to that point. Making sure the right people are involved from the beginning and minimizing changes to this group will provide a better-quality result as they learn together and get a greater understanding of the whole of organization perspective.

It is not easy to make the shift to using these core components. First, you will need the work sizes to be smaller so that your decisions are smaller and can be changed often with minimal impacts. Next, be prepared to get it wrong and have to adapt as you go.

CASE STUDY: PRIORITIZATION IN ACTION

Looking back on one of our more recent engagements with a client, we recognized several pivots in the way work was prioritized as we gained a better understanding of what would work for the individuals involved and the organization itself. By keeping an eye on the backlog order, we were able to reflect on where we had got to and how comfortable we were that the right result was being achieved.

The process began with the very classic steps of functional leaders putting forward an ask, the executive team agreeing to an annual spend, and the spend being proportioned back to the functional leads who were then held to account for what they had bid. In the end, it resulted in very little value reaching the customers, very little being finished, and too much in flight at once. Therefore key resources were never available for the important work. Work that crossed function boundaries came with cross charging, and each time it happened, the receiving team would add its own priority to the work. A single outcome could be broken up and spread across the organization with each piece being prioritized by the function that received it. It was very difficult to bring all of the pieces back together.

Our first radical attempt to simplify this process was a simple handout of 10 green dots to the leadership group. We visualized all of the work on a wall and allowed them to place their dots on the work they felt was important. After some debate, a result was achieved; however, afterward, everyone went back and continued to work on the same things, and a lot of the work that received green dots remained unstarted because it was too difficult to stop the in-flight work. It was easier to keep doing what teams were already doing, especially when it was the work that they wanted to do anyway. It was also a very adversarial process, argumentative and unpleasant for participants.

The breakthrough came during an off-site in which we combined a number of techniques to power through prioritizing 80 large programs of work within about four hours:

It began with the concept of "agile poker," in which each participant had a deck of Fibonacci cards of ?,1,2,3,5,8. The CEO was also given a 13, which she was allowed to play only once. We then added some of the concepts of Weighted Shortest Job First (see Figure 5-2), which gives the owner of the work a few minutes to describe the work and its value to customers. Then we counted to three, and on three everyone raised a card. If there was a great discrepancy between cards, those two were given a short time to explain their position. Finally, we recounted the cards and recorded the mid-majority number.

We repeated the process for the elements of cost of delay (does time change the value) and risk/opportunity. We later added the element of job size or complexity. The group was in great spirits and had a lot of fun; everyone gained valuable knowledge of one another's work and was able to more holistically evaluate the priority of work.

The safety factors were also important: we added a regular cadence in which we could come back together and reassess previous scores based on changing market conditions or add a new item to be evaluated against the current backlog. We also did not fixate on the weighted score; after the backlog was visualized in order, we asked a simple question: "How does that feel?" Then we gave the participants the opportunity to physically swap items around a bit until everyone felt comfortable that the proper order had been achieved, for now.

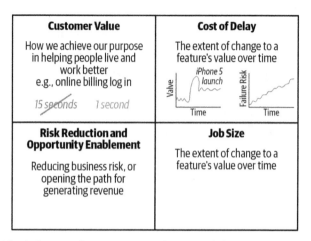

Customer Value	Cost of Delay
How we achieve our purpose in helping people live and work better e.g., online billing log in *15 seconds 1 second*	The extent of change to a feature's value over time
Risk Reduction and Opportunity Enablement Reducing business risk, or opening the path for generating revenue	**Job Size** The extent of change to a feature's value over time

Figure 5-2. Weighted Shortest Job First is not a tool to give a definitive answer, but a way to make conscious decisions

One of the great moments of the session was when one of the leaders became tongue-tied while trying to explain the customer value for a piece of work and had to admit, "Actually there is none." This funny moment led to a valuable conversation about why the work was still critical. Customer value or not should not be good versus bad, just a conscious decision. The key win was to give everyone involved a broader perspective in a safe environment in which everyone could be transparent about the work in progress and the work they wanted to do, and as a team, they could then make the best call for the business. This is just one example of a client journey, but to be honest, the more mature the organization becomes with transparency, visibility, and its use of data, the fewer issues you will have with prioritization.

PIVOTING TO A SIMPLER PRIORITIZATION MODEL

There is a transition point at which the need for these formal prioritization processes are replaced by a simpler identification of value, and everyone begins working on the next most valuable thing. This would mean functional boundaries need to be ignored, and the use of data as a pointer to measurement and a culture of experimentation need to be refined. Most important, the organization would be creating more regular reflection moments at which you could evaluate whether the work was achieving what you expected, and you could decide when enough is enough, as we described in Chapter 4.

The truth is that an ROI calculation's margin of error in the fast-changing digital world is going to be so big that anything after a T-shirt-sized guess is not going to be much more valuable. There is also no need to understand the exact impact. You need only know the relative potential impact between the bets and initiatives.

It needs to be an informed, educated guess. The best way to conduct the prioritization is to make sure that you have enough knowledge in the room in most of the critical areas—customer behavior and expectations, market, product, technology, and finance—and that this knowledge is evenly used in the process without one area overwhelming the rest.

The prioritization process shouldn't take too much effort because you will be doing this a lot more frequently than in the traditional process. As work progresses, end-to-end solutions will be tested and validated as early as possible in real customer environments, and new information will become available on the value delivered to the customer and key measurements as well as the effort required to build and deliver the solution. You will frequently reevaluate the bets and initiatives based on the new information. If the process involves too much effort, it won't be as Agile as the work requires it to be.

There are almost always more ideas than you have capacity for, more experiments than you have time for, and more initiatives than you have funding for. Prioritization must be ruthlessly focused on keeping fewer streams of work in progress and maintaining a lean backlog. Sometimes, valuable ideas and initiatives grow from unexpected places or adjacent work streams.

PRIORITIZING AT EACH CASCADE LEVEL

You should take similar prioritization approaches at each level of the cascade, and all levels need to be addressed on an ongoing basis, although at different frequencies. The first-level work needs to be done as frequently as possible. Most Agile delivery teams work on weekly or biweekly iterations or sprints. Every two weeks could be a good time to review the results and progress of the teams under one bet to ensure that proper adjustment of prioritization as well as work direction, team size, and resources allocation can happen as early as possible if not in real time. When it gets rolled up into the next higher cascade level, a series of bets needs to be reviewed similarly by a steering group looking after the outcome that consists of these bets at a slower frequency—perhaps every month or every six weeks. Similarly, in the next level up, where multiple outcomes are reviewed, the frequency becomes bimonthly or quarterly.

There are often cases for which a stream of work makes good progress and delivers a lot of value early on, but begins to provide diminishing returns as the work progresses because the needle of measure begins to move more slowly after the highest-impact work is completed. A more frequent, lightweight prioritization and governance model can help to catch these situations to redirect the team to the next initiative on a different stream of work, or to reallocate people and resources to other high priorities.

This is the basic framework of a lightweight governance model to manage the prioritization, work direction, and resource allocation. It's critical to rely on data to make decisions as much as possible to counter sunk cost fallacy, availability heuristic, and other cognitive biases. We discuss how to better use data to make decisions in Chapter 9.

Putting It All Together

Here is the summary of key steps in the cascade model:

- Break the customer outcome goal down to the second, third, or fourth levels of pieces of work and the success measures associated with them. Each piece of interrelated work can remain close to one another, each break down is autonomous, measures are independent.

- Build cross-functional teams around the work identified and adopt Agile and other iterative and continuous delivery methods at the team level.

- Examine the in-flight work with fresh eyes to see whether the intent of any of it matches the work that you have just identified. If yes, apply the four questions to bring the current work into the new way of working.

- Adopt a lightweight prioritization and governance model to make sure that all of the work, new or in-flight, is reviewed regularly so that resources and capacity are optimized for work streams with most value delivery.

Cascading your work provides a clear line of sight to the outcome for teams doing the work. It can help to identify the leading indicators for real-time decision making and faster feedback on our progress toward the outcome.

It is the cascading and interrelated breaking down of the work that will simplify measurement, work dependencies, and team composition. In Part II, we examine some of the challenges you will experience when adopting cascades, aligning the rest of the organization to the work that comes out of this model needs careful consideration.

Before that, though, we can look at best practices for making things visible and transparent in the organization so that decisions become more obvious and the associated mental models create an impetus for change.

Key Points

Following are the key points that we hope you take away from this chapter as well as two actions for you to take to begin implementing the ideas we've discussed:

- Setting outcomes in customer terms as the company level organizing construct helps those doing the work clearly see why they are doing the work. A cascade model is a great way to remove friction and ensure that all work is aligned and focused on achieving the intended outcome, not just completion.

- Creating a mental model of the cascade and how the new way of working keeps the focus on achieving the outcome. You can then assess the current work in flight to see where it fits into your current strategy.

- Prioritization of work needs to become more lightweight, more frequently reviewed, and more led by data.

Here are two actions to take:

- Create your backlog: Cascade your measures to decide the work to achieve your outcome, build and visualize a mental model of this cascade from your strategy to "the work."

- Realign current work to the backlog: Assess work in progress to see which of these fit the new way of working and will help achieve the outcomes. Assign those aligned to your first thin slice into that team, along with those working on it.

6

Visibility and Transparency

When we talk about visibility and transparency, we do not mean reporting and governing, although these can be drawn from it. We are talking about the use of physical visual cues and big visible charts that bind teams together around a common cause. We call them *information radiators*.

Imagine that you have the outcome defined in terms of customer value; the work is cascaded, teams are formed, and success measures are defined. Everyone is humming along to get work done, and a proper lightweight governance model is in place to facilitate the test-and-learn cycle. Now more than ever, at this pace, constant communication and information sharing are critical to keeping the leaders and teams aligned and focused, both in terms of the transformation you are going through and the outcomes you want to achieve for customers.

Of course, in the digital world, everything can be displayed on computer screens with spreadsheets, reporting tools, and all the charts and diagrams coming along with them. However, PowerPoint presentations and digital diagrams don't have the impact of physical environments when it comes to changing people's behavior. Visual cues have strong roots in empirical psychology research and in practical case studies and are frequently used in UX design to focus people's attention on what matters. There is no right or wrong way to create them; whatever gives you the insight you need is the way to go, so it means getting creative and using trial and error to find what works for you.

In this chapter we introduce some of the concepts that will help you set up a physical environment in which you can see where to focus your attention, where you need to take action, and, even more so, where "everyone" can see what is happening, and how they can lean in and help. Most important, this is a critical technique to facilitate communication and reinforce the mental model change by helping to achieve the following two main effects:

- Create a safe environment in which success is more about the work itself than about the person.

- Allow leaders and teams to spot the trends earlier and make the correct decisions in real time.

Creating visibility through physical environments and sharing them across teams will result in a higher level of transparency.

Visual Systems

A *visual system* has a tight relationship with the thin-slice approach discussed earlier, bringing visibility across the entire cascade, providing the journey map of the transformation as well as the work. It is the communications vehicle answering critical questions such as these:

- Are we achieving the outcome?
- Are we improving?
- How much value are we delivering?
- Are we aligned?
- How much are we spending to deliver that value?
- Are we being fiscally responsible?
- Do we have the proper skills to do the work we need to do?
- What issues are there and where do we need to lean in?

It uses common visual elements and indicators that make it easy to roll information up and down the system keeping everyone informed and allowing decisions to be made closest to where the knowledge is and where the work is being done.

It's ironic that information abundance in the Digital Age is sometimes better at hiding real insights than revealing them; it's easy to hide behind a computer screen with myriad dancing graphs and charts. But with limited real estate and physical intimacy, people need to interact with one another more directly and transparently. But transparency is also dangerous. By itself, it does not automatically create safety. It could very well be the opposite, as people feel safer behind a veil with less exposure. Making progress, outcomes, and measures of success more visible and shared more broadly could easily make some people uncomfortable, at least initially. In a recent example of creating transparency in a physical space detailing money allocation and progress made, we saw one program manager become very aggressive because they had not had time to "prepare my boss" and manage the message so that the boss could explain the reasons why it was the case to their peers.

It's the leader's job to be a role model in creating a safe environment. Here are a few strategies for doing so:

- Focus on the work rather than the individual or team.
- Share your own decision-making process and criteria.
- Be vulnerable and not overly defensive.

The transparency you create about what is happening and the impact it has is a massive cultural element that will ultimately depersonalize the changes you need to make, making business decisions more obvious as well as less about the person and more about the work. It helps to eliminate biases and politics, giving your organization the best chance to be able to make the more difficult and more courageous course-setting decisions and bringing everyone along the journey together.

Visibility and transparency are also critical building blocks to empower teams. Equipped with the strategic alignment, broad context, and data from other work streams, individual teams will have more confidence in making the correct logical decisions in real time without having to escalate to their managers or supervisors. Besides their experience, information and context are the main advantages managers would have in making better decisions than the teams close to the work. By pushing the information and context down to the lowest level possible, the ability to make good decisions will also be pushed closer to the work itself and to real time. This will significantly reduce the waste and cycle time in decision making, improving the effectiveness as well as efficiency of the test-and-learn cycle.

There are a few aspects to consider when thinking about how to create the appropriate level of visibility and transparency:

- How to set up the space?
- What information to show in the space?
- How to use the space as an effective storytelling tool?

We explore each of these aspects in more detail here.

Spaces

There are several types of spaces that you can create to generate the visibility and transparency that both informs the work and drives your digital transformation. They all operate at different altitudes from the organization, through outcome or program levels and down to the team level, each bringing a finer granularity of information and informing one another.

OBEYA ROOM

The engine room, or *Obeya* room (a term from Lean manufacturing describing a "great room") is the central nervous system of the organization (see Figure 6-1). It is where you find the visualization of the organization from its purpose and strategy through to the work being done to achieve the outcomes. It is often compared to the bridge in a ship. It's not a place designed to dispatch orders; rather, the room is designed to help leaders understand whether they are meeting the intent of the outcomes they are driving toward. It reduces departmentalization by viewing the entire system of work and measures in one space and using prompters to call out significant insights and decisions to be made.

Figure 6-1. An Obeya room narrates the connection between strategy and work

This resonates well with David Marquet's intent-based leadership concept: "The captain cannot be expected to know everything about a nuclear submarine, so should not be giving all the orders."[1] An Obeya room makes sure "many brains" are problem solving and working through how to capitalize on opportunities rather than one or a few. It sets the guardrails that allow teams to make aligned decisions in the moment.

As with all spaces, the more time spent inside an Obeya room, the more it talks to you and the more obvious decisions become. For this reason, executive meetings and team meetings should be held in there surrounded by the information at hand. When setting up an Obeya room, you need to think about the aesthetics of critical meetings, comfort, and the ability to see and walk around the information. Access to the room will vary by company. For some it is an open room available to all. This has benefits that all teams can use it and be immersed in the information and insight. They feel connected to it and can see their work's relationship to everything else. For others, the information contained in it can be highly sensitive, so they might restrict access for a time as leaders build safety and comfort in the transparency.

Building an Obeya room takes both creativity and information. There will be many changes over the first few weeks as knowledge grows and new ways to create insights are found. We suggest including the following elements in your room:

- Think about your space in relation to the frequency of change of the information as a starting point. Begin with the purpose and strategy of the business and the outcomes you want to achieve. Because these won't change that often, they can be embedded into the style of the room and represented more graphically big and bold. This graphic should be the North Star for the digital transformation.

- Next represent the work being done to achieve the outcomes. How you represent the work can include key insights like what is in-flight, what is next, and what work was born from the outcome cascade versus work that was already in-flight and allocated to that outcome after the fact. A key measure we have seen used successfully as a guide to whether your organization is changing is the amount of work being done that was prior to the transformation versus new work born from it. Seeing new work deriving directly from outcomes tells you that people are rethinking the way in

---

1 See his Leadership Nudges video (*https://youtu.be/pYKH2uSax8U*) for more.

which they approach work. These work areas change perhaps monthly, so they are set up using cards and icons that can be updated regularly to show progress against measures and issues to be resolved.

- Make a space for measures of your transformation—big visible charts that track the change and improvement in the reasons why you began your digital transformation. You can also add mental models and vision anchors. This will be a great space to keep track of the overall change management: are we creating a sense of urgency? Have we formed a powerful coalition? How are we communicating the vision? Are we creating enough short-term wins? Have we anchored the changes in corporate culture?

- We highly recommend making working spaces available where you can riff in the moment with a group visiting the room, or where big questions that come up can be worked on for a few weeks, and then the space reused for something else. In a recent room we were involved in, the tables themselves could be used as whiteboards for real-time collaboration or sporadic, unplanned discussions that the Obeya tends to generate. We keep a section of the wall space painted with whiteboard paint for investigations that last just a few weeks.

- Last, think about making visible the "to-do" list or the things the leaders have front of mind for the next block of the transformation; for example, "setting clear prioritization of the work" or "ensuring that all new work is born from an outcome with a clear measure."

PROGRAM SPACE

The Obeya room serves as a starting point for your visual system and provides the interconnectivity to the more traditional *program space*, as illustrated in Figure 6-2. When the outcome is cascaded down to the next level of bets or initiatives, each of them could consist of several projects or work streams designed to improve a closely related set of success measures. In the traditional program management framework, a program space is designed to track the priority, sequencing, dependency, status, and progress of this set of projects and work streams. Although we won't go into as much detail on setting up program walls (that has been well covered by many books and articles in program management disciplines), the interconnectivity elements of Obeya are worth calling out.

Figure 6-2. Program walls using color to frame the sections

Entry and exit

Having clearly defined "portals" into the other spaces so the altitude of information is understood and consistent. When you start the wall, you should see indications of where it began, and at the end of the wall, where you should go next if you need more information. This can be done using large infographics that indicate the location of the next level of detail, the contact person, and other relevant pointers. The use of photos is another great way to reference other connected spaces.

Colors and icons

This is about consistency and simple identification. When you are in the Obeya room, you will perhaps use color to segment or categorize the work, either a color for each outcome or each work type or even to identify work belonging to a single tribe or line of business. Icons are also critical in that they make information pop and draw the eyes of the reader. They can be used to call out hot spots or wins, to highlight key areas that you want the leadership to discuss, or even as part of the measures to show progress and achievement. In a recent example we saw, participants used a different color of tape in the Obeya room to surround each outcome; this color was then duplicated at the program wall, and each tribe had an icon so that they could identify the work they were doing and know where to head next. Teams then applied large red dots to a card of work that needed attention. This allowed people to float from the Obeya room to program walls without losing context, and they could understand the interrelationships of the work more easily.

Cards and fonts

Those familiar with Agile are likely also familiar with card walls and cards in the Kanban style popularized by the Toyota Production System and

Taiichi Ohno.[2] Using cards applies in the Obeya room and program walls, too. We again are looking for standardization of design and usage to make it easy for people to follow along. Cards can be color coded for different categories of work and tagged with icons to show status, who is working on it, and how it is aligned to the outcome. When thinking of the design, consider the font from the perspective of readability from a fair distance. Princeton University psychological scientist Pam Mueller conducted research that found handwritten notes are better memorized than printed, this needs to be balanced of course with the size of the font, the quality of the handwriting, and by just not putting too much information on one card.

These are just a couple of ways you can create the "system" of spaces, the important thing is to consciously consider how you will do it.

TEAM SPACE

The next layer of spaces is the *team space*. This is the more traditional Kanban way of working that has frequent changes and is the most granular, being very detailed and specific to that team. Team spaces should be a key element when you consider office layouts. You need to make sure that the space is suitable for collaboration and cocreation and has quiet spaces for think time, working spaces for riffing and discussion, and, of course, room for meetings. In a way, it is the reverse of traditional thinking: you want the general area to be noisy and dynamic, ripe for discussing and collaborating, and you want the office space designed for thinking and quiet time. Gone are the days of the noisy ones being asked to "get a room." The interconnection of the team space to the program space follows the same patterns outlined earlier.

Experience tells us that this interconnectedness between the layers of altitudes of spaces is a critical communication tool and will create a different and more valuable conversation than traditional status reporting. The use of visual elements that link them together will amplify this and help align the organization around the same things.

---

2 The Kanban approach is best articulated in James P. Womack's 2007 book, *The Machine That Changed the World* (Simon & Schuster).

Some Antipatterns of Building a Visual System

As with all transformational elements, there are some antipatterns. Let's take a look at a few of the most noticeable ones in our experience:

- Lacking ownership of spaces. It is critical to have clear ownership in keeping them up to date and synchronized. Does one team own the entire Obeya room, or is it a shared responsibility based on sections? Who is responsible for the program wall and keeping it aligned with the Obeya room above and the team walls below? It might mean that a new kind of PMO for your organization, from governance and reporting to insight and guidance. Not having clear ownership of the spaces could quickly leave it out of date and ineffective.

- Falling into the trap of trying to make the current work look right by forcing alignment or overfitting. This could be as simple as deliberately allocating each current work item under one of the new outcomes or rewording something so it sounds like a fit. It's always best to begin with "what would we do to achieve this outcome." Get that designed, then look at the current work and see whether it is one of those items, using the four retrofit questions, of course. It's perfectly fine to have work that does not fit. That does not make it bad. There might be other critical reasons for certain work; for example, keeping the lights on or other necessary maintenance or efficiency improvements. It just makes it a conscious decision, so now we all know the connections.

- Replicating the organizational structure on the walls. This is a very common mistake. Creating headings of lines of business and the work under it only serves to give the false impression that work is perfectly aligned to your organization structure. In reality, this is very unlikely and will only validate that you are designing work from within these structures to suit the skills that are assigned in that hierarchy rather than starting with the customer outcome.

- Showing today's reports and scorecards on the walls. When deciding what to show in the information radiators, it's easy to match up with a report rather than focusing on value delivery. It's better to leave them until the end so that they don't bias your design of the wall.

- Using spreadsheets on the walls. This is a giant *NO*. When it comes to visibility and transparency, spreadsheets are at the very opposite end. For the non-Excel experts, which is most of the population, an Excel spreadsheet is never a visually intuitive representation. When people are putting spreadsheets up, it means either they are trying to justify a position they know is unaligned, or they are void of creative skills.

A common theme in the antipatterns is the desire to justify the status quo and resist any real changes. It's sometimes motivated by a lack of safety to be transparent and make things visible. Again, it's the leader's job to tackle the safety issue early on, focus on getting the work right, as opposed to being punitive toward individuals. It's important to be a good role model in demonstrating vulnerability as opposed to defensiveness when data and results invalidates one's own ideas. There is a difference between the firm conviction on the strategic vision and flexible adaptability on the details of execution.

Reports and Charts

When it comes to actions and practices to improve security, there is an often-criticized antipattern called *security theater*. It's a set of actions and measures that are designed to make people "feel" more secure but does not actually improve their security. We have seen many examples of reporting evolving into some similar kind of reporting theater, albeit unconsciously and unintentionally.

We did some work with a reporting team that was under constant time pressure to produce more reports. We were asked to change its ways to take on a more visual way of communicating. To help build the buy-in for change, one of the team's most important and frequent reported items was studied. We followed the 30 or so people who worked on creating the spreadsheet for six weeks to ensure its accuracy; the manipulation and massaging of the data to create a more "positive" message; and the incredible use of data that was already a month old and would be more than two months old when the report was completed. In any case, given its importance, we wanted to understand how it was consumed and how we could create more visual representations to make it easier to capture important insights. To everyone's surprise, we discovered was that each member of the leadership team looked at the report for no more than two minutes and then deleted it. There was rarely any future reference to the data and insights, and rarely any decisions made differently as a result of seeing this report. It turned out that the report was made because everyone thought there should be such a report—reporting for reporting's sake, not because it was needed to make decisions or adjustments.

This experience led to an overhaul of the reporting team into an insights team. The team asked a leader and teams for areas of interest and analyzed the data from different perspectives to provide narratives and trends that the teams could act on. Over time, leaders grew accustomed to spending time in the physical spaces, like the Obeya room and program walls, and their ability to "read" the walls and identify where they needed to pay attention grew. Their dependence on the traditional reports diminished even further. During a regular quarterly business review, the CEO raised an awkward question for his team: how the meeting could be repurposed or the time better used rather than having teams come and report on information that everyone was already aware of.

To help frame a better conversation, the information radiator should focus on value delivered versus money spent, relevance to customer outcome versus internal preference, new work born out of learning versus in-flight work due to existing commitments. An example, reflecting on our cost versus value delivered graph, could be a poster of easy-to-read graphs that shows whether outcomes and value delivered line is running above, below, or equal to the money spent chart. It could be an instant view of overall outcome progress, or it could be one per outcomes and have a graph for each of its pieces of work shown.

Big visible charts are important in making the insights clear and in making decisions obvious. A pictograph helps you to see alignment of the people to the work, the work to the measures, the measures of the outcomes, and the execution of your strategy while engaging the audience and providing the motivation to act.

Here are some examples of the insights and charts and the way they ended up being used to identify trends and make decisions:

A vision anchor

Figure 6-3 illustrates how value is delivered to customers. It's not a predefined set of new internal process or a customer digital journey. It's a vision that describes the new way of working and what "good" looks like. It gives leaders a GPS of the conversations that need to be had; a common syntax of how to describe the change and the relevant emphasis points. This consistency in language and having leaders all talking in the same way creates an echo through the organization and a rallying point for change agents to know where to lean in.

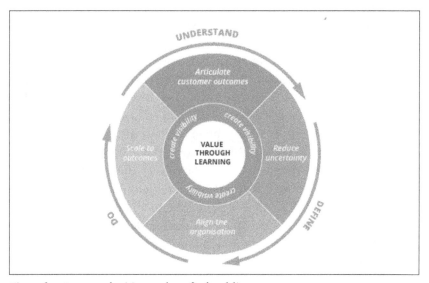

Figure 6-3. An example vision anchor of value delivery

A financial view

In a large financial services company, leadership teams wanted to know how money was being spent and what proportion was being invested into the strategic initiatives versus running the business. The team's estimates ranged from 70% being spent strategically down to 20%. The existing report was done along the lines of functional spending; it did not produce an overall view. It was also only reported on if the money was being spent or not according to the budget, not if it was geared toward certain outcomes. It became clear that one of the investment buckets related to reliability was being used as a catch all. Basically, if you built a business case and showed the work to be in this category it was more likely to be allocated funds.

Over a three-week period a group of four people were able to talk to the program leads and finance teams to unravel more than nine billion dollars of spend, where it was going, and to what outcome. Bubble charts were created in which the size of the bubble represented spend; the color represented the outcome; and the placement on the wall represented the investment type. It allowed leaders to instantly see where the money was. It turned out that only 5% of the money was being spent on the strategic intention. The flaw in the investment process forced teams to fudge the process so they could access critical funds. At the same time, much of the strategy investment was hidden under other categories, making it nearly impossible to make good business decisions using financial data. This created a much different conversation and approach to investment and prioritization processes so that more investment would be made in higher-value work.

In another organization, there was a fantastic illustration that showed the interrelationships between the large infrastructure investments being made in IT with the business strategy and high-priority outcomes. Immediately people walking past the space could understand why investing in a datacenter upgrade was critical to the success of one or two of the business outcomes, making investment decisions easy to justify.

A staffing view

At a large telecommunications company we worked with, we saw a 6 x 3–meter illustration of how teams and work interact. The big visible chart was used to create a heat map of what people were working on to help understand the current business priority. Across the top were the programs of work, down the side were the delivery groups, and the teams were icons at the intersection of the two. This view gave great insight into how team utilization was being spread across the priority areas. Interestingly enough, it showed money being allocated on programs where no teams were active and certain lower-priority programs with less funding being heavily populated with teams of a particular skill set. It turned out that work was being done simply because people with certain skill types were available rather than because the work was prioritized due to value.

A transformation view

A wealth-management organization going through the digital transformation tried to create more work aligned to customer outcomes based on the testing and learning cycle instead of the traditional approach of long planning cycles on program and project work. Visualizing the transformation is a key way to create focus and change behavior.

They began with a giant Kanban wall of all the programs they were tackling in-flight by line of business. In itself this was valuable because they were able to use icons to tag the high-priority programs and through the use of a timeline they could see interesting patterns. At one point, they realized that a range of programs barely got started, while many lower-priority programs were well underway. People were deciding what work to do based on ease and skill availability rather than priority and value. The information radiator exposed the issue early, and actions were taken to fix it.

Next they built a space that reflected the new outcome approach based on key customer personas. This view showed the outcome cascade and measures associated. In the beginning, this wall was empty and only new work born from the outcome cascade process could be placed here. They then came up with a set of criteria that any in-flight work would need to meet to be able to be placed from the old space to the new space (as outlined in Chapter 5 in which we discussed "move across"). A visual imperative was created using an empty to full approach between the spaces, but, more important, a competitive imperative was started as leaders of the lines of business took pride in being able to physically move their work from one to the other, amidst plenty of jibes at their peers who were not moving items.

A program view

We don't want to dive into too much detail about program walls because there are plenty of books and articles on visually representing a program view. But there are some examples that are too good to pass. Our colleague Nick Thorpe of Agile Board Hacks fame has created or been involved in some of the more creative and amazing interconnected spaces. One of our favorites was the now famous Lego wall for which Lego pieces were used to build a multidimensional model. A procurement team was trying to create a visualization of projects through their stages of procurement. Lego pieces were placed on a wall to achieve this. The first was the size of the Lego block to reflect the length of the project. The second dimension was the placement along the wall that reflected how long it had been progressing for. The third was the clincher, the use of the color of the pieces to reflect the phase of the procurement process it had gone through and written on it was how long it took for each phase. By looking at the wall, you could see how long a project had been in its current stage, the stages it has already been through, which stage any given job is at by the top colored brick, and total time versus expected time.

Walking the Walls

Building visibility and transparency is not trivial, and it takes effort and commitment from all parties to change habits and get better at understanding where to look for the information. Putting information on big visual charts is only the first step. The so-called "wall walk" is a key to supporting this.

In this context, the concept involves having a consistent approach to taking people through the flow of the spaces for the purpose of reviewing progress or providing visibility into the "strategy" or how the work is interconnected. A wall tour is a very effective way to engage people. It's physical, intimate, and interactive. As a tool to tell a story and to influence people, walking together through a physical environment is much more engaging than a PowerPoint presentation. It can be used to share with employees what is happening from both a change perspective and strategy execution perspective. It helps them to connect mentally with how their work aligns with the strategy and the important outcomes for the business. Having leaders capable of showing peers, partners, and stakeholders through the spaces can't be underestimated; doing so creates a personal connection.

Just like any effective storytelling approach, walking the wall should be a well-curated experience. It doesn't need to be overly prescriptive and should allow plenty of interactions and discussions. An effective technique we have used is the "follow the bouncing ball" analogy. Placing numbers at the top of each section of the spaces that helps the tour guide (those showing the spaces, including leadership) to keep a check on themselves as to the order in which to tell the story. Early on, you can extend this to include three readable bullet points to be highlighted at each number; rarely do those touring the space recognize the numbering and so on, so it is a great way to help keep the story consistent, allowing several people to learn the art of the narrative telling.

The consistency of the story creates an echo effect where word spreads and everyone is repeating the same message, helping communication and change management. A tour guide simply starts at number 1 and succinctly walks people through each section in a flow, moving from an Obeya room tour to a program wall, even down to a team wall, highlighting the interconnected points through entry and exits. At each level, you can involve the teams from that space in showcasing their work and calling out any issues or successes they are having. A strategy, finance, and PMO discussion in the Obeya room could quickly turn into an outcome and measures conversation at the program wall, and then a granular discussion on day-to-day activity at the team wall.

Something that can enhance the wall walk experience is to add obvious areas for providing feedback. Even going as far as adding feedback boards in each of your spaces allows people to add comments or questions in real time as they tour, or come back later and add in private, shortening the feedback loop on information that might be missing, inaccurate or confusing.

Getting visibility through your spaces right will allow more information to be shared more broadly and quickly. It will create better alignment across the hierarchical ladders and the functional boundaries, empowering teams who are close to the work to make better decisions in real time.

Key Points

Following are the key points that we hope you take away from this chapter as well as two actions for you to take to begin implementing what we've discussed:

- Visibility and transparency create an environment in which decisions become more obvious.

- There are various space types to be considered and keeping them consistent as a visual system will greatly increase visibility and transparency.

- Consideration needs to be given to the role of leaders in creating safety for these spaces so that they are not abused to justify the current state.

Here are two actions to take:

- Design a vision anchor: An image and language that is a way to consistently describe and explain your desired future state, creating an echo for change in the organization. This connects your vision and change road map.

- Create your visual system: Identify spaces and visuals to best reflect the key elements outlined in this chapter, start your tours.

Building a Responsive Organization

The main obstacles to improved business responsiveness are slow deci-
sion making, conflicting departmental goals and priorities, risk-averse cul-
tures and silo-based information.
    —*Economist Intelligence Unit, "Organisational Agility: How Business*
    Can Survive and Thrive in Turbulent Times"

Part II looks at the organization's ability to evolve to the model outlined in Part I. The Digital Age demands responsiveness; the ability to listen, learn, and change. Responsiveness comes from working smaller, changing often, and using knowledge and data to make better decisions on what to do, when to change, and when to stop.

Working this way is difficult because of the organizational and functional constraints that are inherent in an organization's current nature. Your ability to align and manage these constraints and to capture and use data to build knowledge will play a major role in sustaining your digital transformation.

The thin-slice approach will expose the functional constraints that will need to be addressed during digital transformation (see Chapter 3). Common functional areas include the following:

- Organizational structure misaligned to value delivery

- Funding models for allocation of resources more aligned to line-of-business budgeting than spending more on things that generate the most value

- Prioritization approaches that value certainty and completion over value and accuracy

- HR policies and processes that limit team stability and cross-functional collaboration

- Bonus and KPI methods that reward individual contribution over team collaboration, and are not consistent or aligned to outcome achievement where everyone is working in the same direction; if we win, we all win

- Measurement that is either nonexistent, or not related to what is being measured, or so lagging that you cannot show any relationship between the current work and the results

- Legal, regulatory, and compliance policies that hinder and slow down value delivery rather than engaging in it and being an enabler

All organizations have varied influences from this list, with some being rigid and some being totally flexible.

Part I focused on customer alignment; Part II moves to more about the antibodies that will fight your ability to do it and how data can help identify and resolve them. We often use the mantra "knowing what to do is the easy part, being able to do it is what's hard," and doing it sustainably so it sticks is even harder.

The main reason is the "engine" of the organization is like a giant heavy cog that just keeps on turning, and no matter what changes you try to make, the big wheel just comes back around on the next cycle and corrects itself back to the same patterns. Putting a stick into the cog is not the answer; breaking it will only risk irreparable damage. You need to nudge it and gradually change the norm of its motion. You do that by adding lots of little cogs that when connected provide both a speed of redirection while still being able to support the main cog. Eventually the main cog is not necessary, and you end up with a bunch of autonomous smaller engines (cogs), each of which can be upgraded or replaced without affecting the others—engines can be replaced in-flight rather than in surgery. These smaller engines are the analogy for the combination of thin slices we discussed earlier and the supporting functions.

Perhaps that's a bit of overkill on the cog and engine analogy, but we hope it paints a clear picture for you. Let's now have a look and some of the constraints that make that main cog so difficult to knock off its course, allowing it to recalibrate back each time. Here, we examine both organizational and functional constraints that you cannot ignore, without a conscious approach to these, your simplified framework will be untenable and frustration will abound. You need to decide which constraints to accept, which to change, and which to tackle head on if you are to have sustainable digital transformation.

We end Part II by examining the incredible impact data is having on transformational activity and speed of decision making. As the main weapon in the battle of speed and responsiveness, data is the link between ambiguity and the clarity of decision making. In a way, digital transformation is the mental shift from hero-based decisions to exploration and validation so that wiser decisions can be made by the many who are closer to the work and ready to respond in the moment. The combination of your ability to take advantage of data and adopt emerging technology will surely be the leading indicator of your future success.

7

Organizational Constraints and How to Tackle Them

In this chapter, we look at the constraints that are inherent in the way your organization executes as a whole. *Organizational constraints* have to do with how the company behaves, unlike *functional constraints*, which have to do with the processes and policies that exist within functional areas. Functional constraints (which we discuss in Chapter 8) are often more difficult to change because they deal more with people, belief systems, and how one perceives personal achievement. Rarely having anything to do with poor behavior or evil intent, organizational constraints more describe and reflect on the things that influence the way that a company makes decisions.

Although each organization will have different constraints, or at least in different degrees, there are some commonalities that we will highlight:

- Fixed organizational structures
- Obsession with roles
- Compromising change
- Culture

Organizational Structures

Perhaps the most common constraint we come across is the impact of the rigidity of organizational structures. In 1967, Melvin Conway introduced a concept now known as Conway's Law (*https://oreil.ly/3tiPM*) that states, "Organizations which design systems...are constrained to produce designs which are copies of the communication structures of these organizations." Although maybe this was aimed at the realm of software design and delivery, our experience suggests it stands true for all communication and decision-making pathways throughout the organization.

Imagine sitting around an executive table with a group of functional leaders, each with their own budgets to protect and manage, their own KPIs to achieve, and their own staff at their disposal to nurture and allocate toward the functional work. It is highly likely that each executive has their own functional goals and accountabilities. Is it so difficult to understand, therefore, why decision making and planning would not simply replicate this model, giving each leader the autonomy and the faith to execute their own functional unit?

But customers do not think functionally, they do not buy functionally, and therefore value is not measurable functionally. When value measures are challenging to find and count, we begin to look for what is easy to measure and count. These measures invariably exist within our functional lines, validating the structural approach.

In the absence of information about Value, of course the system optimizes for other things. Why should this surprise anyone?

—Joshua J. Arnold (@joshuajames), January 5, 2014

Even though it is logical to group functions together, to put structures in place to help with information flow, staff development and accountabilities, the same does not hold true when it comes to decision making in regard to the work to be done, prioritization, measures, and investment. We constantly see the adversarial environment this creates in which there are winners and losers in the organizational fight for scarce resources, and "decision rights" are used to block the involvement of those who have knowledge. It is too much to expect decisions to be made by functional leaders that would have an adverse effect on their KPIs, their organizations' makeup, or the funding of work under their watch. This kind of sacrifice is admirable but not the norm, especially early on in the transformational journey when everyone is a bit uncertain and the future of their roles and responsibilities is in question.

Earlier, we touched on decision biases; organizational structures are normally the basis of these, and some of these might sound familiar to you; for example, decisions are made:

- To suit personal objectives: "My Achievement"
- Because the work had already started: "Quick start the work—that way they have to fund it"
- To be seen to deliver: "So we can celebrate its completion"
- To meeting the numbers: "Find more work, we are at risk of not spending the money"
- To meet prior commitments: "I will lose face if we don't go ahead with it"
- To suit the skills of the staff that report to you: "We can't have stranded labor; we need to find more Java work"
- To do work that is functionally aligned: "We need to go and talk to the business to get more digital work; our backlog is low"

The conductor of an orchestra stands in a very specific spot. Why? For communication, for it is only from the position in front of the orchestra that you can truly hear the music as it is meant to be heard; if you stood near the percussion section you would hear only drums. From this central location, they can see the leads of each section of the orchestra and communicate through eye contact or facial expression the nudges and rhythms they need to make through the piece. Your organization is the same: decisions need to be made from that same metaphorical spot from which the entire organization can be viewed and work created so that the customer hears the music of your organization, not just from the string section, but as it is meant to be heard, in its entirety.

It stands true then that digital transformation through the eyes of the current organizational structure is unlikely to optimize to the value you are trying to deliver to customers and will eventually find its way back to the current state. Figure 7-1 presents a functional alignment Circos diagram that shows the flow of work through a traditional organization. You can see the spaghetti that is formed as work of all sizes (the thickness of the lines) shoots across the different functional areas of the business. With each one you can imagine the increase in handoffs and dependencies that need to be managed leading to increased wait times, context switching for the individuals as they work on multiple things at once for multiple outcomes, reduced collaboration, and a near impossible environment in which to measure value.

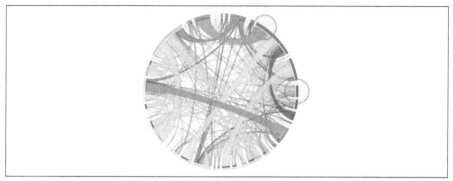

Figure 7-1. A Circos diagram showing the relationships between budget owners and delivery teams

Drawing your attention to the two areas circled on the right in Figure 7-1, you can see in the first case a thick line indicating a strong link between two areas working on this group work, the majority of work is done for each other and a strong signal they should be the one team. In the second case, you can see many thin lines from one area flying out across the organization. In this case, the leader of the team is barely seen by the team because they are off across the whole organization, negotiating and managing relationships in order to get their work done.

It is time to rethink traditional organizational structures and associated project-based formations. At a high level, assess these points:

- First understand the team needed as the main construct of who works together, regardless of reporting or structure:

  — The skills you need in order to complete the work required.

  — Who are the people you need to work together in a stable team for those skills to be present? (Note, it's not one skill per person.)

- Use the lens of the outcome as the "care and nurture" line for leadership. An outcome team should be a collective of the stable teams working together toward achieving the outcome so that it makes sense that the outcome owner acts as the custodian of this group.

- Think of using a matrix style to add a "skills and competencies" development leadership. This could mean that you have a leader who is responsible to build the design competency within the business, for example.

Most important, don't sweat over these points; ultimately you need to work
out what works best for your organization to provide the appropriate way of nurturing and competency building. Just keep the structural decisions and the teaming decisions an arm's length apart. This way you can abstract the organizational
structure from the decisions being made so that it does not bias how you do it.
Don't just form teams to suit the current structure, but instead form them to
optimize value delivery to customers by bringing together the best people and
skills to get the work done sustainably over the long term. Starting with the first
bullet item in the previous list will let the organizational construct form naturally
and as that happens simply continue to ask yourself whether it makes sense to
make structural changes to match or whether it just works as it is. Do not make
structural changes just because different people from various reporting lines are
working together.

To start with the first bullet, use the framework outlined in the earlier chapters to ask yourself what is the backlog of work you need to do in order to maximize value to customers, what skills would it take to do this, where are those
skills in the organization today, and how do we connect them? Organizing
around the outcomes rather than around tasks will better align the skills of the
team to the work needed to be done and give a better line of sight and end-to-end
awareness of value.

Thinking about the work before the structure will allow you to build stable
teams who stay together with work continuously flowing through them—the
thicker lines in the Circos diagram from stronger relationships. The gap between
the work you need to do to maximize value and the current skills and capabilities
of your organization will reduce, a clearer picture of the skills required in each
team will form, and the teams who need to work closely together can move
together closer to where the work is.

Over time, as the more "natural" organization forms, you will be able to
measure things like the amount of work leaving teams in order to be completed
as ways of monitoring team makeup and make small adjustments as you need to.

While building out a 150-person Agile program of work, one of our clients, a
large Telco, went through quite a logical process of team creation. The leadership
team studied the work and identified the skills required to complete its backlog.

The company looked for the scarcest resource pool and found that one particular technology had only eight resources, and so it created nine teams, each team with that skill set except one for which it would expedite through the work that did not need that skill. It ended up with nine teams of 8 to 10 and a pool of functional teams, like infrastructure. It seemed logical and felt right, but a strange thing happened: the new model was imposed on the group from the leadership team, and from very early on it created a lot of friction; teams were having to constantly reach out to non-team members for help. After about six months of trying to push through it, the teams took things into their own hands and reorganized themselves to better match the work. This led to a shift to 5 teams of 30. It was a very natural shift as an unexpected learning that the teams were too small to match the variation in the work; thus, the skill set was not broad enough to complete the next item. At 30, the teams could take on the next most valuable item from the backlog at the start of each release, break it down, and then self-organize into three smaller teams that could take on each piece. The result after two years was a doubling of productivity, a reduction in staff from 150 to 125, and a 60% reduction in the cost per unit produced.

The organizational structure remained constant throughout the first 12 months or so, and the shifting in teams was all learning based and employee led. It wasn't until later that the leaders recognized their more natural place in the new groupings with some becoming "capability leads," whereas others were the more natural "people managers." It was only then that structural reporting lines moved more formally; it was the natural thing to do, and because the teams were already operating anyway, there was no jolt like you could expect to see when a "restructure" is announced.

Stable Teams

Let's take a moment to reflect on team stability, or persistent teams, when it comes to naturally forming organizational structures. This concept of *stable teams* has had a lot written about it, and the benefits are clear. In a recent engagement, we witnessed an average time of 45 days to set up a team; that is, 45 days from the time a project was given a green light to the time a team came together to begin work. Stable teams remain constant and have a continuous flow of work run through them; there is no downtime or setup time. They own their own backlog and are made up of capabilities that, when together, can handle most of the items in the backlog autonomously. As the work demand trends differently, team constructs can be nudged to add new skills, either through adding new members or teaching current members new skills.

Stable teams form more naturally to suit the backlog of work. It means thinking more broadly than an organization's structure in terms of who has knowledge to contribute, who is impacted, and who has the skills. This creates a far richer input and ideation. Getting this right will help to align people to the work.

Creating stable teams leads to higher performing teams as it:

- Builds autonomy and empathy with purpose

- Reduces context switching

- Doesn't create stand-up and stand-down implications

- Limits handoffs and dependencies of teams

- Creates higher engagement, allowing members to get to know each other well, truly gel, and adjust personalities and communication styles

High-performing stable teams become more effective the longer they work together. They are constantly learning each other's strengths and needs, forming better tolerances, trust, and resilience to one another. They provide greater certainty to the business, allowing for accurate capacity funding rather than project projections and simpler ROI measures. They encourage individuals to bring forth their talents and build expertise that is more generalist so that they can contribute more broadly. Teams become more flexible and spend more time thinking about innovative ways to achieve outcomes rather than just doing what the scope or their job titles say.

The altitude of stability is up for question, and something you will need to experiment with a bit to find what works best for you. Remember, by "works best" we mean delivers more value more often to customers at a sustainable cost, not what builds the best empires. You could start at the outcome level, grouping the teams required to deliver the outcome. At this level, stability can be binary, it would be the equivalent to a line of business. As per the earlier Telco example, the next level down feels a bit like teams of 30 or so that are very tightly correlated, and although there would be some movement, the stability would be fairly constant. At the team level you expect a degree of self-organizing. Even though this might feel like it flies in the face of the "8- to 10-person Agile team," it is an adaptation that you might need to make when the outcome is not as distinct as a feature of a story. You will likely still have the Agile team structures, especially in some areas of technology-specific work; this further signals a mix of teams styles that's needed for balancing stability and value delivery.

The nonnegotiable part is that you need to reverse the order from the organization's structure determining the work and the decision rights to the work determining the organizational structure. A structure must be designed to optimize the flow of value and be robust enough to be able to support a degree of change for when work needs changes in response dynamics.

Role Obsession

Perhaps the tougher of the organizational constraints, or at the very least the most emotional, is the obsession with roles. This is not too surprising given that, for the majority of people, roles are how they identify within the organization; they are what they applied for to get a job there, how they sold their attributes to the organization, their talent credentials, and was the reason to be hired. It goes directly to the heart of feeling valued: "If my role is not needed, I am no longer valued."

But "roles" can be your worst enemy during transformation; the obsession companies have with tightly defined roles and functions can bring down sustainable change. Early on in a large-scale transformation, the lead of a project management community once gave a 40-page presentation to a leadership team outlining the role that the project management team would play in the future state. It described in exact detail the parts of the transformation and future state the team would own. Even though it was of interest to see how the function thought it would add value, it assumed what the future state was and what it would need. Rightly, one of the leaders pointed out, "Not once did you challenge if your role was even required." It was a pitch caused by fear and rumor mongering that the "role" would not exist in the future—a counter punch, if you like.

We have seen it everywhere, across all functions:

- The finance lead who pushes back on financial model changes because they don't understand what their job would be in a world where teams have autonomy over an investment limit rather than project budgets
- The head of a call center who avoids investing in fixing the reason customers call because their call center would not be required if the calls didn't come and thus their role and team not required
- The head of digital who balks at reorganizing around customer value because "I only want to do digital stuff," and if value could be delivered without digital tech, they were not interested

Of course, it is also more grassroots than these examples. In its simplest form, role obsession is people fearing losing their jobs in a time of organizational change. As a result, we see many digital transformations start with role conversations and discussions over "the new role of the project manager (PM), the new role of X and Y," or worse, the mega spill of all roles—"everyone must reapply because your role has changed." We see the opportunity for real change fail because the starting point assumes that current line-of-business leaders and existing role types remain. So change happens within these preexisting boundaries of functional lines; for example, the ever common "IT transformation." But making change and work-based decisions based on roles and job titles is antiquated and illogical; people's talents are not limited to their current role or past experience, so you end up with a suboptimal result.

We can avoid all of this if we stop the misinterpretation of the meaning of role to be job title rather than a grouping of things that need to be done. We are not saying clearly defined roles and responsibilities don't help; they give people a strong sense of how to contribute their talents and an understanding of accountabilities. They can empower collaboration or even better cocreation by removing friction between teams and individuals. Accountability can be a motivator and give clarity to get things done fast, as long as it is not overused as a "one throat to choke" excuse to point fingers in times of failure. However, where the concept of roles falls down is when you make fragmented, one-off decisions about a job function, title, or role scope. These set artificial boundaries and constrain input. The tying of roles and responsibilities to job titles can increase friction and create adversarial behavior around winning and losing, function versus function, role versus role, and decision versus decision. In the end, the customer is forgotten.

So let's redefine roles by thinking about what they should or should not be:

A role should not be a one-off decision.

A role should not be a one-off decision like that of an employment contract. Instead, roles should be decided on a more frequent basis to suit the work, and by the members of the team focused on achieving a common outcome. A role should simply identify common groupings of work capabilities and be used for developing those capabilities in individuals. This conglomerate of similarly skilled people might even form a community to share and learn from one another. Yes, we are deliberately describing what seem like the way you describe roles in your organization today, but we are also deliberately avoiding the link to structures and formal job titles.

Don't let a one-off decision about a job title turn into a fixed, long-lived role. Even more important, don't let long-lived titles and structures be the basis for designing your transformation. Allow a degree of fluidity that lets roles evolve as the work does.

A role should not be the same as a job title.

A job title is irrelevant; what is important is how an individual can contribute to the team. Placing less emphasis on job titles and descriptions pushes people outside of rigid structures, and allows them to unleash their talents to move the entire team forward. The reality is that roles are not who you are, they do not describe your talent, and they run the risk of serving as a boxing of what we can contribute in the eyes of the organizational engine. Often, the mistake is made of describing people and their skill set by the archetype of the role we gave them, that they "sold themselves" to you to get. In doing so, we fail to unlock true individual talents and constrain the environment for those who might be able to contribute in ways we were unaware of.

Once, when looking to help a client align its work to its strategy, a graduate developer came forward offering to help. At face value, it would be difficult to see how a person with this role could contribute, but, in fact, unknown to many, this person had spent several years in a strategy consulting firm, only later deciding to go back and get developer experience to round out their skill set. They were in fact very well placed to provide valuable input regardless of their job title. At ThoughtWorks, we actively practice this separation of roles and skills. We don't just look to hire a developer or a BA: we routinely and deliberately hire people into a technology company that have no technology background at all and who become great technologists. We look for a willingness to learn, ability to adapt, for those who look for new challengers and can embrace their faults and limitations to find ways to contribute.

The key to managing this role obsession in your digital transformation is to create an environment in which the fear of losing one's job is minimized, especially early on, while you are learning what change will work for you. This is why starting transformations with a restructure creates a tsunami of activity that is rarely beneficial to the change that you are trying to make. It sends everyone into a scramble of trying to be valuable, jockeying for new role appointments, and takes away from the focused, aligned approach to change. It's an easily recognized state; there will be multiple transformation efforts, the battle to the top, where "my way" needs to be better than "your way" rather than teams working together to achieve common outcomes. Facade change becomes rampant as it is safer to look like you are changing rather than actually risking change itself.

Take away someone's dependency on the security of their role and its place in the organizational structure and you create the environment in which to unleash the natural talents of people, not the roles they're constrained by. You make it safe for people to be curious, to be OK with not understanding, and to seek knowledge and clarification rather than conformance. You encourage an aligned effort toward sustainable change.

Here's our advice for building the desirable roles environment for change:

- Let changes to structure evolve naturally over time. Don't make long-standing changes until you have the knowledge of what works.

- Build a new muscle: teaching teams how to form and how to build into their cadence a reflection on current role responsibilities so that they can adapt. Armed with a clear outcome and measure, you should be able to come together and identify what work is needed, what skills are needed, and who is best positioned to do it. This is how you will learn to form your first thin slice. You should use a regular cadence to change who is responsible for what based on actual knowledge and learning.

- Abstract titles, roles, and skills from one another. Skills are what individuals have and learn. Roles are what is needed at the time to meet the outcomes. Skills are applied to the role by individuals. Titles are patterns of roles we learn over time as the likely responsibilities and accountabilities, the roles are learned over time but still are ever evolving.

- Avoid job title conversations early on in transformations.

- Work on providing clear career path and progression opportunities based on existing skills. Which roles could people lean in to and what titles are more likely to need those skills. This will build a view of archetypes that you can use as your learning pathways and team allocations.

The challenge of the role-obsession conversation is to find the precise balance of being able to release talent in a time of ambiguity, reducing fear so that change can thrive.

In our interview with the senior vice president that we referenced earlier, they also highlighted the "air cover" leaders need to provide to make people feel safe during the transition:

You need to build a rockstar team of diverse, smart, passionate people, and then be prepared to blow that team up and allow another team to carry the ball over the goal line.

This type of transformation is a marathon, not a sprint. It is very rewarding but also very difficult for the team given the opportunity to lead it.

Be prepared to ask very talented, highly successful leaders and associates to step out of their current jobs (and their comfort zone) and join you on this journey, but also be prepared to find them a great place to land when it's time to hand the baton to the next team—if they're doing their jobs well, they will be pushing teams and individuals to change their mindsets and skill sets, and without a doubt there will be some broken glasses —don't let the team take the hit for this, but instead ensure they have the "cover" to bravely push, knowing that their jobs aren't at risk at the end.

Death by Compromise

Transformation isn't easy. It takes courageous leaders and a steely resolve to resist the traditional mindset of the Industrial Age that no longer applies in the knowledge economy. To stay the course, you need to avoid becoming stuck in transition, the constraint of compromise, cutting corners, and convincing yourself it's "a step in the right direction." Like technical debt, you will likely forget to go back and fix it. You can get so caught up in the implementation of the transformation that you look for wins where they don't exist. For example, we have seen organizations trip up by being seduced by the perceived simplification from bulk standardization, as if having everyone doing things the same way or using one tool is the success measure rather than teams working out for themselves how to maximize value. As a guiding principle, if you are making transformative decisions to suit yourself and not the customer, you not only risk being convinced by a facade or improvement internally, but also risk making customer value less attainable.

A classic example is the way digital transformations seem to exclude the technology infrastructure teams because it's "too big and too hard" for that pet program that you don't want to interfere with at the moment, so they get given an exemption on changing. Avoiding the difficult things just delays the sustainable change that you are trying to achieve. Reflecting on the thin-slice approach as an example, you want to be able to identify the company's antibodies as early as possible so that they can be consciously managed or eliminated. Avoiding the challenging, important, difficult, or complex can mean you don't get to flesh out the things that will ultimately determine your success. This leads you on a path to a false sense of change that does not impact on the outcomes that you are trying to achieve; you implement change rather than actually make change.

Note

There are also critical technical reasons why leaving infrastructure teams out of digital transformation is not sustainable. We discuss that in detail in Part III.

One way to try to avoid falling into a compromise constraint is to be very conscious and visible about the trade-offs you are making, almost like capturing a backlog of the business and technology debt as you consciously make them and forcing yourself to go back and readdress it. Using the example shown in the following table, you can begin to get a picture of some of the trade-offs we have used with clients to get a view of the tolerance for change you have in particular areas. Map yourself as a low, medium, or high appetite for change in key elements of your digital transformation. Then, start in the high-appetite areas (these axes are just for illustration, you can add your own elements to it). This way, you are not avoiding difficult problems; instead, you're tackling them in areas where appetite is high first as a way to build organizational muscle:

	Low appetite	Medium appetite	High appetite
Strategy	Long-term sacrosanct strategy in place; an immovable object. Strategy was recently set so the last thing they want is for us to change that—the justification game.	Strategy is in place but isn't getting traction; execution lethargy. Looking to reinvigorate the strategy—the fixing game.	Strategy exists with tangible outcomes and buy-in. Uncertainty exists in how to execute effectively. The execution game—the fastest way home.
Ways of working	Everyone is fixed in their ways.	There are some sacred cows that can't be moved, and you need to identify what they are (this is hard!).	Completely open to anything we want to do.
Funding	This is the money we have: the budget is fixed.	Flexibility to change business cases and prioritization. Money can be held at a certain level rather than being allocated all the way through.	Completely open to redesigning how money is allocated and how budgets are set.
Planning cycle	All plans are in place, all they want to do is execute.	The plan has a sunset clause—leave what is in flight in flight, and change in the next period.	Happy to replan.
Team fluidity	People must sit in these teams and report to the people they report to today.	Flexibility to move groups of people together to colocate and become a cross-functional team.	Completely open to redesigning organizational structure.
Measures	Profit, customer acquisition, cost reduction. Everyone has a KPI; no one is willing to change it because it's tied to bonuses.	Sunset clause—flexibility to change KPIs in next period.	Open to thinking about new measure types, learning about customer measures, flexibility to change KPIs in place to adapt to these.
Architecture	Leave it alone, we can't do that here. We have a predefined set of rules and process everyone needs to follow.	Look to improve practices and experiment with emerging technology.	We must redesign, decouple and modularize the architecture. Let it emerge.

A trade-off slider type of approach is a good starting point to get a feel for where your organization stands. At the one end, you have "go ahead and completely redesign it," and at the other "that is not touchable, we can't change it." From this position, you can begin to work through which constraints can be removed, which can be remodeled, and those that have to be lived with and will influence your ongoing evolution. This uniqueness is another reference point as to why blindly copying those before you will not work, it is unlikely that your company would have the same trade-offs in the same degree as the one you try to copy. Of course, there is much to be learned from others, and something that worked for another organization would be a great starting point to explore your transformation journey. The catch is that it starts as an exploration, not an implementation, so use it to learn and adapt your way to what will work for you and be prepared to change course if you see things not working.

As a result of the trade-off conversations, you can set up the initial comfort position of your digital transformation, the guardrails for teams to be aware of as they tackle constraints. If your sliders are all to the left, you are likely in a very conservative mode and change will be very difficult. If you are all on the right, you are in an anarchy mode and change might be too fast and overwhelming. As Figure 7-2 depicts, understanding the mix of these sliders is, in a way, a snapshot of the nature of your organization. It is not a one-and-done, though; it's more a temperature check on your change profile. As the organization learns and builds trust in change, you will find the sliders move.

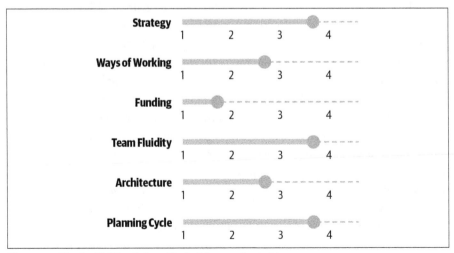

Figure 7-2. Trade-off sliders help guide decisions and priorities

As teams look to innovate and rethink how work flows and how functional activities are done, they can make priority calls based on the appetite for change in certain areas. You can then set up a cadence, as part of your lightweight governance, to reflect on the comfort levels and change the sliders as new knowledge and understanding is gained, acknowledging that your organization's comfort with change will grow over time.

Evolving Culture

The final organizational constraint worth touching on is the culture of your organization. Organizational culture loosely describes how a company does things and how people behave. It could include the kind of taxonomy that is used to describe things: how people dress, how decisions are made, how work is planned and done, and how conflicts are resolved. A company's culture is influenced by a variety of factors including the founders' philosophy, societal culture, values and beliefs, the successes and failures from the past, and the CEO and management team's style. Culture could be an awkward thing to change given that it is often considered to be like the personality of your organization, and personality is difficult to change.

Societal culture changes slowly. It evolved to what it is today over thousands of years. To some extent, an organization's culture is still heavily anchored in the society in which it lives. Most governments and militaries are still strictly following the traditional wisdom of command and control—power is channeled through a hierarchy with formal roles and reporting lines. When a business decides there are better ways to do things and begins to change, it starts to shape its own distinct culture that is different from the social norm. Because it's not the social norm, it takes effort to just to maintain that culture—ceremonial activities, policies, trainings—to make sure that new hires and external influences don't dilute the special sauce and change people's behavior back to be mediocre.

But the opposite is also true when you try to change your culture. Sometimes, you need to bring in new ideas, thoughts, and experiences to challenge the status quo and break through current norms. You can also never stop trying to discover new and better ways to do things. For example, nurturing people to unleash their productivity and creativity, decentralizing decision making to improve responsiveness and effectiveness, or communicating and collaborating horizontally to empower and encourage teams to innovate.

Often attempts to make these changes to evolve to a better culture will meet resistance in the name of "protecting" the (existing) culture. You might have heard the well-known story about five chimpanzees, a banana, and a ladder. In an experiment, scientists placed a banana on the ceiling of a cage with five chimpanzees in it. The banana could be reached by a ladder in the middle of the cage. Every time a chimpanzee tried to climb up the ladder to reach the banana, before reaching the top, the scientists would spray cold water on the rest of the four chimpanzees. After a while, whenever one chimpanzee tried to climb the ladder, the rest would pull it down and force it to stop. This behavior continued even after the cold-water spraying was removed. A new chimpanzee joined, saw the banana, tried to climb the ladder, got pulled down and beaten, but without knowing why. Slowly, but steadily, all old chimpanzees were replaced by new ones one by one. No one would have experienced the cold water, but they knew climbing up the ladder would get them punished.

Maintaining a successful organizational culture is difficult. Developing it to cope with the new environment is even more difficult. The reality is that you need to treat culture like home water storage—kept hot enough to avoid bacteria growing and cold enough not to scald you. You need to provide an environment in which great culture thrives and the constraining elements are constricted or strangled when you need to do things differently. The most important behavior is to always ask why (why do we do things this way here?), and never settle for the norm and just follow it blindly.

> The most dangerous phrase in the language is, "We've always done it this way."
>
> —Grace Hopper

If we look at some of the big callouts from previous chapters, there are some obvious culture shocks for which you will need to prepare. We have covered things like your approach to roles and hierarchy, creating the safety for transparency, measurement as a decision tool, and being open to learning and having the courage to respond to those learnings. Following are some other high-level elements to be considered when nurturing your culture. Think of them a bit like a manifesto as culture is a balancing act, and recognize that not everyone can go to the extreme of the goodness. Some organizations will thrive with a bit of both, but none will with all of the bad side:

Purpose versus profit

Having collective purpose as your guiding light over the focus on profit or cost reduction. Yes, it's important to be accountable to the bottom line, but growth comes from maximizing the delivery of value to customers. Having managers who are more accountable for delivering profits than supporting innovation and value delivery will not move the culture in the proper direction. You will know it is evolving when investing in value delivery takes precedence over making the numbers and your purpose is more likely to motivate than to provoke cynicism.

Openness and trust versus cloaking

How your organization responds to conflict or failures is critical in building the muscle to respond to change. A rigid approach that dictates process over outcome will lead to hidden results and false representations of actuals. Work that is not achieving the intended value is dressed up in reports to look good for fear of losing staff or budget. Organizations will thrive where accuracy and transparency is celebrated, regardless of what it tells you.

Heros versus collaborators

How does your company celebrate success; how do people feel valued? The collective-over-self trait has been shown to be a key enabler of sustained success. Heros like to achieve personal success and recognition and are more likely to look for the route that brings them personal success versus the one that achieves organizational success. Collaborators value the achievement of the collective and seek group success. Often, we mistake collaborators as not being self-driven and that somehow they don't put in the effort or intensity of a hero. But this is rarely true. The power of a collective is also a powerful motivator because people don't like to be seen as not pulling their weight toward the team goal. There is more evidence of better performance from a team with a single goal than a team with individual goals. This does not make individual goal setting bad. Individual goals should be about improvement and results measured at the team level. A collective culture is about cocreation wherein someone does not need to lose for another to win. It's one in which everyone is working toward the same definition of success.

High- versus low-risk attitude

We examine the legal and regulatory functions in digital transformation in a bit more detail later, but certainly the risk aptitude of an organization is an important cultural consideration. Note that we use the word "aptitude" not "appetite." Digital transformation is often mistakenly thought to be higher risk, but in fact is about reducing risk—the risks of not dealing with change. The Digital Age brings with it more uncertainty and ambiguity. These are unavoidable facts, so an organization has two choices: ignore them and continue the charade of making things look certain and in control, or learn how to operate with these new characteristics. Rigid policies make it difficult to respond quickly to customers. Traditional governance models are too heavy and time consuming, constantly looking for milestones, dates, and certainly, and interfering with moving from a project mindset to an outcome-based one. A good risk aptitude shows an understanding that experimentation is not risk taking but risk mitigating, so we make longer-term financial and team commitments only to things that we know will work.

Perfection versus learn through fast feedback

The cone of uncertainty is a favorite of ours: it explains the relationship time has with knowledge. The more time passes, the more we learn. It goes on to say that the quicker we get started, the sooner we learn and the more likely we are to achieve the outcome by doing the high-value work first. Many traditional firms are hamstrung by the need to know everything before they begin—approvals, specifications, scope, solution architecture sign offs, business cases, and so on. All of these things lead to time wasted without knowledge gained. Again, there is a time and a place for which specifications and planning are crucial to success, but these are in the minority, such as surgery or network planning for Telcos. Ambiguity now rules over certainty; when a need for certainty is more likely to slow the pursuit of new opportunities. Your culture needs to make it safe to experiment and learn. Trading future certainty for current accuracy means being able to create and capture feedback quicker and adapt to what you find to be accurate.

Top down versus bottom up

Culturally, both have their pros and cons. Top down turns sour when it's all command and control: "Do as I say." However, left unguarded, bottom up can lead to anarchy with everyone making their own decisions about the work to invest in regardless of the overall organizational outcome pursuits. Oddly, many organizations do a form of this today with their bottom-up planning. Line-of-business managers plan work based on the utilization of their teams and bid for money using multiple layers of buffers on cost and inflated promises of returns. Loose coupling to "strategic imperatives" allows them to make the work look as if it will fit into the strategic funding buckets. It's often done with the local optimization mindset in order to get the budget approved. The middle ground is about guardrails of autonomy, giving people enough autonomy to use their talent but aimed toward the customer outcomes. It is about equal worth rather than hierarchical decision making. It's important to recognize that those closest to the work have the knowledge to make the appropriate decisions. Hierarchy is an organizing construct to facilitate and optimize global outcome, not a knowledge hierarchy. Getting this wrong sees individuals simply shaping their opinions to fit the biases of managers where few individuals feel empowered to initiate change.

Frederick Taylor and his contemporaries have a little bit to answer for here, or at minimum we deserve a whack for our obsessive use of their Scientific Management Theory (*https://oreil.ly/vI9Tt*) long after its use is outdated. Their idea is to separate thinking from doing, thus they create a role called "manager," and try to make everything and everyone as controllable, predictable, and efficient as possible. Rigid structures, budgets, timesheets, performance planning, and hierarchies were conceivable in an industrial age aimed at mass production with efficiency. But in the Digital Age ambiguity reigns, the pace of change makes prediction cycles much smaller and accuracy more valuable than certainty. We live in the age of mass customization for everyone at all times. Decision making needs to be redistributed based on where the knowledge is so that weaker signals can be captured, feedback loops shortened, and decisions made in a timelier fashion by those closest to the work.

Unlike functional constraints, the organizational constraints are subtler and hidden from sight; they inform decisions and actions more than define them. Learning to make them visible and being conscious of how to live with or mitigate their impacts will be critical in sustaining change, and failure to do so will result in rolling back to old habits.

Key Points

Following are the key points that we hope you take away from this chapter as well as two actions for you to take to begin implementing what we've discussed:

- Organizational constraints are those that represent the norms of the company that will try to reverse the changes you make. For sustainable change, you need to create an environment in which great culture can thrive and change is seen as an opportunity not a threat.

- Organizational structures and roles need to be decided after the work is known or implemented separately from decisions about the work and investment. Digital transformations cannot be sustained from the lens of current structure and roles.

- Taking half steps creates the business equivalent of technical debt, convincing yourself that any move forward is good and resisting the sustainable change steps. You need to ensure that your environment allows great culture to thrive in a way that supports the magnitude of change that will occur.

Here are two actions to take:

- Use trade-off sliders to help plan and manage "transformation debt": Create your trade-off sliders for your digital transformation; discuss the implications of this and how you will transparently manage compromises and shortcuts.

- Identity the culture constraint: Understand the culture blockers and articulate and spell out how the culture should evolve.

8

Functional Constraints

Now that we've discussed the constraints that affect your organization as a whole, it's time to shift our focus to functional constraints. Functional constraints are those brought on by the individual corporate functions of the business. They occur when traditional organizations operate from a functional lens, be it IT, finance, HR, legal and regulatory, or marketing.

Often the tensions and struggles between these units are obvious, either between themselves or more generally with the delivery of value to customers. They each follow their own processes and methods using domain expertise, experience, and best practice, supported by years of university studies in the functional roles. When it comes to digital transformation these tensions can be amplified as change, pace, and ambiguity put pressure on these traditional activities. For this reason, it is vital that you understand that transformation includes everyone; functional units cannot be exempt. Functional representation in every element of the transformation is critical so that you can see in advance where tension will be and be conscientious in how you approach it.

When it comes to functional involvement in digital transformation, no organization is the same, and as such, no approach to each of the functional constraints can be prescriptive across the board. What you need to be able to do during the transformation is identify which functions will cause the biggest heartburn and which will best "oil your engine." Which of your functional units is most rigid in its ways and which is most open to explore new techniques and approaches that might speed and increase the delivery of value to customers.

We begin by introducing a general philosophy on functional alignment, and then we have a look at some of the prime functions and the constraints that you will likely need to deal with.

General Functional Alignment

The loose process we have been discussing of test, learn, and scale what works is generally the same one you want functional units to use to learn and adapt processes and procedures to support value delivery and organizational protection. The simple rule of thumb to apply is that all functional units exist, whether they are there to manage risk or provide services, to add value to the value chain of the organization. This means that their primary purpose is to operate their function in the support of the delivery of value to customers. Their success should be measured on that. Although at times it might be OK and necessary to have a neutral impact, under no circumstances should they degrade it. For example, a legal and regulatory compliance function that takes eight weeks to approve releasing value to a customer after it is complete degrades; one that can approve it a day or so after completion is neutral; and one that bakes all compliance into the design adds value. An HR function that limits the talent and role of employees to their employment contract stipulations degrades it. Job flexibility is neutral. Separating roles and job titles can add value. And so it goes.

Overall you need a way to engage each of your functional units early in the transformation process without disrupting the entire unit, remembering that they will be in a confusing world of transition in which they need to keep the entire organization moving while some of its parts begin changing and speeding up.

Often we see organizations fall into the trap of having functional teams be the sole input to changing themselves. Transformation requires a new skill set in and of itself, plus the bias we tend to place on our own thinking, knowledge, and experiences makes it unlikely that you would get the best result. We often see functions looking for ways to justify the things they do today, why the tasks need to continue, and the policies need to be enforced. Examples might include business cases still called for on every initiative, long-winded approval processes to tick boxes, managers doing performance reviews for people on whose work they have no visibility. So, you need to think more consciously about change in functional units and how to involve them all in the broader transformation efforts.

THE DOUBLE-TRIANGLE MODEL

One way you could approach this is the double-triangle model, which a method you can use to help bring functions along the journey and ensure an inclusive change that takes advantage of rather than isolates the expertise within the function. In Figure 8-1, the left-hand triangle perhaps represents your transformation team; this is a group you look to provide the expertise you need to identify, explore, analyze and test new ways of working. They are specialists in this muscle. The right-hand triangle represents any of your functional lines of business—they have the expertise in understanding the functions processes and policies. They understand why the constraint exists. The red box is the "Pod" with which you test any prospective new ways in order to see whether you can scale and institutionalize the innovation. A Pod is made up of a team or group that you identify as a suitable candidate for the new way of working, combined with members of the functional group and the transformation team. The Pod is how you validate that the change you want to make will have the desired impact and not negatively affect the delivery of value to customers.

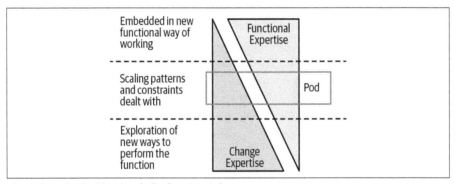

Figure 8-1. The double-triangle for functional change

As you can see from the diagram, there are three stages to consider. Also, there is a variation in the makeup of the two areas of expertise at each stage that will be needed as part of the transformation journey for a given function. So the total working group includes the following:

- People with experience in implementing new ways of working
- People with knowledge on how to explore new ways of working through research, experimentation, and validation
- People who don't have a functional bias that might resist change or skew the best outcome in favor of a safe outcome for their functional team
- Functional expertise

Stage one

In stage one, you are exploring the optimal way in which the function can provide value to the transformation. Here, you would expect to spend time studying other organizations, seeing what has worked and failed for them, reading whitepapers, and perhaps visiting some conferences on the topic. You then would form some hypotheses about what "good" might look like for you and maybe run some small experiments to validate your thinking. Clearly, then, in stage one you need more of the expertise in those activities and less functional knowledge; the functional knowledge you do need is to articulate the guiding principles and to provide the intricacies of the organization's current setup.

An example of stage one might be looking at performance management, researching the optimal way for team motivation, looking at the *Harvard Business Review* on how companies are significantly changing the face of individual performance management, and visiting organizations like Deloitte, which have reinvented how they do it. You might choose to prototype some new ways for your organization and talk to relevant stakeholders in the process to get their feedback. The functional representation could map out the current steps and gather feedback on how it is working for individuals. They could provide the compliance requirements by which the organization would be legally bound, and so on.

Stage two

Stage two is where you look at scaling patterns in the organization, and how you implement your findings from initial experiments to a broader group so that you can find both what works and any upstream or downstream issues it might cause. For this, you might form a Pod structure whereby the change expertise and functional expertise come together in equal parts along with representation from a broader stakeholder group. Following the previous example, you might choose a number of teams with which to roll out the new performance management process. The Pod in this case would include representatives from each team as well as other affected stakeholders like their manager and perhaps payroll. You are now building muscle into the functional unit, their involvement in the change process, the experimentation and the roll out is lifting their capability, preparing them for talking on the new ways.

Stage three

Stage three is where the new way becomes the norm for that functional unit: new policies and processes are embedded into the day-to-day operation of the function. The functional unit is now better prepared to start to analyze other aspects of their unit to see where improvements can be made. Using the performance management example, you would expect to see planning underway for the following year's KPIs using the new methods and education for the rest of the functional unit. A small check in style support is left in place from the transformation team just to nudge the functional unit and make sure it doesn't roll back to the old ways. They will also gather great feedback for the next change.

Let's now look at some specific functions.

Finance

For years managers have methodically set target numbers and budgets on an annual basis and worked tirelessly in a mire of KPIs, performance plans, and forecasts. In the company-wide drive to "make the numbers," visibility and transparency are left in the wake of the "gamers"—those who put more effort into the numbers balancing than value delivered. Money becomes such a scarce resource that managers are forced to do what it takes to get their share of the pie so that they have enough to do their job for which they are being held to account, for the entire fiscal year. This leads to classic behavioral issues:

- Pumping up the importance and value of projects

- Making projects look as successful as possible

- Making everyone seem busy

- Doing what you must to make it appear that you made the numbers at the end of the financial year

These practices make the information we have to make decisions useless. Predictability, transparency, and visibility are lost in favor of muddied waters that allow leaders to hedge their bets when it comes to reporting progress.

We are not about to say that the numbers are not important or that being financially responsible is not something we should all commit to. But we do believe that fiscal responsibility is being lost in translation as it permeates the chain of command. This is further validated by constant grandstanding and motivational speeches that ignore customer value as the key indicator of profit instead evangelizing the merits of making the numbers.

We have all witnessed the huge number of proverbial "deep dives" in our organizations during which hoards of people bury themselves in spreadsheets looking for that elusive silver bullet as to why the forecasts are tracking above plan or below plan, trying to solve where and how you are going to cut back or reassign money in order to make a number that is clearly too low to cover the cost of the work you are being asked to do. It's amazing how many events can happen in a single company over six months that trigger questions about the numbers that can only be answered by a deep dive...of the same data...in the same way...trying to find a different answer. It is almost predictable: the first half of the year overspend, the hiring freeze, the EBITDA rise, and the slowing of work to slow spending toward the end of the financial year.

A fiscally heavy organization shows signs of cultural degradation. As we covered in Chapter 4, the decisions you make, your behavior, and how you spend your time all bias toward the number-making goal, and then when you attach a bonus structure to it, you begin to forgo collaboration and "doing the greater good" for making "my" number. The focus on the work disappears, spending becomes more important than finishing, and slowing more important than stopping. You start everything and finish nothing, keeping everyone utilized as a sign of efficiency and inflating the value of work so that it is looked at more favorably. All of the measures are about progress toward the number rather than about whether you are delivering more value more often.

Somehow being on budget has become a key indicator of the success of a company. Although this can be true in a literal sense—that is, the company is spending within its means—it translates to managers as, "Do everything, but only spend this much." Then, the budget decreases each year, causing a never-ending spiral of "do more with less" until what is left is "do everything with nothing."

In the digital world this just won't work. There has been much written about funding in the Digital Age, so much so that it can take up an entire book; in fact, it has in *Beyond Budgeting: How Managers Can Break Free from the Annual Performance Trap*, by Jeremy Hope and Robin Fraser (HBR Press). In our book, we want to focus on highlighting the key constraints of the traditional models that lead to the aforementioned symptoms and the style of approach you need to prepare for.

ANNUAL CYCLES

A great analogy often used for this is to imagine if your personal bank decided to open for only a day or two each year. What would it be like for you if you had to decide so far in advance how much you were going to spend in a year, what you would spend it on, and for what benefit. Thinking about life in general, how difficult would it be to even know what you would need the money for, let alone decide what you were going to do or how? Yet we still see this scenario playing out in many traditional organizations for which a cycle of planning, bidding, awarding, and monitoring drives the company and takes up leadership's time far more than the stewardship of value delivery.

There are so many anecdotes that we could come up with to discuss the impact this has on the success of a business in achieving its outcomes. Here are two classic examples of how this annual thought pattern is counter to the focus on customer value delivery and responsiveness that you need in the Digital Age.

The first is around *slowing the work in order to make the number*. In a large Telco we worked with, the IT budget was being eroded in a typical "actuals minus 5%" each year. This put pressure on the leadership from two directions: the cost pressure to complete work, and the fight over what actual "actuals" should be used from the previous year as the baseline. The closer the company got to the end of the financial year, the greater the pressure became. Each and every day, a team of 30 people stayed buried in spreadsheets managing the flow of money across the portfolio of projects and reconciling each expenditure to within an inch of its life. As the risk of cost creep increased, the work was slowed and spending deferred; in other words, managers delayed value delivery and deferred expenditure to the following year. So here is where it all falls apart. It got to the point at which years of accumulation of this technique meant that at the start of the next financial year, 70% of the budget was already committed spend on work that had already started. Managers had no recourse to stop the work; they could not ask for more money for that work as it was already approved in previous budgets, so they expected to be well funded. They were left with only 30% of the annual allocated budget for new work in the coming 12 months.

The second anecdote relates to *the budget negotiation process* where, during a leadership meeting, someone commented that "we are at risk of not spending the budget." Unbelievably, the pressure created from the financial cycles had turned not spending the budget into a "risk" to be managed. This leads to a whole negative conversation about where they might be able to redirect funds to stranded labor (underutilized resources) who could start work on a lower-priority item for which the actuals were not short. Underspending would have led to less final end-of-year actuals, so when the following year's budgets were calculated on "last year actuals" with a cut baked in, the team would end up with a smaller budget than if they made the number and had the cut applied.

But it's important to note that it is not the annual cycle itself that is the issue. It's how you treat it and tie individual performance and KPIs to it that causes issues. Combining these things creates a situation in which failure, being wrong, or changing based on what you have learned is impossible. You would need to forgo personal success and bonuses to do the right thing for the organization. The annual cycle is a reporting cycle—it should be a simple snapshot in time to close out the books and record results. The information should always be available and visible, easily accessed, and full of insights captured through the year, but it should not take loads of planning time and massaging of figures to reach. The company should not slow to a grinding halt leading into the end of the financial year only to have to jump to hyperspeed in a mass ramp-up the following month.

Although there are antipatterns, there are also organizations—especially digital-native businesses—that have done it better, where everyone feels valued, the highest-valued work is done, and people and money are available to support it. They generally embrace a more dynamic funding model that works within the annual cycle and has the ability to change as knowledge is gained. This flexible funding model is generally enabled by the following:

- Smaller work sizes and smaller decisions so that change has less risk associated with it and being slightly wrong does not have large financial implications.

- Budgeted money not given in its entirety to the team from the start. Money is instead dropped in line with value being delivered; as one small chunk is complete and value is validated, the next drop happens.

- Moving the outcome needle when an initiative is successful to make sure more money is available for it. This means that you might need to stop something that is providing less value. Working in a way that supports stopping early without implications is therefore an important component.

- A venture capital–style approach to funding experiments and exploration. This is where you fixate on the outcome, provide a small amount of funding to multiple options to achieve it and scale only the ones that work. It might mean increasing the money available to ambiguous smaller pieces of work. But you will save way more than this by providing large funding amounts for only the ones that work and stopping those when you have achieved enough rather than completing the full scope.

- Funding capacity rather than projects, having stable teams with fixed costs to provide operational predictability, and simple ROI calculations. Measuring value delivered as the source of return, not work completion.

- Rewarding managers and staff for changing course to meet customer demand. Stopping work that is less valuable and providing accurate visibility so that better fiscal decisions can be made more often.

OPERATING EXPENSE AND CAPITAL EXPENSE

This is a touchy subject, largely in the realm of a country's accounting and organizational constitutions, because businesses need money to be money. The separate treatment of money once delegated to day-to-day decision making again sets off a chain of poor decision criteria with conversations like, "Can we make this an operating expense (OPEX)," as capital expense (CAPEX) budgets run low. We certainly don't want to lead you away from the rules and compliance of your organization, but we want to highlight constraints that need to be dealt with consciously and carefully so as to not get in the way of value delivery from your digital exploits.

Imagine, for example, a large project that has been going on for a year. You identify that perhaps the work being done is now outdated, no longer needed, or is not achieving the value that was intended in the business case. What do you do? What we see is program managers choosing to spend budgets at the expense of delivering value. Stopping the project before it can be capitalized causes unintended consequences: if a deliverable can't be capitalized, it might consume the OPEX budget rather than the capital budget from which it was approved. This is the same bucket that pays for staff, so now you are faced with the choice of continuing with low-value work or risk having to cut staff. Instead, it's likely that if you choose to continue, we now have the resources and money tied up in low-value work, whereas work that could be moving you toward achieving an outcome remains unstarted.

We have seen several organizations manage this through the separation of accounting and the day-to-day operations of the business—the finance team worries about OPEX or CAPEX; everyone else worries about value delivery and fiscal responsibility. But this is not always possible. This is where the modern software delivery methodology can actually help. By using Agile techniques, you can break a large effort into smaller chunks and deliver work in autonomous pieces that provides value continuously and incrementally as these small pieces go into production one by one. This allows you to capitalize, if needed, much earlier and more often. This also creates many more stop points at which you can reflect on progress and make decisions whether to pivot or discontinue the work with far fewer consequences to budget treatments. (We discuss this in more detail in Part III.)

Figure 8-2 illustrates an example of a $20 million program of work. The work is broken up into five smaller pieces of work of varied size and value. We start on the highest-value piece, allocating teams to the smaller initiatives of that first. If there is availability, we might start the next piece, too, but the remaining pieces remain unstarted. This is often where the big mistake is made. Teams can understand the concept of smaller work but still start all of the pieces at the same time; this makes it difficult later on to stop any of them. An issue that traditional funding can create is if we give this team the entire $20 million, they will do anything to keep it knowing a likely future funding cut will happen. Starting each piece concurrently makes the capitalization issue arise and perhaps forces the organization to commit to spending the money on all of the started pieces.

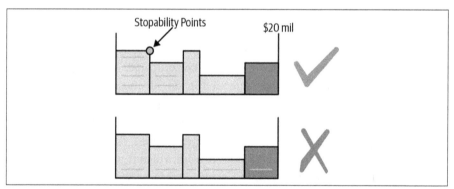

Figure 8-2. Creating stopability through true Agile approaches

What you should be trying to achieve is finishing the first piece before the next piece begins so that you can decide when enough value has been delivered from the money available. You give yourself the option to reallocate a portion of the money that would be used on say the fifth piece to another more valuable program of work. If the inevitable budget cut happens, it's easy to show what will not be complete (the unstarted pieces), and the business consequence is a lot easier to understand. Additionally, you will have already completed some pieces, so you'll have achieved value for the money spent even if you don't end up finishing any more pieces; therefore, less sunk cost without a return.

As was mentioned earlier, to encourage this, you should drop the funding only for the initial pieces and make sure value is being created and previous pieces finished before dropping funds to start the next one. Each of the stop points is then an opportunity to reflect, pivot, and capitalize early, avoiding the OPEX trap.

BUSINESS CASES

Business cases provide two constraint challenges: first, they can lead to a "bigger is better" attitude; and, second, they are often fanciful documents. Breaking work into smaller chunks comes with undeniable value such as improved flow, stopping when enough, and generally more agility to respond to change. However, budgets require big assumptive business cases to justify an allocation of funding sometimes more than 12 months in advance. This conflict forces people to cram all possible scenarios and buffers into the business case to allow for contingencies for things that they don't know about.

The magnitude of a go/no-go decision from a business case means that they are often full of overambitious claims on returns, corresponding with over inflated buffers on cost, leading to a totally unrealistic sense of the case to proceed.

Often it is a battle to the top for access to scarce resources, so the document writers are encouraged to seek out related benefits to add some candy to the story. We once witnessed an entire business case that was simply an aggregation of many other business cases. It literally offered the aggregated benefits of these other documents but with a slightly reduced cost due to a volume purchase that could be achieved. It was approved, as were all the other ones, spending twice on the same promise of returns. In another situation, we looked at all of the business cases claiming to reduce call transfers in call centers, and the total number added up to more calls than were being transferred. If we were to believe the business cases, we would have a negative number of calls being transferred in call centers. Nevertheless, these business cases were also all approved.

What is worse, of course, is that the business cases are rarely reflected on in hindsight to see whether the value was achieved. After they're approved, organizations usually switch into completion mode, and the focus and measures are all about whether the money is spent, the scope completed, and the people utilized. By the end of it, the people are all redispersed to other work or the original case writers have all moved on, so it's nearly impossible to know whether it achieved the benefits it was supposed to anyway.

With or without the business case, what you should be checking against is how much knowledge you have prior to starting and therefore applying the appropriate working style and investment to match this. If you know exactly what to do and are certain about the value it will bring—for example, if you input $1.00 you know you will get $5.00 out—why business case it? Just invest the money and save time and effort. If, however, you are unsure whether it is of value or whether what you are going to do will result in the value, you shouldn't ask for all the money in the first place. Experiment instead and see whether the value is achievable. In doing so, you'll build up your knowledge to where you don't need to business case it. In either way, the rigmarole you go through to create the business cases often seems over engineered and unnecessary. The experimentation leading up to the investment should take the place of the detailed business case and is full of validated data to base it on.

Again, you do not want to rid the organization of governance and cross-checking. There is still the fiscal responsibility side that needs to be covered and the need, at times, to prioritize across different pieces of work. What needs to happen is a much more transparent and lightweight sense check that uses data as the basis of decision making with a more frequent cadence of review and opportunity for change. In a recent example, we saw business cases abolished within the first seven months of the digital transformation and replaced with a streamlined template that allowed them to both ensure a fiscal diligence was taking place and also that they were driving behavioral change. Here's the type of information you could include:

- What steps is the team making toward working differently? What challenges has it encountered? How can the senior team help?
- What is the (clearly stated) value to the customer and how do you know?
- What is the underlying hypothesis?
- What is the data source for measuring and what is the baseline measure?
- How is the work broken down into its smallest pieces of autonomous value?
- What leading indicator will we watch to signal us whether to continue versus pivot?
- What validation/learnings do we want to get from customers?
- Are we building a stable team (dedicated, autonomous, persistent)?

- What resource risks exist (skills, level of commitment, location, etc.)?
- What are the key financial drivers and needs?

PROJECT-BASED FUNDING

Project-based funding is at a microlevel and can put the greatest limitation on change. It is a one-shot funding approach in which a decision is made at the beginning and then everything becomes about execution of the plan. It was designed by consultants back in a time when things were predictable and more certain: you scoped out a piece of work and then executed it and measured its completion. Teams were stood up and stood down project by project as work was completed functionally without much thought or consideration, simply following a plan written by someone else. It was designed mainly to satisfy the functional units of finance and project management, and its main benefit is as a reporting construct.

Even though this method isn't one that we want you to focus on, we raise it because it is the motive of most of the previously described functional constraints, as in, it is because of the desire for project-based reporting that all the aforementioned issues arose. Project-based funding leads to a significant hidden cost and a black market of financial trade-offs in middle management as they scrap and fight to complete work and find resources. This is the cycle we so often see:

1. A project is funded.

2. Headcount numbers are applied rather than a cost, meaning that teams can't source more resources at a lower cost.

3. Scalability, maintenance, automated testing, infrastructure costs, and so on are either left out or undercooked in the hope it comes from someone else's budget.

4. The project is completed over time and over budget.

5. The cost to maintain it comes into the operation bucket for the following year that is already under year on year reduction cycles.

6. The inability to sustain leads to corners being cut and quality sacrificed until something breaks.

7. A new project is created to fix the work.

8. Begin the next loop.

For many, the alternative feels like anarchy, ungoverned and uncontrollable, but the opposite is in fact the truth. Outcome-based funding, more prevalent in the Digital Age, is more controllable, more highly governed, and less risky because the information is real time and more accurate. We work in much smaller pieces for which the implications of failure are smaller, the ability to adapt is higher, and the realization of benefits more measurable. Decision making happens on faster feedback loops rather than forecasts and manipulated figures. When combined with a visibility and transparency mindset, the organization can now operate in a customer lens rather than a reporting one.

Funding outcomes over projects lets you be more flexible in moving around the buckets of money and results in less upfront commitments until you have the knowledge that success is most likely: *Make decisions at the last responsible moment.*

FUNCTIONAL BUDGETS AND PLANNING

Functional budgeting also tends to lead to functional thinking and functional execution. It suggests that the organizational structure is the most optimal way to deliver value to customers, which is not always the case. It can lead to functions doing their piece and then a bunch of handoffs or wait time for others to do theirs. It can also create an adversarial environment when plans are made separately in order to optimize the success of the function.

Functional budgets are an adjunct to project funding. The answer is the same: fund the outcome, recognizing that there is still of course the operation expense of the function that needs covering separately. But this needs to be considered after the outcomes are planned, not prior, for without the knowledge of what it will take to deliver the outcomes, how are you to know what you need functionally? Often in IT, you have a budget "IT for IT," and a separate funding source paying for IT to do strategic work aligned to outcomes. These two budgets are a source of great tension within IT: the IT one stays under constant downward pressure, whereas the other tends to be much larger. The strategic budget covers the business outcome but rarely takes into account the impact on IT assets, putting further pressure on the IT budget. The impacts can be a disconnect between the business need and the IT capabilities (architecture, capacity, stability, scalability) and lead to IT having to hide asset work within the strategic budget. Again, we see an adversarial environment being created; for example, to deliver great outcomes from the strategic budget, IT needs to use automated testing, but the business unit for the work does not want to pay for this as it impacts everyone not just them.

To illustrate this, take a look at Figures 8-3 and 8-4.

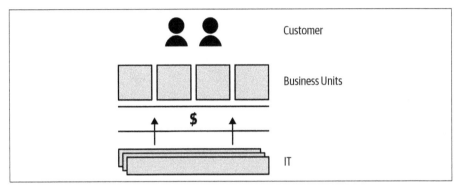

Figure 8-3. Traditional model

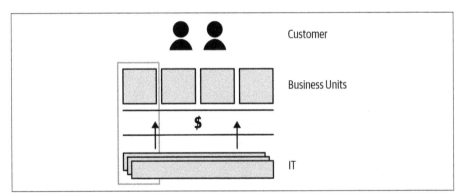

Figure 8-4. Cross-functional model

Figure 8-3 shows a more traditional perspective. The business is the conduit to the customer and IT is subservient to the business, so the only frame of reference they have is money. In this case, they optimize horizontally for efficiency of scale in order to save money, IT starts to treat all of the business units the same, optimizing around lowest-common-denominator services that it can provide to them. The business unit's unique needs are being trampled and ignored, which implies an ignored customer need. Meanwhile the business sees IT as a cost center, and budgets are allocated to the business unit and IT individually.

Figure 8-4 illustrates an alternative: a cross-functional IT and business team, with direct access to the customer and a single budget for an entire outcome. It has responsibility for its own technology capability, maintaining it and covering the cost of the "ilities" previously mentioned. The trade-off here is standardization and the overhead of managing many more moving parts. (We discuss this more in Part III.)

The role of a functional unit is to add to the value delivery to the customer. At worst, it should have a neutral impact, but never a negative one. This needs to be measured. For example, a basic value chain for an organization could be this:

1. Understand customer need.

2. Know how we can uniquely solve it.

3. Have the best people solve it.

4. Solve it well.

5. Begin next loop.

So, in this chain, the functional unit must ensure its processes and practices do not reduce your ability to understand the customer need or solve for it.

MEASURING COMPLETION

We have discussed measurement in earlier chapters, but it's important just to remind ourselves that this is also a finance constraint brought on by the obsession with measurement for fiscal governance sake rather than value. Governing too often means ensuring people did as they were supposed to (spent the money, finished the work, delivered the scope). These are all lagging measures that are internally focused and do not tell us whether we are delivering value for the customer. Getting back to one of our key premises in this book, the more value you deliver more often, the more profitable you become. Focusing on lagging completion measures drives a culture and behaviors of focusing on the wrong thing and often leads to doing low-value work.

In the traditional world of finance adapting to change can become onerous. It includes reworking business cases or resubmitting approvals. In many cases, it's just easier to finish what you're doing and go back later to make changes in the next budget cycle. These constraints and biases need to be mitigated so that the organization can focus on value delivery. It means separating reporting, compensation, targeting, and budgeting, and using them for their intended purpose rather than tying them together and creating a false economy from each. Begin by measuring the impact on the work of a financial decision made by things like "make the number" or "my functional budget." It could be as simple as making the work that won't be started as a result of the decisions visible or looking at the change in the date that value from the work will be made available as a result of decisions—the true cost of delay.

HR

One of the important purposes of the traditional role of the HR function is to reduce risk and exposure for the business. This is often achieved through managing the workforce using rigid job definition policies and procedures designed to enforce compliance. Another is to maximize productivity and effectiveness of people, often achieved through standardization of process and structure.

However, a highly defined work structure that optimizes standardization will at the same time limit responsiveness and cause unnecessary delays when edge cases come up or changes are needed. In some extremes, job descriptions go so far as to confine the work an individual does to the bullet points of their employment contract. A business analyst we worked with in an IT group at a client once stood their ground against proposed cross-functional teaming because their "job" was not about having to talk to the business. Of course, role obsession, as discussed earlier, is an institutional symptom not just caused by HR policies, but it's often reinforced by that group. In such environments, teams are deprived of autonomy, instead following predetermined instruction, and any deviation is done at risk of disciplinary action, and motivation is instilled through pay and incentives.

EXAMPLE WARNING SIGNALS: EMPLOYEE SATISFACTION SURVEYS AND THE BELL CURVE

There are many examples of how you can spot the warning signals. Take for example, the annual employee satisfaction survey charade, the annual "Kit Kat moments," which goes something like this:

1. First, the survey result is tied to the leadership team's bonus, which they then have to sign up to a random guess of the satisfaction change year on year as their target.

2. The same leaders get up at the next all-hands meeting to announce the timeline of the survey, intertwined with positive reinforcement messages of the year's achievements.

3. Employee completion rates are then tied to the performance of middle managers, incentivizing them to find ways to get people to fill it in.

4. Next it is the middle managers' team meeting where you all sit together with Kit Kat candy bars in the middle of the table and fill them in as a group as part of team bonding. Again, the manager will talk about how great the year has been.

One year a person dressed in a bear suit went floor to floor handing out lollipops to remind people to fill their surveys in. Of course, the worst part of the charade is that the survey is normally only a reflection of how the person is feeling that day. A recent bad conversation with a manager, and the survey is poor; a recent pay rise, and the survey is great. Our experience is that leadership teams rarely need a survey result to know whether employees are engaged.

Another example is the *bell curve*, created in the mathematics field to show normal distribution of a variable and then adopted by HR practitioners as a method to manage individual performance. You know the drill: each year staff get a rating so that they are placed across the curve to identify the underperformers, overperformers, and normal performers. Pay raises then are allocated by where you land in the curve. The problem is individual performance is not evenly distributed, especially in small teams. A bell curve is a statistical tool that could be useful at the aggregate level, but at a more granular level, it would force ranking people into a category they might not deserve, hyperperformers mixed with good performers, average mixed with poor.

We witnessed this constraint in action in a large enterprise during a most disturbing conversation. An HR manager chastised a manager who was not prepared to force rank her team, instead choosing a group rating because she had not worked with the team for long and didn't feel there was a distinction between them. In the rather angry exchange, the leader was accused of naivety and lacking in courage, so the HR manager ranked them herself. As one example, a person who had the worst attendance was put in the bottom ranked, attendance being the differentiation point. It turned out that, instead of negligence, this person was a good performer and had to take time off for the passing of a family member. We could only imagine how the person felt after receiving this ranking.

As Figure 8-5 demonstrates, it could be comical if it weren't so potentially detrimental.

Figure 8-5. A lighthearted Dilbert view of the bell curve issues

There was a reason that the HR manager was uncompromising about applying the ranking. That was her functional responsibility and priority. Although this is an extreme example, it illustrates the functional constraint where blindly applying method and process optimizes for the completion of functional activity instead of the business outcome of delivering value to customers. The doing becomes more important than the achieving, and the function's success becomes more important than the whole, which results in conflicting goals and behaviors across the business.

We paint perhaps a slightly unfair picture of the function as such issues are often influenced by the entire leadership team, not just the HR function. But, certainly, this is where the execution and enforcement lie, and today we still see this perspective playing out in real life.

In the Digital Age, to maximize productivity and effectiveness, you need to break away from the constraints of this rigidness. The need to find a balance between protecting the organization and the employees with the required speed and adaptability means digital transformation just cannot be done without the full buy-in of HR. As with most functional units, HR must be proactive and be in front of the changes that need to be constantly explored and nudged. In many cases, instead of reinforcing rules and policies, we have seen HR become a custodian of culture, organizational structure, and employee engagement.

TALENT MANAGEMENT

This new role of HR in the digital sphere takes more of a talent management shape, a unique blend of employee experience and dynamic capability planning. (In Chapter 12, we discuss in more detail how to grow and empower talent.) It necessitates moving from the rigidity of policy and process compliance to providing the value add of supporting a world in which change is constant and ambiguity is the given. In fact, we have seen more and more digital-native businesses redefining the head of HR role to become the chief talent officer. Following are four of the key components to the new chief talent officer.

Capability planning

As an enterprise goes through the digital transformation journey, the type and volume of work flowing through the outcome-based teams will be a key indicator of the skill set and capabilities needed by the organization in general. The HR department needs to increase its ability to first understand the skills currently in the organization, where they are, and in what volumes. Next, HR needs to be able to interpret the likely skills demand given the backlog of work needed to achieve the outcomes, creating an organizational gap analysis of the current skill disbursement versus that needed to maximize customer value. This is an interesting reflection point because it's likely that today's work will match the current skills purely because work is created to match the skill. In the Digital Age, we need to build skills to match the work needed to achieve the customer outcomes. It is a nuance, but an important difference in the way work is born.

For example, the resignation of a PM in one location, under a specific line manager, should not automatically trigger a like-for-like replacement. What is the status of the PM role across the organization? Is there an excess elsewhere that can be used? Does that team need that PM, or is there scarcity of another skill that we see as a better replacement? These smaller, more frequent changes to the organization are often better ways of upskilling and managing capabilities than relying on functional or line-manager hiring.

We see the HR role being a source of data and insight to manage the capability profiling of teams and supporting both more effective supply planning but also a more efficient management of work alignment with teams. This alignment comes not through heavy upfront design or a complete reassessment of all the teams, but incrementally and iteratively through constant observation, questioning, and small adjustments. This way, in the future, mass restructures are replaced by constant nudging and adapting to changes in the work from changing customer value perceptions.

Employee experience

Employee experience is clearly one of the critical factors in general talent management (in fact, we discuss in detail how to acquire, retain, and develop digital talent in Chapter 12). The rise of the millennial workforce is a game changer for the HR team. The workforce of the Digital Age is motivated differently and is more likely to assess and seek out companies they actually want to work for rather than simply applying for jobs. The old adage of "work–life balance" is no more; it has been replaced with *work-life synergy*, in which the things you love in life are intertwined with the workday. There is a need for flexibility to engage with our lives throughout the day, whether that be taking kids to school, playing a sport, having pets at work, or friendships, social engagement, rest and relaxation, and so on. The workplace of the future is a "life place," or an authentic living environment in which excelling at your job does not cost you your interests, family, and health.

Dan Pink's 2010 book *Drive: The Surprising Truth about What Motivates Us* (Riverhead Books) was a bit of a game changer in this field with the introduction of the autonomy, mastery, and purpose (AMP) concept as an explination of personal motivation. From the book's Wikipedia page (*https://oreil.ly/4F8MQ*):

> *Based on studies done at MIT and other universities, higher pay and bonuses resulted in better performance ONLY if the task consisted of basic, mechanical skills...If the task involved cognitive skills, decision making, creativity, or higher-order thinking, higher pay resulted in lower performance...To motivate employees who work beyond basic tasks, give them these three factors to increase performance and satisfaction:*
>
> - *Autonomy—Our desire to be self-directed. It increases engagement over compliance.*
>
> - *Mastery—The urge to get better skills.*
>
> - *Purpose—The desire to do something that has meaning and is important. Businesses that only focus on profits without valuing purpose will end up with poor customer service and unhappy employees.*

Although Pink points out that you need to pay enough "to take the issue of money off the table," the theory of AMP has become a widely accepted truism for rethinking the role of HR. It means creating the working environments to engage with employees, allowing them to be themselves and intertwine their lives into the day. It is also about creating a learning environment that encourages and supports continuous improvement and development, allowing employees to master their craft. HR even has a role to play in teaching leaders how to articulate the mission and the purpose of the organization in ways that help employees connect meaning to their day-to-day activity. It's not easy to make everyone feel connected to the purpose of the organization all the time. It takes both effort and creativity to create that belongingness.

The concept of "autonomy" is perhaps the most difficult part for the HR team as it could be perceived to run against accountability and discipline. A lot can be done through sharing context, pushing decisions closer to the point of actual work, and designing KPIs and targets at the team level instead of individual level. Individual performance "management" should be turned into individual performance "enhancement." Peer reviews and continuous feedback should be used to boost performance as opposed to measure performance.

Leadership through ambiguity and experimentation

Leadership development sometimes sits under the HR department. We would certainly advocate it to be a first-class capability, if not hierarchically from a reporting perspective, certainly from a strategic perspective. Leadership development plays a crucial role in the empowerment and autonomy afforded to employees. After all, it's all the leaders, not just the HR department, who need to shift away from command and control to steward, mentor, and culture custodian. Broader, more systems thinking and soft skills become even more crucial when the questions being asked are less about completion, achievement, and disciplines and more about returning problems unsolved and giving "orders with minimum constraints" It's a new type of leadership style and we cannot underestimate how much learning leaders will need to go through in order to thrive in an environment of ambiguity and customer value.

When running leader workshops, we see some consistent topics that are more difficult to work through than others. Perhaps old habits die hard, but for some, the new habits are just too foreign. A first step that is often tripped over is using the lens of customer language in the syntax of the organization. Simple examples include being able to describe company outcomes in customer terms, adding customer value measures, putting programs in customer lenses and of course creating the organizational strategy from customer insights. It can be really challenging to make the mental shift and make it permeate into how you talk in the hallways, the questions that you ask of teams, and the conversations around the board room. It is so important for the belief system of the organization during your digital transformation that people hear the leadership talking the talk and walking the walk. Leaders cannot just say the words of customer centricity and then turn around to ask for their project to be done on budget and on time. A simple, "How do you know that will move the needle?" or a "What could we do first to validate that before fully investing?" are gentle shifts that will make the change far more sustainable.

Another topic we see challenging leaders is the concept of smaller chunks of work. It is difficult to resist making a large, bold, upfront plan or decision and instead make lots of smaller ones that can be validated along the way to ensure they will achieve the outcomes intended. It's counter to the instincts of those used to making the annual declaration, building a portfolio of projects, funding it, and managing its progress. Now we need to talk about outcomes, and be explicit about how we would know whether we are progressing toward it and allowing teams to self-organize. Leaders need to be more comfortable with ambiguity—be the custodian of the outcomes, as opposed to driving process and activity.

So it's clear that to transition into new ways of working, leaders need help, too. A client of ours recently had a team create an MVP that would test the water and see whether current high-value customers would take up some new functionality. After six weeks of effort, it was delayed by a leader because he felt it was not "pretty enough." The team was sent back to work on adding what was originally researched with customers as being low-value requirements and unnecessary for the testing and learning stage. It was simply because the leader misunderstood the outcome measure and hypotheses to be tested by the MVP and was viewing it through the lens of a mass production roll out.

Leadership development programs should be designed and provided to help leaders transform themselves effectively first and foremost.

Technology for employees

To build a responsive organization, collaboration and communication are paramount. The global nature of the workforce requires strong tooling for real-time informal interaction as well as planned collaboration activities. Increasingly, we will see adoption and merging of social media platforms into the workforce as well as more targeted collaboration applications like Slack, Trello, or Google

Docs. Teams need to be able to work simultaneously on one thing, whether it's a line of code, a document, a presentation, or a program.

The millennial workforce grew up in the Digital Age. Millennials are comfortable with digital tools and also have high expectations due to the digital experience in their personal life. After being used to the intuitive user interfaces and responsive functionality of their favorite social media platforms, shopping apps, or games, using the corporate applications and tools could feel like a ride on a time machine back to the last century.

With the technology expectations, the HR department needs to drive the adoption of better tools and experiences that connect employees' work and life. A better technology experience is becoming a differentiator to attract and retain millennial talent just like acquiring and retaining customers. The challenge for HR will be to work closely with the technology teams to ensure the exact balance of productivity, collaboration, and employee engagement with the constraints of policy and compliance.

Legal and Regulatory Compliance

Although we all want to maximize the value we deliver to customers, we are also responsible for protecting the interests of the organization, including not breaking the law and maintaining a tolerable risk profile. The LRC team plays a crucial role in ensuring that.

However, the LRC team is often inherently and appropriately conservative. Its role often involves monitoring other people's work and actions to make sure that things don't go wrong. In the Digital Age, there is tension between the speed, creativity, and perceived risk-taking approach and the more traditional, conservative, manual-auditing process.

When we think about LRC, there are a few dimensions and it's important to recognize each in the context of constraints. Not all of them are the sole responsibility of the LRC team but fall under a compliance banner:

LAWS AND REGULATIONS

These are the constraints that you must live with. They are the things imposed on you from countries, government bodies, industries, and law enforcement that you cannot change and with which you must ensure compliance. In the next decade or two, we will generally expect to see an increase of regulatory constraints due to the complexity introduced by digital technology; for example, the European Union's General Data Protection Regulation (GDPR) for data and privacy protection, Payment Services Directive (PSD II) for customer protection, and stress testing regulations like Basel III to mitigate systemic risk. At the same time, the emergence of new technologies like AI, surveillance and tracking, drones, and new social media applications add a whole new dimension to compliance among a wide range of digital footprints. Even something as simple and obvious as allowing employees to bring their own devices into the workplace has blurred the ownership of data and the use of company assets.

POLICY AND PROCEDURES

This is the how; the ways in which people should behave and the necessary steps you have to take while conducting business. The goal is to reduce the possibility of stepping into the wrong side of law and regulations by accident. They are created by the organization and largely are changeable. The issues that organizations need to face is that policies and procedures, after they're created, are typically long lived and seldom reviewed. For the most part people are simply trained to follow or enforce them.

In reality, any policy or procedure that is more than two or three years old needs to be able to be challenged for fit for purpose in the Digital Age. Otherwise they might be unnecessarily constraining your capabilities. These could be functionally led policies like the use of internal transfers that limit the flow of talent to where it is needed, or the use of internal money exchange where one department must pay another for the use of its skills rather than money allocated once and holistically to complete an outcome. They could be legal policies such as the need for approval. A recent client's LRC team had a three-week service-level agreement (SLA) with the delivery teams. Three weeks to get back to delivery teams on approvals! How will that work with an increased volume of high-value, smaller pieces of work that you want to release weekly?

There are policies that you might need to add or update to be able to promote diversity and attract talent; we talk more to this in Chapter 12. Effective, well-written policies should serve as decision making guides rather than a prescriptive list of things employees can and cannot do. There are inevitably going to be some definitive things people cannot do, but a policy should not try to be (nor pretend to be) exhaustive.

As your organization goes through digital transformation, it is important to flag policies and procedures along the way that constrain or restrict value being delivered. You must resist the "you can't do that because the policy says so" reaction, and instead question the suitability of the policy. Policies and regulations need to become more about enablement than enforcement, safely removing roadblocks ahead of time rather than applying the handbrake. The one thing you won't be able to do is hold back the pace of change. The flow of water will find its way around policies if it needs to, and that could create greater challenges.

STANDARDS

Mostly external benchmarks or community-developed standards are specifications and procedures that are used to provide a level of uniformity that can be obtained by using prescribed methods and materials. They provide business benefits such as interoperability, safety, government legislative support, and economies of scale through market adoption and contribution. Compliance of standards is very much a yes-or-no answer and might also come with a level of accreditation.

Standards exist in many functional areas of your organization; for example, technology standards for uniform engineering practices, LRC ISO standards around compliance and risk management, HR standards for people management, and financial reporting standards.

Some standards can be overbearing and provide more constraint and cost than benefit. Standards communities can have a degree of blind bigotry that distort the adoption into areas it was not designed for or create more work than perhaps would be of value. Standardization can lead to mediocrity and constrain innovation; the collective is unlikely to be able to move as fast as the market conditions, so it's important to stay active in the standards you use and to measure their impact so that you don't fixate on the accreditation over value delivery.

Leaning on the Cynefin framework (*https://oreil.ly/mHD7W*) for a minute, standards play a role when things are known and easily specified, but in the Digital Age, and even more so in your digital transformation, you are often in the unknown realm of the complex and chaotic. In this state, it is difficult to know what standards to apply and simply following a scaling framework or what has worked for others is not sustainable. You can't apply something that has worked in one complex environment and to another complex environment and expect the same result. Never let implementation of standards override the outcome!

GOVERNANCE

The biggest impact in the area of governance comes from providing visibility and transparency of the aforementioned LRC conditions in a way that defines necessary constrains but does not constrain value delivery We refer you to Chapter 12 for the key aspects of this. Governance needs to become less about reporting and more about sensing; less about control and more about insights.

Digital transformation raises some interesting operational challenges for the LRC function. The pace of change, the size of the work loads, and the frequency of change are all antipatterns of more traditional set and monitor LRC operations. We need LRC to lean in and help create an environment in which we can manage through the ambiguity and take advantage of technology to accelerate value delivery. It should define the upfront guardrails for the laws and regulations and embed them into the design of the work rather than enforce them after the fact, to help measure the processes and policy implications on the work, the indicators of trade-offs, and the impacts of noncompliance.

We have seen some successful steps taken by the LRC team in various organizations to become a better business partner in the Digital Age.

JOINING THE DIGITAL TRANSFORMATION EARLY

Because the digital transformation is mainly about growing the business and customer value delivery, LRC is often left out of the change management team until the last stage. The benefit of the thin-slice approach is the opportunity to involve LRC from the very first experiment. The early visibility and exposure will allow LRC to better understand the risk profile of new ways of working and evolve the compliance policies and procedures side by side. LRC could become a collaborative partner for the transformation journey as opposed to the handbrake at the last minute. It will be better prepared for the why and not just the what—a position of strength for LRC decisions.

The LRC function will need to better align itself to the work types of the outcomes, ensuring the right amount of subject matter expertise in the right areas. It will need to better embed itself into the outcome teams so as to provide more upfront contribution of compliance guardrails so work is designed to meet it and less time is spent afterward checking the work. With lots of smaller pieces of work going into the hands of the customer, the days of approving are just not scalable. The focus of the function must be on how LRC can contribute to organizational agility by ensuring policies and procedures are created to suit the various work types and risk profiles. Smaller work means smaller risk, faster feedback, and more data points for monitoring.

DIGITIZATION OF COMPLIANCE ITSELF

Yes, it's about using new technology to better monitor risks introduced by technology. Instead of conducting risk and compliance activities in a manual, ad hoc fashion, invest in new automated capabilities to help streamline compliance processes and help LRC teams make more accurate, informed decisions. Although the digital transformation is mainly about delivering better products and services to customers, the digitization of internal functions, including LRC, cannot be underinvested. There is no way the business can provide better digital services and products without the digitization of risk and compliance management.

You need to bake into your policies and procedures a greater ability to manage change and drive ethical and appropriate decision making. Contracts and warranties should be less about perfection and more about visibility, responsiveness, and providing a framework for prioritization and trade-off decisions. Contracts, like policies, that are too prescriptive have limited usefulness in a rapid-change environment. Good contracts align expectations around the big-picture desired outcome. Many customers will understandably want the contract to include some detailed deliverables, but we think it is more important for the contract and contracting process to align the parties around priorities and to provide mechanisms for making trade-off decisions. In the Digital Age, an organization wants to be able to make lots of small bets or experiments where the output is about learning, not delivery, so LRC should be more concerned with managing the risk of frequent change by expecting automation, tooling, fall-back positions, and by having "contracts as tests." Contracts as tests is a concept that brings the proper constraints or guardrails of the LRC function into the upfront design, making it part of how work is done rather than an approval process that begins after the work is completed.

FOCUSING ON ANALYSIS AND REMEDIATION

Using advanced analytics, LRC teams can have a better enterprise view of compliance risks, and be able to prioritize areas to monitor. A better understanding of the risk profile will help the teams to rely less on enforcing process and policy to achieve prevention and be able to apply more LRC talent on predictive analysis and remediation. This will give business teams more freedom to experiment without tripping over policies and procedures while making sure that the overall risk profile of the enterprise does not exceed the threshold with early and fast recovery.

Avoid big upfront decisions that create long-term commitments to direction, scope, or end states too far in the distance. Teams need the freedom to learn and change, and that includes external partners and vendors. Contractual arrangements that hold external parties to account for a predetermined position without the flexibility to change will only lead to you getting what you paid for, not what you asked for. Relationships need to be win/win, not in a compromised position, but in a newly discovered end state that achieves the outcome in a way you might never have expected. In return you should demand unprecedented transparency of activity toward the outcomes that identifies risks much earlier and allows the organization to be better prepared to manage them.

This chapter has highlighted a few of the more influential functional areas that need to reassess and align themselves with the digital transformation along with a more general approach to functional change that can be applied across the board. All functional units need to focus on outcomes, not completion, and on enabling change and exploration over long-term commitments. When it comes to functional change, the intent is to build adaptability and agility into the organization rather than changing from a static process A to a static process B via big upfront design and change programs.

Using the cascade mental model that we discussed earlier, you should begin with the outcomes the organization is trying to achieve and then define the functional activities required to make that real. You should use this knowledge to design the function's role in advancing the outcome. This is quite the opposite of the more traditional activity we normally see in which each function has its own goals and plans and bids for money to do those things independent of the overall outcome achievement.

The implications of not doing it are like the dam wall in a storm; the pressure will build as a rush of work flies at the functions, who will be unable to drink water from the fire hose, and something will break. It is fair to say that one of the repeated patterns in failed transformations is the inability of the supporting functions to adapt to the new world of small, fast, and adaptive.

Key Points

Following are the key points that we hope you take away from this chapter as well as two actions for you to take to begin implementing what we've discussed:

- Change means everyone. You can't have new ways of working surrounded by old processes and rigid policies. Functional units need to understand that they too need to align to value delivery.

- Experience says one of these functional units will be a stronger influence on the operations of your organization than others. Knowing the angle your transformation needs to come from and constraints that you might need to live with is critical to sustainable change. Using a model like the double-triangle model helps you methodically evolve functional units rather than a big upfront design.

- Combining this section with Part I says: let customers decide the value, value decide the measures, measures decide the work, work decide the capabilities, capabilities decide the people, and people decide the team; then functional units provide support to make it happen.

Here are two actions to take:

- Plan your approach for functional inclusion: Using the double-triangle or other methods, avoid policy and process constraints by ensuring functions are a part of the broader transformation and are transforming themselves.

- Identify the skills needed: You now have a full backlog of new and existing work that you "want" to do to deliver customer value. Use this to create a skills map of what you need and the skills gap against what you currently have in the organization.

9

Letting Data Decide

Historically the need for certainty has slowed the pursuit of new opportunities. The preplanned financial years with all of the work and the spend decided before companies have even begun the work have provided a false sense of surety that allowed them to provide stakeholders with a sense of certainty about what the company would do. Today the pace of change is such that this foundation of guesswork will no longer suffice; organizations need to become more adept at moving forward with imperfect information.

In a world of ambiguity and constant change, certainty has to be traded off with accuracy. Data has become the new economy and a critical component of sustainable digital transformation. Digital transformation demands responsiveness, and responsiveness can be measured by your ability to capture and use data to build knowledge. The organizations that are consistently able to adapt to industry disruption are the ones that are successfully using data as the basis of what to do, when to do it, and—more important—when to stop doing it.

Across nearly all industries, we are seeing transformation driven by the availability of data; for example:

- The retail sector using omnichannel data to drive sales and customer understanding, creating differentiated personalized experiences for their customers

- In agriculture, the use of sensors to monitor crops and livestock so that producers can maximize production and manage the quality of outputs

- Manufacturing organizations using data to provide predictive maintenance or take preventative action, increasing service levels and providing information as a value add to customers

- Government creating smart city strategies, using data to better connect with citizens and optimize the management of assets for traffic flow, utilities, government services, law enforcement, and so on

- The health-care industry providing more connected health services for better patient engagement and monitoring, especially helpful for self-management and remote area patient care

Still, we constantly speak to organizations that are overcommitting resources and work before they have proof that doing so will achieve the outcome, relying more on the highest paid person's opinion (HIPPO) and functional department heads than on evidence. The classic bottom-up bidding wars are also more likely to lead to a result that optimizes for the current work and the current skills of staff than for maximizing customer value.

It's time to let data decide rather than the HIPPOs or the status quo. We explore this topic from two perspectives:

- What kinds of improvements data analytics has made to give us better insights and how we need to change our thinking and process to let data help us make better decisions to guide the transformation

- Using data to help us better understand and deliver more customer value

Data as a Source of Knowledge

Organizations have always tried to use data to improve. Relational databases were a revolutionary change in the 1980s, making it much easier to administer data and make changes. Databases allowed companies to track and manage transactions with high integrity, consistency, and safety, but they also made accessing data at scale more difficult and slower due to the need to maintain high-consistency and integrity. The NoSQL database movement was a response to that. It focused more on horizontal scaling so that companies could easily ask a lot of different questions and get the answers back faster.

Now we have entered the new age of big data and machine learning. There is more data available and more ways to extract information and intelligence from the data. New capabilities include the following:

Scalable storage of any type of data through models like data lake
Cloud storage and distributed file systems allow us to store large quantities of data in its raw format beyond the capacity of the traditional structured relational database.

Real-time analysis of data
New tools allow us to get sophisticated intelligence from live stream of data in real time.

Asking different questions instead of asking the same questions again and again
Independently scalable compute capability allows us to run ad hoc queries on a variety of large sets of data more efficiently. Instead of being forced to come up with a list of static questions to generate the same report regularly, hoping to get a different answer some day, we can now ask different questions and explore the data more freely.

Machine learning
Humans are inherently cognitively biased. Machines can now learn and obtain intelligence with less human influence. This starts to give us surprising findings that the human brain would have struggled to discover.

These modern data approaches present greater opportunities in how we build knowledge and derive insight that can be used to improve business decision making, including the following:

Early response
In some cases, the value of data diminishes quickly as time goes by. For example, in health-care, early response is critical for timely treatment. T7, a UK-based startup that provides care for the elderly at their homes, is helping improve lives by placing devices around a patient's house to gather data via an engaging interface to the elder's caretaker or next of kin. The platform reduces the need for frequent visits by the family or caretaker as well as provides the ability to identify an emergency in real time.

Predictive warnings
A large financial institution was reliant on running large calculations through applications built in-house running on thousands of servers, databases, and messaging queues. System failure led to business disruptions that could cost millions of dollars. The company used machine learning algorithms and statistical techniques to analyze the "telemetry" data

captured from these infrastructure elements (databases, queues, servers) to come up with "early warning signals" for application failure.

Leading indicators unavailable to us before

Clickstream can track data on all of the clicks from visitors on a website. It enables us to understand visitors' navigation patterns, their buying pattern, and their abandonment pattern. Shopping cart data can track visitors' behavior regarding when and how they put items into shopping carts or take them out before checking out. This allows us to study how the website design and functionalities influence consumers' shopping behaviors beyond just what they end up buying in the final stage.

Visualization

Insights gathered from a broad set of data are best represented through graphical representations that help inform decision making.

IMO Market Pulse was a web application that cut through the complexity of the Western Australian electricity market. It provided a real-time dashboard and a set of historical trend visualizations. Market Pulse comprised 15 custom-built animated visualizations of core datasets that provided a snapshot of the market and its history on the IMO public site as well as providing an operational dashboard to industry stakeholders. Market Pulse provided the following interactive visualizations:

- Map of live power generation by facility

- Map of live wind generation across the southwest of the state of Western Australia

- Live graphs of current price, load, and generated power across the network

- Outage and generation information for all facilities

- Animation of generation market diversification over time

- Graphical comparison of weekly market metrics over the life of the market

Figure 9-1 shows a screenshot of real-time data for live wind generation. They used the number of turbines, the speed at which they turned, and its size to represent different information. You could then hover over a turbine to expose real-time statistics for that facility.

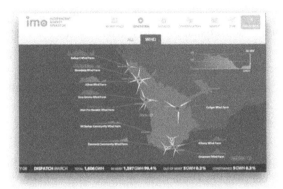

Figure 9-1. IMO Market Pulse gave a visual representation of consumption

Technology advances have opened up a world of opportunity in the amount and type of data available across industries and are driving the adoption of analytics, machine learning, and AI as sources of new value creation. Whether for process improvement and efficiency, more intimate customer engagement, or better business decision making, the breadth of the role of data is critical in future proofing your organization and business model.

Data as a Decision Point: Choosing What to Do

We have mentioned before that digital transformation includes a trade-off between accuracy and certainty. Given the rapid pace of change, you should acknowledge that you are less certain about the future and how to go about getting there; at the same time, you should be able to more accurately know where you are at the moment and the impact of your work. The real-time knowledge gained from data can help you to better track progress to guide and prioritize what you should do with the current work. It can even help to better predict the forward-looking trends to allow you come up with better hypotheses on what you should do next.

For decades, decisions have been highly influenced by factors outside of what data tells us, largely due to the difficulty in getting access to data and the inability to analyze data in ways that generate insight for decision making. Decision makers simply haven't known where true knowledge sits. They have had to deal with other organizational factors like structure, status, fear of failure, and so forth that muddy the water and make it difficult to know which way to move. But by addressing the organizational and functional constraints from the previous two chapters and taking advantage of new technologies, decision makers can gain the visibility and transparency they need to learn and respond to change.

To create this type of work practice, you first need to have a clear understanding of what knowledge you have today, or could have. Being introspective about what knowledge you have is a critical muscle that organizations need to build. For example, as you are about to invest in the next piece of work toward an outcome, evaluate the likelihood of this work moving the needle by asking yourself. Do I know this will be worthwhile, think it will, or hope it will?

In the digital era, you need to be able to adapt your ways of working based on knowledge, to combat the challenges of speed and ambiguity. The more knowledge you have, the more you can confidently invest, and the more successful you will be. This is how you prioritize work, still following from the Agile adage of doing the most valuable items first, using data and knowledge to more accurately identify which items are most likely to help achieve the outcomes.

Borrowing from the terminology of *Lean Enterprise: How High Performance Organizations Innovate at Scale* (O'Reilly) by Jez Humble et al., begin by using work descriptors like *explore, exploit,* and *sustain* to categorize work based on knowledge. Then, adding the context of data will help establish a framework and provide transparency on how decisions are made.

Note

The labels are not the relevant discussion here; you can replace them with whatever works for you organization's taxonomy, but the categories are important.

EXPLORE

This first category refers to when you see an opportunity but have little knowledge whether it will work or be worthwhile. Traditionally, it is the category that would be laughed at or miss out on funding; imagine a business case that honestly said, "I am not sure whether it will work." But this type of work happens more often than we are prepared to admit: we overhype the case for it, convincing people it is bound to succeed. Then, as per all projects, we complete the scope, stand up a team, and go about delivering it safely in the knowledge that no one is likely to check whether it worked.

However, by being upfront about having minimal knowledge to go by, you can reset your thinking to being more of a goal of testing if the opportunity is real. You can constrain the time, cost, and resources invested, create a hypothesis, and design the smallest thing to prove or disprove it. Answer questions such as "is there a market demand" or "is it viable for us to offer it to market," using data to inform the truth rather than opinions.

It also means a change in how you use data and what and how you measure. Many organizations have made the transition to where an experimental pathway is acceptable, but they constrain it with a traditional measure like revenue to judge success. Using revenue as a measure for explore mode will likely lead to a fail mark every time, because explore measures are about whether the hypothesis was proven to be true, or whether we have learned something new—that's it. Understanding the relationship between data and capturing leading indicators of success is what's important.

For explore mode to work, you must apply the principles of the scientific method: have a hypothesis, a fixed time frame, and minimal commitment of money and people that would otherwise lock you in to proceed. Knowing where the data source will be and being able to point to the baseline before you start is essential. Using this method makes it safer to fail and less risky to try, encouraging a lot of ideas to achieve an outcome. If it works, exploit the opportunity; if it doesn't, walk away with new knowledge and the satisfaction that you saved the organization a lot of money.

So rather than saying, "I am not sure it will work," in explore mode, you might say, "I think this feature will change buyer behavior and increase profits."

EXPLOIT

Exploit mode is for when you now know you have a good idea or opportunity but need to work out how to carry it out. In this stage you have seen positive results from explore activities. There is evidence of success, but only in small doses, and you want to see what it would take to scale it out. Will the benefit still exist at scale?

In exploit mode you are basically figuring out how to capitalize on an opportunity. Measurement moves to more growth and scale indicators such as knowing whether you can build capability, attract customers at scale, or support it functionally with suitable funding models and team structures. All while still seeing the same positive results from the early experiments. You can be more confidently investing and committing resources to the activities but must remain cautious about being capable of taking advantage of the opportunity.

In this mode you might say, "This feature changed some buyer behavior and increased profitability in this segment, I wonder whether it would change everyone's behavior and if we offer it to everyone whether we could support it affordably."

SUSTAIN

You reach the sustain mode when you have knowledge such as empirical data, mature clients, or consistent revenue.

Sustain means you should have predictability about investments, target clients, and behaviors. It is the work that you can build your business around reliably and therefore deserves the most attention and effort. It is important not to become complacent with sustain work; you must continue to invest in nurturing it, perhaps adding new features or tweaking usability, in order to keep ahead.

Measurement becomes more traditional because by now you should have a solid link between inputs and outputs, a clear understanding of success measures, and be seeing a direct impact on revenue and/or profitability.

It is fair to say that most organizations treat all work like sustain work. We think what we know is true, so we just commit everything to it and use traditional measures as if they were directly relatable. It's a false sense of sustain driven by an inability to be introspective enough to assess or validate our own knowledge, perhaps some ego gets in the way here, too.

In this mode you might say, "This feature changes buyer behavior and increases profits; we need to take care of it and make sure it continues to deliver on the value expected."

Categorizing the work this way gives a unique view of the portfolio of work and helps to focus the organization on what matters. Many of the clients that we have seen adopt this perspective are able to then balance the portfolio across these categories to make sure they are always exploring and always looking to exploit opportunities while investing the majority of their resources in things known to be true. A general guideline for this balancing act is 15/25/65 as percentages of investment and focus across the three categories.

Use Data to Create an Intelligent Enterprise

We just discussed how we can use the insights gained from data to make better decisions on investment portfolio management and prioritization. Next, we explore some patterns to take advantage of data insights to help people in the organization make better decisions in order to provide better products and services to the customers or create new business models.

The explosion of data now available is driving a digital ecosystem that sees us reshaping organizations through the creation of new data-driven products, enhanced personalization, and customer service value add. The McKinsey Global Institute (*https://oreil.ly/iqNZG*) indicates that data-driven organizations are 23 times more likely to acquire customers, 6 times as likely to retain customers, and 19 times as likely to be profitable as a result. Organizations are evolving themselves at a rate unprecedented in history because the digital interactions we have with our customers is uncovering new meaning and insight into what customers value is and how to best deliver on it. Let's look at a few.

DATA DECIDING FOR ITSELF

Andrew Ng, who led the development of deep learning and artificial intelligence at both Google and Baidu, wrote in a 2016 HBR article (*https://oreil.ly/vJWCP*):

> *If a typical person can do a mental task with less than one second of thought, we can probably automate it using AI either now or in the near future.*

Instead of a second, some argue that it can be done for all tasks that take less than a minute of thought. In any case, there is no more doubt that AI is going through a phase of explosive growth. With proper algorithms and enough data for training, machines can make very good decisions similar to what an experienced human can do. Although these are simple and narrow tasks, the benefit from volume and accuracy can be significant for a business or an entire industry. There are well known examples: facial recognition, speech recognition, grammar correction, and language translations.

Anomaly detection is a particularly useful area. Traditional methods of data analysis have long been used to detect fraud. They often require complex and time-consuming investigations that deal with different domains of knowledge. AI and machine learning have proven to be very effective at detecting spam emails. The application of AI and machine learning for anomaly detection has been since expanded to credit card fraud detection, diagnostic radiography, and system breach detection in information security.

PERSONALIZED CUSTOMER EXPERIENCES

Product recommendation is another category that has been well documented in case studies of Amazon and Netflix. A lot of their fantastic revenue growth is built on their product recommendation engines, which are powered by AI algorithms and massive amounts of online data. But you don't need to be an internet giant to leverage AI and machine learning to recommend better and more relevant products and services.

One of our clients in the real estate industry had successfully built one of the largest digital assets in its market. The downside was that the enormous percentage of anonymous users on the site restricted the company's ability to understand those users and provide valuable insight to its partners. The company's response was to run a machine learning exercise. It asked anonymous users as they entered the site whether they were a first-home buyer. Although you would expect a low response rate, the company was able to gather enough data to train the machine learning algorithms. The algorithms were able to detect patterns from the clickstream and other navigation behaviors to predict first-home buyers rather accurately in real time. This gave the business new opportunities to generate first-home buyer offers and products that are highly relevant to this target audience.

When consumers give us the permission to access more of their data—for example, sensing data like location, voice, movement, temperature, and personal data like calendar, email, and social network—we could infer more accurate and specific user context; for example, their activity, environment, mood, and even stress level. Designers will have a lot to work with given this wealth of context. The individual, as opposed to the target group, is what defines user experience in the age of machine learning.

MAKE BETTER HUMAN DECISIONS

AI and machine learning are very good at finding a needle in a haystack. Humans are much better at looking at the needle and deciding what to do with it. Apart from simple, narrow tasks, most business decisions require good judgment, empathy, intuition, and creativity. But humans are actually very poor at pattern recognition due to our cognitive biases. Our brains are extremely poor at predicting statistical trends.

Our brains can be tripped by things as simple as a coin toss. After getting heads five times in a row, most of us would be thinking, "The next time it must be tails!" Statistically, it's still 50/50, even after we get 100 heads in a row. With a little mental effort, most of us can counter that cognitive bias and come to the proper conclusion.

But here is a slightly more challenging question. Behavior economics pioneers Amos Tversky and Daniel Kahneman conducted this experiment:

A town is served by two hospitals. In the larger hospital, about 45 babies are born each day, and in the smaller hospital about 15 babies are born each day. While about 50% of all babies are boys, the exact percentage varies from day to day—sometimes over 50%, sometimes lower than it.

For a period of one year, each hospital recorded the days on which more than 60% of the babies born were boys. Which hospital do you think recorded more such days?

1. *The larger hospital*

2. *The smaller hospital*

3. *About the same*

The result: 56% of subjects chose option 3, and 22% of subjects respectively chose options 1 or 2.

The correct answer should be 2, the smaller hospital. That's because a larger number of events should lead to a more average daily outcome. It takes a lot more mental effort to counter this cognitive bias.

This is not a trick question. This happens all the time in our daily activity. If we need to set a price for a product, besides competitor's pricing, historical pricing, essential versus discretionary nature of the product, we need to predict potential future demand from consumers for this product, and the potential future supply of this product from providers and supply-chain data. AI and machine learning will become, if it's not there already, much better at predicting the future trends based on data. It's our job to use the data and algorithms and apply the insights to make better and more rational decisions.

For important business decisions like pricing, inventory management, supply-chain management, people and equipment scheduling, maintenance scheduling, and so on, we will need to unpack these decisions, identify the parts that are information processing, pattern recognition, and prediction, and let data/AI/machine learning give those answers. The parts that require empathy, creativity, and common sense should remain in the realm of human judgment.

Data is incredibly effective at helping to build a responsive organization. By reacting early and effectively to weak but telling signals coming from the market, the customers, and the internal organization itself, you are better placed to do the following:

- Move forward with imperfect information.
- Make decisions at the last responsible moment.
- Increase your ability to change.
- Be able to generate new sources of value.

On one hand, business leaders need to understand the organizational constraints and our own cognitive biases and learn how to remove or mitigate them, both personally and institutionally. On the other hand, we need the technology capability to collect clean data, put it into the appropriate place, and apply the correct algorithms. We explore this in more depth in the next section as part of the overall technology strategy in a digital transformation.

Key Points

Following are the key points that we hope you take away from this chapter as well as two actions for you to take to begin implementing what we've discussed:

- In the trade-off between accuracy and certainty, data helps you better understand where you are at so that you can speed up the decision-making process, becoming more responsive.

- Being introspective about how much knowledge you have in regard to the impact of your work helps you to make smarter investment choices and do the work more efficiently.

- The availability of data and the technology to analyze it allows you to make better decisions, create new products, and serve your customers better.

Here are two actions to take:

- Use data as a strategic decision-making asset: Rethink your data strategy to include the use of data to speed up decision making and drive your digital transformation road map, knowing which levers to pull and when to pivot.

- Invest in work that you *know* will succeed: Categorize your current portfolio/backlog into explore, exploit, and sustain. Balancing your investments and priorities based on the amount of knowledge you have will move the needle.

PART III

Building Technology at the Core: A Tech Perspective for Business Leaders

In a recent Forbes CIO Summit, Walmart's CIO, Clay Johnson, talked about an inspiring moment during a 2017 Walmart leadership team meeting. When someone suggested that the technologists should make the technical terms in the IT strategy more accessible to business line managers, Walmart CEO Doug McMillon instead said, "Business people need to start speaking the language of technology." We too believe that business leaders also need to become more technology savvy. After all, digital transformation is about how to better take advantage of the new information technology capabilities in executing your business strategy.

However, we did not want to start this book from the technology perspective. The most important lesson we have learned is that during the digital transformation, digital technology transformation is the means, and business transformation is the end. We want to highlight the importance of the changes needed on company alignment, business processes, organizational structure, and operational constraints because these are needed to be able to take advantage of your new technology capabilities.

In the first two sections, we explored some key concepts that will allow technology to create more value:

- A focus on customer outcomes
- Smaller and incremental work loads

- Measuring value end to end
- Frequent changes
- Capturing data and insights for decision making
- Creating visibility and transparency into the work and the impact it is having on outcomes
- Work with, around, or remove constraints

It's now time to examine the enterprise technology landscape to understand what changes we need to make to support these new ways of working and further unleash the potential of technology as a new value creation center for customers, a differentiator for the business, and an enabler for new business models.

In this section, we discuss how to build a world-class technology capability at the core of a modern digital business. It is not just more product innovation and insights from data analytics and machine learning; we are seeing a complete shift in the way IT departments are viewed. Technology investment is now part of strategic initiatives rather than tactical spend. The line between business and technology is now blurred more than ever, with shared goals and a tighter appreciation of what technology can do for the business. Perhaps it's time to consider that there is no line at all.

Many of the improvements and changes technology teams should embrace in this new Digital Age are not groundbreaking new ideas. Some of them have been around for a while, just not broadly adopted. As notable science fiction writer William Gibson once said:

The future is already here—it's just not very evenly distributed.

Our goal here is to summarize the most important lessons we have learned through observing how enterprises build technology capabilities facing the increasing demand from the new Digital Age. We hope that this advice can be useful for business and technology leaders in the middle of building a new digital capability or transforming a traditional enterprise technology team into a modern digital team. It's not just the technology leaders' job; business leaders have an equally strong influence on the build out of technology capability. For example, technology excellence is not something that only the technologists are accountable for: it is first and foremost a business decision, a decision that business leaders and technology leaders should make together consciously. So part of our goal is to share these important lessons with the business community, too, so that everyone knows how to work together to build the best technology capability for the future.

We believe that there is a minimum set of technical concepts that all leaders need to be aware of, even if you happen to know very little about this area to begin with. So in the first chapter, we are going to summarize the entire section at the very high level. It's important to have this basic level of understanding to know what changes need to happen in the technology area, what questions to ask, and what your role is in helping the technology teams to transform. Then, we break out each topic into more details in individual chapters. Think about this next chapter as a TL;DR (too long; didn't read) summary. You can then move in and out of the details, in the chapters that follow, with each topic as it suits your interests.

10

Technology Concepts Every Executive Should Know

This chapter gives a brief summary of the entire technology section of the book—from Chapters 11 to 16. This is the minimum set of concepts that we believe all leaders need to be aware of in order to achieve business outcomes in the Digital Age and beyond.

Technology Excellence Matters

Internal software quality, achieved through technology excellence, is the key to giving a software system a high level of changeability, adaptability, and responsiveness. This will of course have a direct and immediate impact on your organizational responsiveness.

However, in many people's minds, IT is still treated as a commodity and a cost center. Software systems are often viewed as a utility and compared with water and electricity. You turn on the tap and expect water to come out. If you want to use more water, you open the faucet more or use more taps. All water is the same, so you try to find the cheapest provider. You are not going to change what kind of water you want that often, so the biggest risk of the system is the risk of failure. The system just needs to perform with low defects, high throughput, and high availability.

However, unlike a utility, a software system is often a strategic asset for a business. All software systems are not the same; they are not "one and done," and they need to constantly evolve and adapt. Your risk is not so much in what a system is doing, it's more what it is not doing as it tries to keep pace. Customers might be demanding new value that's not being addressed. New technology might make it possible to remove some friction and create more convenience. Competitors might be adding some new features that you thought not possible. Therefore, getting your business to stand out requires you to have the ability to continue delivering new differentiating features from your software systems. Faster delivery cycles, responsiveness, and adaptability of software systems are becoming the new ground of competition. Internal software quality is the fundamental indicator and driver of system responsiveness.

INTERNAL SOFTWARE QUALITY

Internal software quality is the measure of design and structure of a code base, which is generally not visible to an end user. A clean, well-designed, and easy-to-maintain code base is like a clean and well-organized room; it's much easier to find stuff and be productive in such an environment. A messy code base, especially in a large software system, will slow everyone down, and make adding new features or making changes time consuming, expensive, and economically unsustainable. At some point, you might be forced to rebuild from scratch instead of extending the current system. This is counterintuitive—when a physical item such as a car or other consumer good is higher quality, it is more expensive because it is made with higher-quality materials and to a higher standard. With software, higher quality actually means the software will be *cheaper*.

SOFTWARE DESIGN AND TECHNICAL DEBT

Good design is often appreciated by both business and technology leaders. Experienced, highly skilled technologists can apply the patterns and knowledge they've learned before and create good upfront software design that is well structured and scalable.

However, contrary to most nontechnologist's beliefs, good upfront design is not enough. Design deteriorates over time, whether we like it or not. When new requirements come up, they could introduce exceptions to the original intention of the system design; when developers write code, they could introduce messy solutions; when the team is under pressure to deliver more features, they could be forced to take short cuts. All of these little things happen almost on a daily basis, and they are properly referred to as *technical debt*. As the name suggests, taking on debt means that you must make interest payments, the equivalent of which in software development is the extra effort required to develop new features or maintain the system as a whole. When there is too much technical debt, there might come a time when the extra effort required will make it economically nonviable to extend the software any further.

SKILLED ENGINEERS

It's important to maintain a high level of technical skill across the entire engineering team. The traditional software factory model is about surrounding a few senior technologists with an army of low-skilled staff (often from low-cost vendors), hoping that the thinking (design) is done by the senior people, and the simple coding tasks are done by the less-skilled staff. That model might work for utility software for which change requests are at a minimum, but it will quickly break down when your organization, and therefore your software, needs to be adaptive. There are no simple coding tasks in strategic digital assets when the software continues to evolve and extend.

Even when you have a highly skilled technology team, technology debt will still build up; we talk about the reasons for this in Chapter 11. It's critical to have the discipline to maintain low technical debt. Through constant review and refactoring, it's possible to spend a small amount of effort to pay down some technical debt. If the development team does this early and frequently enough, it's entirely possible to keep the technical debt at a low level and reverse the decay of the software design.

BUSINESS AND TECHNOLOGY LEADERSHIP

The most difficult part of managing technical debt is to have a constructive relationship between business and technology leaders in order to do the *right* amount of work on software quality. Instead of focusing on and measuring only the number of features and requirements delivered, ask the team to measure the internal quality (often not visible to inexpert eyes if you don't measure it) at the same time. If internal quality falls too low, or developers find the code difficult to work with, or the speed of delivery is affected, leaders should support the team's efforts to improve the code base and pay down technical debt. Balancing feature development with the technical health of the system is a constant challenge and requires trust and a healthy relationship between the technical and business experts. The amount of effort going into features versus code quality will be a dynamic equilibrium in which there is no static "right" answer. This is a difficult balance because it is often at odds with the constant pressure from the business to deliver more and faster. Both business leaders and technology leaders need to constantly remind themselves: the discipline of applying a small effort now to pay down the technical debt is worth its weight in gold a few months later.

We cover this topic in greater depth in Chapter 11.

Growing and Empowering Talent

Technology excellence requires highly skilled technologists. CD and DevOps require more polyskilled generalists. Platform thinking and modern architectural techniques demand knowledge of the latest technology trends. At some point, all of these come down to people. Do you have the quality and quantity of talent required to accomplish all these asks?

Whether we like it or not, the entire technology industry is in a position of a net shortage of digital talent, and will remain so over the next few years due to the high demand. This is the same across different countries and business domains. No matter which organization we talk to, acquiring and retaining digital talent has become one of the highest priorities in the digital transformation journey.

When the majority of technology assets are viewed as utilities, the conventional management wisdom leads to outsourcing as much as possible. As a result, many businesses outsourced most of their IT functions—including core software development capability—to third-party vendors, especially the large-volume, low-cost service providers. Not only did this build up large amounts of technology debt that made IT expensive and slow, it also depleted the business of critical technology expertise and system know-how.

Despite the heated battle for talent, we don't see any option to ignore it—the need to build more digital capability internally is stronger than ever. If digital technology is a future differentiator, you will want to own it in-house or co-own it with partners, and certainly not outsource it completely anymore.

When it comes to building digital capability, the question we are asked most is "Where and how can I hire digital talent?" We believe that's actually not the most important place to start: the place to focus on first is within the organization, not outside.

Despite the outsourcing or the changing of roles (many moved from practitioners to vendor managers), there is still an unbelievable amount of raw talent in most organizations.

There are two key aspects to focus on to unleash this potential:

- Build a culture of learning so that your people continue to develop and become better over time.

- Build an environment that empowers people so that they are more productive.

BUILD A CULTURE OF LEARNING

In this Digital Age, the ever increasing pace of technology improvement is pushing all of us into a lifelong learning mode. Technology is progressing at an exponential speed, so technologists are required to gain new skill sets every few months or weeks. Learning is not just something you do in school or once in a while through some on-the-job training program, it's becoming a part of everyone's day job. Although that sounds daunting, it also means that it's never too late for anyone to learn.

There are many things leaders of an organization need to do to create a learning environment. Here are some areas to consider:

Create a safe environment to provide feedback.

Although training is a great opportunity to learn and improve, the majority of learning for most people is done on the job from advice and feedback from colleagues. It is thus critical to create an environment in which it is safe to provide constructive and effective feedback. Detach feedback from performance reviews so that the intention is to help and support, as opposed to judge or criticize.

Encourage continuous feedback.

Feedback doesn't happen naturally without facilitation and encouragement. It should certainly not be given or collected only during formal annual or quarterly cycles. It should be done regularly and continuously. Team leads should be trained on how to give and receive feedback and facilitate it regularly with team members.

Create an environment where it's safe to fail.

This is especially important in the Digital Age in which the ability to experiment quickly and learn fast will separate the winners and losers. No matter how well you research and design your experiments, most experiments fail instead of succeed. The key is to learn through the failures instead of trying to avoid them. This is very different from the traditional risk-averse operational mindset. Many organizations are committed to learn from failures and many have processes and efforts dedicated to it—loss review, postmortem analysis, and so on. But the mindset is "It's very bad that we failed;

Someone did something wrong; Let's find out who did what wrong, and make sure that we, and others, don't make the same mistake again." We should change that mindset, and view failure through a positive lens— what new knowledge (about the market, about technology, about the customer) we have learned from it, and celebrate that new knowledge.

Don't cut the training and development budget under operational pressure.
Most businesses have some kind of training and development budget for their employees. Value from the training budget is difficult to measure and the return is not immediate. It shouldn't be viewed as discretionary spending and be the first item to be cut under operational pressure. That sends the exact wrong message; that is, that learning is optional and can be stopped at any time.

Build a world-class learning and development function.
A great learning and development function can help to design a capability model for each role and its disciplines that outlines the progression/learning path to achieve mastery. There should also be coaches and mentors identified for each discipline at different maturity stages to provide help for people who are engaged in learning activities. Training, lessons, workshops, and other activities should be organized to achieve these learning goals on the learning paths, as opposed to training "benefits" randomly assigned to employees based on the available budget or as a reward for good performance.

BUILD A CULTURE OF EMPOWERMENT

In Dan Pink's book *Drive* (mentioned earlier), autonomy is listed as one of the three key factors that most motivates modern knowledge workers, together with mastery and purpose. Human beings need to feel that they are in control of their own behaviors and goals. It's a powerful and deeply buried reason why people choose the places they work and what they work on. When a person feels that they have more autonomy to make work-related decisions, they become more productive, innovative, and motivated to do better and do more. Here are some common practices that can help to create an empowering environment:

Communicate and share information.
Information shouldn't only flow up and down the command chain, like a pyramid. It should be able to jump nodes and layers, and it should also flow horizontally. Leaders can influence this by creating additional

processes, tools, and networks to facilitate more channels for information flow through the organization, like the big visible charts and other information radiators mentioned in Chapter 6.

Delegate decision-making authority.
Command-and-control style of management philosophy puts most decision-making authority into a leader's hand, partially due to the extra context that the leader would have over the team members. If the proper amount of information is fully accessible to *everyone*, more people will be in a position to make good decisions, not just a few leaders. In a self-organizing team, the leader's role is to facilitate discussions about new patterns and behaviors that emerge from the work, to combine the information and context everyone has, and to let the correct decision emerge. This is in stark contrast to a command-and-control style in which they would specify in advance what that correct decision should be.

Nurture a sense of ownership.
Besides having the authority to decide how things are done, a stronger sense of ownership will come from being part of the process of setting goals and targets. Leaders' efforts on communication should help to create a clear understanding of key objectives of the company and business units. The effort of further cascading key objectives down to smaller divisions and teams should involve the teams themselves so that they are engaged in setting the goals and targets for their own divisions and teams.

When it comes to the recruiting and retention part, we actually don't have much more to add. If you focus on building a nurturing and empowering environment, not only will it help to unleash untapped potential from existing employees and make them better at working with digital technology, it should also make it much easier to recruit from outside of the company and retain talented employees after they join.

A company known for developing and nurturing digital talent is more likely to attract aspirational talent than its peers. People who feel that they are learning new skills and are being empowered to make an impact are less likely to leave for a higher salary.

Our main suggestion on recruiting is to focus more on passion and potential than skill set. The willingness to learn, the commitment to learn, and the ability to learn are more important than a head start or an existing level of experience.

This approach will open more channels and create more sources for excellent hires that might seem unconventional by traditional standards.

Last, we want to address the issue of partnership between organizations, which is driven by two factors:

- First, the technical landscape has become so broad and complex that it becomes increasingly unlikely for any one company to have deep expertise across all of the possible disciplines—from development to automation to infrastructure to data engineering and machine learning. There is a limit to how many of these specialties a single organization can feasibly encompass.

- Second, even when companies successfully build a differentiating core digital capability internally, scalability will like remain a big challenge in the foreseeable future. The need for this new kind of capability is growing exponentially, more than the industry can provide at the moment, and probably so in the next decade. The appropriate kind of digital consultancy will create a different, if not necessarily better, environment for developing digital technology talent. This source of digital know-how and capacity will complement the insourcing strategy by providing capability uplift, specialized expertise, and talent scalability.

These two factors call for a different type of sourcing strategy—which part of the capability is to be built internally, which should we cosource, and which should we outsource? Although there is no one-size-fits-all solution, the traditional cost-driven outsourcing approach is outdated when it comes to scaling digital capability outside of the organization. A digital partner needs to be able to work closely with your digital teams, almost seamlessly, to form a one-team environment. We suggest examining the following aspects of a digital partner most:

Culture alignment
   Dive deeper into the partner's organizational culture, ideally through interviewing people on the ground (rather than just listening to presentations) and getting references from former employees and former clients on clearly defined cultural behaviors to understand the alignment (or gaps) between the two organizational cultures.

Process compatibility

Although most organizations have adopted or started to adopt an Agile process, many are struggling to include the large number of external contractors and vendors as part of the Agile and continuous delivery process. Avoid the trap of "skin deep" Agile practices; look under the hood at real development teams to find out whether processes and practices are properly understood, as opposed to just ceremonially followed.

Technology excellence

Besides the system design, every practitioner's coding skills and coding quality will significantly affect the internal quality of a software system. Good design could quickly deteriorate into unmaintainable code through bad implementation. All practitioners in the organization should aspire to continue to improve and become masters in their own fields. This applies to digital technology partners, too. When looking for a digital technology partner, be sure to examine their technical excellence across the organization, especially the majority of the practitioner community. Don't focus solely on the partner's quality control process and the capability of a few senior people.

We cover this topic in greater depth in Chapter 12.

Continuous Delivery and DevOps

If we want the entire organization to be realigned to the purpose of quickly delivering the most value to customers, business and technology teams need to work together to complete the build-test-learn cycle end to end. The key technology capability is the ability to deliver software solutions into production early, faster, and to be able to quickly respond to changes. The traditional heavyweight software development approach is simply not capable of doing this. Unfortunately, as much as lightweight iterative software development methodologies have been around for almost two decades successfully supporting those goals, they are still not consistently adopted by large enterprises.

If you are not familiar with the Agile software development approach versus the traditional Waterfall software development approach, that would be a good question to ask the technology team. If Agile is not adopted properly, it *will* be a major roadblock for digital transformation. It's quite likely that even if your IT department believes it is doing Agile software delivery, in fact it might not be, and it might require significant help to take on the technical, cultural, and organizational changes that enable true Agile delivery.

CONTINUOUS DELIVERY

The continuous delivery (CD) concept within Agile is the key enabler to changing the software delivery process from slow speeds and long release cycles to a faster, more incremental and iterative approach. With CD, teams ensure that every feature that has been developed can be released to production at any time, and that the decision of when to deploy is a business decision. Changes can be released at the push of a button with no need to wait for a long testing and release cycle.

There are some important techniques and practices that product teams need to adopt to build the capability to continuously deliver customer value:

- Build smaller, cross-functional teams including business people.
- Break requirements into smaller chunks that are valuable and releasable.
- Work in "iterations" to finish a few small chunks of requirements end to end (into production) before starting the next iteration.
- Write fully automated tests to create a safety net so that the small release cycles can be properly tested without a heavy manual process and effort.
- Use automation to enable "one button" deployment in a consistent manner through all environments, from development through to production.
- Manage infrastructure "as code" so that it's easier to create and re-create environments on demand, to help with removing bottlenecks as well as helping with scalability and disaster recovery.

Another important concept is to build more general skill sets and create more generalists in a product development team than relying only on specialists.

In most technology organizations, building the software and running it are viewed as two entirely different types of activities with different skill sets required. As a result, there is generally a different team operating the software system after it goes into production. This team will be managing and maintaining the production environment, configuration of the software, monitoring performance, and escalating any production issues or user complaints. If we want to release software frequently and update it continuously, the development and operations teams will need to work side by side in close collaboration. The handover, communication, coordination, and departmental barriers today create many delays and defects.

DEVOPS

DevOps is a cultural movement aimed at solving the "build versus run" problem by getting development and operations functions working closer together, often by having an operational expert as part of the development team. This allows the operational expert to provide early feedback to the software development process as well as actually owning the operation of the software product as part of the development team.

Many people in the DevOps communities also support creating a new type of role on the team: the DevOps role. The idea is that instead of trying to figure out how to coordinate and handover better, we should get the same person to do both jobs. Hence, the name DevOps—the combination of development and operation skills in one role. According to Glassdoor, on the list of top-10 tech jobs in America for 2018, DevOps engineer is the runner-up after data scientist as the most sought-after job in terms of earning potential, job satisfaction, and number of job openings.

This is a double-edged sword. We don't like DevOps as a job title. It can lead to the behavior that there is only one person who should care about the connection and collaboration between development and operations, whereas the rest of the team are still siloed developers, or siloed operators.

But we do like the philosophy that people can have multiple skill sets across development and operation. The technology industry, like many others, has been strongly influenced by the "division of labor" concept aimed at improving productivity in a mass-production environment. In the Digital Age, productivity is about mass customization and collaboration to achieve speed, agility, and responsiveness to changes. In the Digital Everything Age, we can set up and change software systems at machine speed. The slow part, therefore, is getting the humans to do the complex thinking and expressing their thoughts in software. The faster we can be at going from concept to code—an entirely intellectual exercise based on humans collaborating—the faster we can deliver value into production.

We cover this topic in greater depth in Chapter 13.

Digital Platforms

The concept of a "platform business" has captured the interests of many executives across different industries. Some of the most successful companies in the Digital Age are known as platform businesses (or API businesses)—Apple's iTunes, Alibaba, Amazon's Marketplace, Salesforce, Uber, and Airbnb, just to name a few. A platform business connects ecosystem participants together and exhibits nonlinear scaling characteristics.

Connecting ecosystem participants is not a new concept. Marketplaces have existed throughout human history, from ancient bazaars to modern shopping malls where merchants and shoppers meet and trade. Newspapers have also existed for a few hundred years, from which advertisers get benefits from a large captive audience. Beside capturing a large audience, a modern platform business also provides a foundation for someone else to go faster. For example, Salesforce and Amazon provide client relationship management and fulfillment capability for small- and medium-sized businesses to get up to speed quickly and focus on their core value creation.

What's common about these modern platform businesses is the digital and online infrastructure enabled by advances in information technology. Digital technology makes connecting people a lot easier and cheaper. The increasing amount of data captured by the platform also allows more value creation opportunities to all parties through new analytical techniques.

The digital platform we are going to discuss here is not the platform business itself. Rather, it's the digital technology platform that preludes the business model revolution. Although necessary, it doesn't have to always lead to a platform business. In fact, we don't think the majority of large enterprises need to become so-called platform businesses to differentiate themselves. A platform business accelerates growth, but it's still going to be a small part of the overall economic landscape.

Regardless of whether you are going to expand your ecosystem to become a platform business or not, in the long run, this digital technology platform is always going to be a crucial step to take now for any modern business to be able to deliver new value to customers faster, with higher quality, and at a lower cost.

We believe there are three key pillars supporting a digital platform:

Modular, API-enabled architecture
> Instead of a monolithic architecture, enterprise systems should be built up from granular services—often known as *microservices* in the technology

community—that correspond to business domain capabilities that a business person could identify and relate to. For example, a business capability like "find in store" is identifiable as a valuable retail domain capability and is reusable in both online shopping and in-store shopping. These services are independently built, deployed, and run by stable teams and expose these business capabilities as APIs in the digital world.

Self-service data

Data within an organization is often locked up in silos (either intentionally or through accidents of technology) and is inaccessible across teams or departments. Modern organizations need to enable team autonomy, and one critical area is enabling teams to "self-serve" access to the data they need to create value. Self-service data can be enabled through a coherent enterprise-wide data strategy or through simple API-based mechanisms. Self-service ensures that teams can quickly focus on delivering value to customers rather than becoming bogged down in organizational red tape in order to access critical data.

Delivery infrastructure

Teams are often held up waiting on infrastructure such as servers, databases, networks, and firewalls. Today's best IT organizations improve delivery infrastructure to remove any friction that technology teams experience. These infrastructure services include fast self-service access to computing environment; elastic scaling of compute resources; provisioning of development environments; provisioning of development tools; and provisioning of runtime environments. The goal is to allow product development teams to have fast and easy access to the tools they need so that they can run their experiments with less overhead, get feedback quicker with fewer communications, and handover barriers in their path.

It's often helpful to set up a dedicated "delivery infrastructure" team to build these services and tools for the development teams incrementally over time.

These three pillars seem to be full of technical details. But at the higher level, they all share the same philosophy. Package the digital capability, data, and delivery infrastructure into services that can be easily accessed by all teams within the organization. These three types of services form the concept of the marketplace or platform. When done well, if a customer outcome–based team decided to experiment with a new idea and test it with the market, it would have quick access to the necessary business capabilities, the data it need for insight, and the delivery infrastructure required so that it can begin coding and releasing its new ideas immediately.

In a large enterprise where many technology solutions are already in place, we usually don't have the advantage of everything being built in a modular, reusable fashion with high quality and low technical debt. In fact, we often have monolithic legacy architectures in isolated silos. The challenge of platform thinking is not the new capabilities, it is how to package, transition, or replace these legacy systems to work in the new platform style.

You will likely need to do some amount of legacy modernization in order to support the thin-slice approach to digital transformation. But modernization efforts should be driven by these thin-slice requirements rather than some overall imperative to simply replace all of the legacy assets. In general for each legacy system there are a number of modernization patterns:

- *Replacement,* either by custom code, a new package, or Software-as-a-Service (SaaS)

- *Augmentation,* by adding a new system alongside the old one and mediating requests between the two, adding a service interface that all new integrations should use

- *Continuation,* by keeping the legacy system running but making modernization improvements such as adding better testing, more automation, or industrializing it via APIs and making it easier to reuse across the organization

The exact approach to legacy will depend on a variety of factors including the current state of the technology, risk level (of both keeping or replacing a legacy system), and likely future needs based on the current business climate and road map. In the end, a legacy modernization strategy will need to include a close partnership between business and IT in order to make the best decisions.

We cover this topic in greater depth in Chapter 14.

Products over Projects

One of the significant buzzwords in the IT industry at present is *product*. Companies that make physical goods are familiar with the word, of course, but now we're being encouraged to apply "product thinking" to all manner of things—

digital services, customer experiences, internal applications and even flows of data from business to business. Even though most people intuitively grasp the concept that treating a customer-facing "thing" as a product is a useful idea, non-customer-facing parts of an organization are typically a lot further behind.

If we were to treat many more apps, services, and data as products, what would that look like? Key characteristics of products include the following:

- Products solve a problem or satisfy a need. The best products solve a need that people didn't even know they had (remember the iPod? Who knew that people needed a thousand songs in their pocket?).

- Products uniquely differentiate against other, competing products. The best products might solve the same need as other products, but distinguish themselves through feature set, speed, ease of use, or cost.

- Products are built with a clear customer (or set of customers) in mind. Feature set, build quality, and price are all tuned to appeal to a particular target customer. Often, a product team will do significant market research as well as create prototypes to ensure a product will be desirable with the intended customer.

Critically, products contrast heavily with IT's customary "project mentality" in which any initiative is broken down into a series of projects with defined scope, budget, and dates. Whereas a project is intended to be completed in a set period, a product might live for a long time if it is creating value and solving a customer need. Timing is just one of the ways products differ from projects:

- Projects bring people together for the duration of the project, with the specific skills needed to complete the project. After it's complete, a project team is reassigned to other parts of the business. Products are built by product teams comprising the skills needed to design, build, support, and evolve the product. Typically a product team will be stable; members stay together working on the product for the long term.

- Projects are usually funded by estimating effort, adding a large contingency, and then managing to the overall budget. Products are generally funded by estimating the size of the team you'll need to build a useful, valuable product, and then funding that size of team for the long term.

- Projects are oriented toward *completing the project* over anything else. Usually, projects are kicked off in order to contribute to some larger strategy of value creation, but after they're running, most projects focus on hitting their deadlines and scope. "On time and on budget" is usually the measure of project success. Products are laser-focused on creating value for their customers, and as long as a product is valuable, more effort can be put into enhancing it.

These differences cause a deep and profound change across an organization when every team is working on a product, knows who their customers are, and can plan for the long term. One key benefit is that teams working in product mode can often redirect their efforts to deliver value faster than project teams, which must often wait for a formal planning and budgeting cycle.

Enabling product orientation is a big shift and will not be accomplished overnight. We see four key steps in the journey:

1. Determine what constitutes a "product" for your organization.
2. Connect product teams with your thin-slice approach.
3. Create long-term funding for your products.
4. Create empowered, cross-functional product teams.

Shifting to product orientation is definitely challenging. Organizational structure, funding, and success metrics all need to change, and you'll need to work hard to find the right product owners to shepherd all your new products.

We cover "product thinking" and its implications in greater detail in Chapter 15.

The Future Shape of the IT Department

According to a 2017 study by the Hackett Group, based on a survey of 160 executives in companies with annual revenue of $1 billion or more, 64% of respondents said they lacked confidence in their IT organization's capability to support digital transformation. The study also suggests that there is an increasing demand for IT capability, but the largest actual increases in workload and IT staff are happening outside corporate IT. Business groups appear to be investing in their own IT capabilities.

This is both a challenge to IT departments and an opportunity to better support these demands and add more value to the digital transformation. Besides a lack of technology excellence, CD, platforms, and talent management, we have seen two more antipatterns that are working against IT's ability to deliver more value and help drive more business transformation. We want to call them out here:

- Teams are built functionally around technology and systems
- The so-called "Two-Speed IT" notion

1. BUILD TEAMS AROUND BUSINESS CAPABILITY OR CUSTOMER OUTCOMES

In the Digital Age, with heightened customer expectations, more and more systems need to coordinate to deliver the desired services and experience to customers. In the delayed-flight situation mentioned earlier in the book, different systems like flight operations, aircraft routing, airport operations, crew scheduling, baggage tracking, customer care, loyalty, and even hotel booking must work together to deliver the optimal solutions for passengers. Real-time information from these systems will need to be dispatched to flight crews and passengers to reduce anxiety and allow preparation, often through multiple channels including the web, mobile apps, text messaging, and phone calls. Getting the systems to integrate with one another is both a technology challenge and an organization challenge.

We have seen many airlines moving away from this siloed technology-oriented structure to a business capability or outcome-oriented alignment. To better handle delayed flights, new teams are built around irregular operation to support the customer journey as opposed to distinctive systems, including all the relative functions of both business and IT. Although this does not completely remove the need to have a core development team around a particular IT system at various times, the knowledge and skills of developing and integrating these systems are spread much more broadly across the organization than concentrated in one place.

2. "TWO-SPEED IT" IS NOT SUSTAINABLE

During the adoption of Agile software development and other new digital techniques, there are always excuses for why the new techniques could not be applied to the mission-critical core legacy systems where safety, stability, and accuracy were deemed more important, even at the cost of speed and adaptability. Facing this dilemma a few years ago, some organizations embraced the concept of *Two-Speed IT* (advocated by McKinsey) or *Bimodal IT* (advocated by Gartner), in which the fast speed, or mode 1, approach can be applied to new greenfield digital products, whereas the slow speed, or mode 2, approach can still be kept to run the large core legacy systems.

At ThoughtWorks, we welcomed the willingness to make changes and try new things, but disagreed with a risk-averse approach that keeps the status quo in ring-fenced areas. We accepted the fact that two speed might have been a necessary compromise at certain times in certain situations dealing with major changes in a large enterprise. We also believe that now is the time to move on from the two-speed or Bimodal IT concept.

The glaring issue facing most businesses is that systems are more and more interconnected in the digital world in which consumers expect to engage with the business anytime, anywhere. Almost all of the frontend customer engagement software depends on core backend systems to deliver value to customers end to end. For a consumer to order goods on their mobile phone and pick them up in-store, besides the mobile and ecommerce system, the store inventory management, forecast and replenishment, customer service, and loyalty systems all need to be updated to enable the transaction.

We have seen too many examples where the rapid development and release cycles of digital product delivery meet the rigid and slow traditional long-release cycles of the backend system. The two-speed organization ends up moving at the speed of the slowest common denominators. With heightening customer expectation and the digitization of more and more customer engagements, no part of the organization and systems can hide in the "backend" any more. Everything must work together to deliver the end-to-end value to customers at a faster pace. Although certain systems might be able to move faster or slower—and with good reason—*all* systems need to move at a proper pace to support rapid customer value creation. As we discuss in detail in Chapter 11, there are now many success patterns and case studies to help navigate the "legacy modernization" complexity. It's time to embrace the inevitability and come up with plans to speed up the entire IT organization, not just part of it.

Last, we have some advice for business leaders on how to work better with technology teams.

As mentioned at the beginning of Part III, "Business people need to begin speaking the language of technology." Now is the time to make progress on that journey. We have seen more business leaders understanding enough technology and technology leaders understanding enough business. If we push the generalist-over-specialist principle further, we believe that a new breed of business technologist or technical business person will emerge and become better leaders of such modern digital business.

Finally, we have some "old" suggestions for the CEOs. CEOs have a great deal of influence on the effectiveness of IT departments, both in the old world and the new digital world. As early as 1994, there was a well-researched study done by MIT *Sloan Management Review* on how CIOs could add more value, be a strategic partner to the business, and "create competitive advantage and enable business transformation."[1] When it comes to advice to the CEOs, the following were highlighted in the study:

1. Position IT and the CIO as agents of change.

2. Focus on achieving effectiveness, not efficiency, from IT.

3. Institutionalize business values for IT.

4. Build an executive team that includes the CIO.

5. Manage IT as integral, not as an adjunct, to the business.

This was true 30 years ago and is still true today. We cover this topic in greater depth in Chapter 15.

This chapter was a summary of all the topics we think executives should be familiar with. You don't need to be an expert in each topic, but these technology issues are central to today's digital transformations, so at least a passing familiarity is important. Having read the summary, we encourage you to dive into the topics that most affect your organization. If a particular topic comes up on your digital transformation journey, you can refer to that specific chapter for more information and some good questions to ask your own teams. Let's now explore each topic in much more depth.

---

1 Michael J. Earl and David F. Feenu, "Is Your CIO Adding Value?" (*https://oreil.ly/phktu*) MIT Sloan Management Review, April 15, 1994.

Key Points

Following are the key points that we hope you take away from this chapter as well as two actions for you to take to begin implementing what we've discussed:

- All leaders need a minimum baseline of technology awareness with respect to its impact on digital transformation.
- Understanding basic key technology concepts will better prepare you to respond to increasing customer demand and the pace of change.
- All leaders need to support teams adopting more rigorous technical discipline.

Here are two actions to take:

- Set up tech sessions for leaders: Give your leaders a baseline in key technology concepts, and add these to the vision anchor of how they discuss the need for change and what success looks like. Include regular interaction between leaders and technology teams so that leaders can learn and help support the adoption of new disciplines firsthand.
- Build internal technical capability: Develop internal technical talent through capability uplift and recruitment. Be an advocate for enforcing delivery disciplines that ensure quality of output.

Technology Excellence Matters

In a message to shareholders in 2015, General Electric Chairperson Jeff Immelt stated, "We believe that every industrial company will become a software company." GE has set a goal to become one of the top 10 software companies by 2020—among software giants like Microsoft, Oracle, and SAP.

The exponential growth in technology is driving heightened customer expectations, new competitive advantages, and market changes at an increasing speed never seen in the Industrial Age. To thrive in the Digital Age, business leaders need to be able to operate comfortably surrounded by ambiguity and use technology to redefine the value delivered to customers. In this new era, technology no longer sits on the sidelines supporting the business—technology is becoming the business.

Almost every company in the world uses some technical solutions already. Just adding more devices and applications don't make you a technology company. Building technology at the core means that you view the world through the lens of technology. Technology should be at the heart of your business strategy.

In a business for which technology is a differentiator, technology excellence matters. It's the foundation to deliver the most engaging UX, fastest response to market changes, and the most innovative solutions to customers and partners.

However, technology excellence is defined differently in different contexts. For some systems, excellence could mean it doesn't break; for others, it could mean the system needs to be flexible and easy to change. In this chapter, we must first define the context we want to focus on—the strategic digital assets for which flexibility and responsiveness are important, and what technology excellence means for those systems.

Which IT System Is a Utility Asset and Which Is a Strategic Asset?

Our observation is that for strategic assets, the internal quality of the system is highly critical. By *internal* quality, we mean the maintainability, flexibility, extensibility, understandability, testability, and so on. High internal quality will allow the system to extend and upgrade constantly with a higher speed and at a lower cost, which the new digital business strategy depends on. This high internal quality can be achieved only through technology excellence.

However, we are surprised by how difficult it is to pin down the criteria that separates an IT system from being a utility or being a strategic asset.

In the FedEx example early on in the book, Fred Smith recognized the strategic importance of package tracking information as early as the 1970s and built the information system that differentiated FedEx from its competitors. By the 1990s, more and more businesses were using information systems as a strategic asset to provide competitive advantages against their competitors.

At the same time, the view that information technology is just a utility—a cost center—never ceased to exist. As late as 2003, Nicholas Carr came out with his book *Does IT Matter* (HBR Press). And his answer was: "Not much." IT was a commodity, like electricity. You turn it on, you turn it off. You dial it up, you dial it down. IT was seen as a cost center: you need to constantly squeeze it for efficiency and you want to outsource as much as possible to low-cost vendors.

How can we make sense of these seemingly contradictory notions? Our conclusion is that it really depends. In theory, it depends on the business strategy, it depends on the view of the CEOs, it depends on how the business wants to compete. In reality, it also depends on whether IT is delivering value to the business, how IT expertise is included in setting the business strategy, and how IT teams relate and align to the business teams. To some extent, at the practical level, we are almost seeing a chicken-or-egg conundrum—if our IT capability is good enough, we will position it as a strategic capability, and many IT systems as strategic assets; if our IT capability is not good enough, we will treat IT systems as mere utility, build business strategies that do not depend on IT effectiveness as differentiation.

But if we take out the practical constraints and begin with a "good" level of IT capability, the business strategy should be the most important factor driving the difference between utility and strategic assets, not system design, tenure, or other technology aspects of the IT system.

After taking the thin-slice approach (see Chapter 3) to align work and teams, including both new work born out of the cascade or existing work moved across, there will be plenty of work, teams, and technology assets left in the "old world." When we examine these systems, a lot of them belong to the technology infrastructure category; for example, the management of corporate telephone systems, network, laptops, mobile phones, emails, video-conferencing rooms, and so on. We often refer to these systems as *utility assets*.

An airline is not going to provide a better online flight-searching experience to travelers because it has a world-class laptop serial-number tracking system for its employees. Asset management needs to be reliable, stable, and accurate, to some extent, not so different from what we expect from electricity and water supply. A business depends on a utility to run a smooth operation, but it will not differentiate itself from competitors or provide a better experience to customers by having better electricity, water, or laptop serial-number tracking system.

Strategic assets, on the other hand, are what a business uses to provide products or services to customers that could be innovative, better, or cheaper than the competitors. For an airline, the online booking system, self-check-in kiosk, and baggage tracking system are all strategic assets. Work or teams engaged in these systems will eventually be aligned closely to and organized around specific customer outcomes or business goals. These systems will continue to be developed and evolved. New capabilities and changes will be deployed into production continuously fueling the innovation and differentiation the company needs to win customers over.

SYSTEMS OF RECORD CAN BE HIGHLY STRATEGIC

The line between utility software and strategic software is not always clear. Gartner makes the distinction between "systems of record" that store authoritative data and "systems of engagement" that interact with customers. The idea is that systems of engagement can (and must) move faster than systems of record. Many people automatically classify systems of record as utility and systems of engagement as strategic. A similar distinction is made between "new" versus "legacy" software, with many people classifying older software as a utility simply because it hasn't gone through a lot of changes recently.

Quite often in fact, systems of record and systems of engagement are closely connected when it comes to serving the needs of customers. An electronic medical record (EMR) system keeps track of a patient's medical history, diagnoses, medications, immunization dates, allergies, lab results, and doctor's notes. An EMR system is more than just a system that tracks these records: it's a critical building block that enables effective communication and coordination among the members of a health-care team for optimal patient care. It is a highly strategic and differentiating system for a health-care provider.

LEGACY SYSTEMS SHOULD NOT BE TREATED AS A UTILITY

Whether it's the financial service industry, airline, manufacturing, retail or health-care industry, any early adopters of information technology would have a few legacy systems written in COBOL and running on a mainframe system. Even though these systems are old, large volumes of critical transactions are still flowing through them on a day-to-day basis. Many of the highly interactive consumer-facing applications depend on these systems to provide crucial information or complete the transactions. There, systems are often compared with the utilities because they are highly critical to the smooth running of the business and it's very messy when they break. That said, reliability and availability don't automatically make something utility software. When a system is part of the critical path to provide value to customers end to end, it is subject to the same challenge coming from heightened customer expectations and accelerating technology change.

Theoretically, there is no reason why Agile software development and other modern practices cannot be used in COBOL and other vintage languages. Indeed, there exist unit testing tools developed by the community for this purpose. But in reality, there are few good examples available for people to follow, and most of the systems were written before the modern techniques becomes available and would thus take a lot of effort to modernize the internal code base.

It's becoming increasingly challenging to maintain these systems so that they don't break, let alone update them frequently to cope with the new requests coming from the business. Many of the people familiar with these technologies are reaching retirement age. Few universities still offer COBOL courses. The developer community around these technologies is dwindling.

Legacy system modernization takes a lot of time and effort. A big rewrite project could take hundreds of millions of dollars and years to complete. There are also ways to gradually replace a legacy and monolithic system with a modern modular, API-enabled architecture. The *Strangler pattern* (*https://oreil.ly/rK3Kq*) is just such an approach that's proven successful in many enterprise scenarios. It's entirely possible and much more preferable to incorporate legacy system modernization into the thin-slice approach when the system is considered a strategic asset and is critical to the end-to-end value creation for customers.

UTILITY SYSTEMS CAN BECOME STRATEGIC DUE TO CHANGES IN THE BUSINESS LANDSCAPE

As industries evolve, utility assets can become strategic. Innovation in technology creates new possibilities. In the airline industry, available seats are commonly referred to as *inventory*. In the '60s and '70s, the airline inventory management system was like water and electricity. Inventory management was critical to sell tickets, to not break, and to scale to customer demand, but it was not strategic because there was not much customer segmentation or discounting in airlines' revenue management strategy. To compete against a new wave of lower-cost airlines, premium airlines needed to be able to offer lower fares. In theory, if an airline could accurately forecast passenger demand, it would be able to give deeper discounts on seats that would otherwise not be sold. In 1985, American Airlines built a dynamic inventory management system to do just that. This allowed the company to introduce "Ultimate Super Saver" discount fares that matched the low-cost airlines. This quickly drove the low-cost airlines into crisis because they couldn't respond effectively. In just a few months, PEOPLExpress, a low-cost airline, saw its load factors drop from 85 to 30%, and losses piled up month after month. It was forced to merge with Continental Airlines in 1987 to avoid bankruptcy.

Today, most airlines have highly sophisticated inventory management systems that give them tremendous flexibility in offering a wide range of fares based on time of booking, seat availability, travel pattern, customer loyalty, and many other factors. Today's airline inventory management system is highly strategic and no longer a mere utility.

The criteria to gauge whether software is a utility or strategic is therefore not tenure, language, technology stack, backend versus frontend, or system of record versus system of engagement. The *function the software provides* and its relation to the business's overall strategy determines whether it is strategic or not. It's a conscious choice for the business to treat a piece of software as a utility or as a strategic asset. This is a decision that the executive team and the CEO have to make. The same software could be a utility in one company, but strategic in another company. Very often, the choice cannot be made in a vacuum without understanding the underlying realities of the technology. This choice is often a balance between what technology differentiation a business could leverage and what technical capability the organization can provide. The need to deeply understand both the current realities and future possibilities of technology is one reason that business and technology leaders need to work much more closely together. As we discuss in Chapter 16, business leaders need to know more about technology, and technology leaders need to know more about business to succeed in today's Digital Age.

Build Versus Buy

Organizations constantly face the question of whether they should build software tailored to their specific needs or buy an off-the-shelf package, instead. Prevailing wisdom is to "buy for parity, build for differentiation" —that is, if a piece of software will be a utility, you should seek to buy it, and if the software will be strategic, you should consider building it. But software vendors will muddy the waters, claiming that their packaged software can provide strategic value.

For packaged software to be successful, the vendor needs to create software that can be sold to multiple customers and supported and enhanced over time at a cost to the vendor that is lower than the total licensing and support costs paid by its customers. The economics of packaged software drive a few behaviors:

- First, packaged software never actually encompasses "best of breed" or "best practice"—it's more accurate to say it encompasses "good practices" that are widely applicable and useful across a range of organizations. Many buyers of packaged software can get a big boost from this, even if the software cannot take them to "best."

- Second, packaged-software vendors have significant incentive to include customization options to tailor their software for a wide variety of organizations across different industries and to downplay the effort required to customize the package for any particular customer.

- Third, packaged-software vendors typically sell related software components or modules and will try to sell more than just a single function to each customer in order to increase their licensing revenues. In some cases, they might employ architectural or technical patterns that increase the chances that a customer will want or need to buy extra modules and often increase "lock in."

There are many factors that could influence the decision to buy off-the-shelf software or to build a customized proprietary system: cost, time to market, internal technical proficiency, flexibility, growth potential, and more.

If software is going to be a utility asset, then it's probably better to buy an off-the-shelf package or use a SaaS solution. In this case, you would want to apply the best practices from the industry and the lower cost resulting from the software vendors economy of scale. Because this is a utility asset like water and electricity, as long as it doesn't break and is delivered at a reasonable cost, it's fine for the process to be exactly the same as your competitors. When executing an off-the-shelf software solution, it's always better to change your process to fit the software product than to customize the software to match your process. By design, the package embodies good practices that will work across a wide variety of businesses, but it will be constrained in how far you can flex it from these core use cases. Although a vendor will *claim* that its package can be customized to fit many situations, we repeatedly see high costs to customization and problems with upgrade paths. In some situations, a package vendor has, quite seriously, quoted a *billion-dollar, eight-year* upgrade cost to an organization that is using its software. Given that for utility software the process or workflow is not a differentiator, the impact of changing it and keeping it similar to the industry standards should not be significant and will often be justified by the low cost of implementation.

If software is going to be a strategic asset, it's probably better to build a customized proprietary system than buy an off-the-shelf product. The argument is exactly the opposite for that of a package. For a strategic asset, the unique processes and workflows will be a key differentiator, and the software will need to be customized to match. It's highly likely that the system will need to be constantly changed as customer expectations evolve or as the business improves processes to pull further ahead of competitors. Flexibility and faster reaction time are easier to achieve with a custom-built system than an off-the-shelf product. There are often two main constraints of custom software: lack of internal technology proficiency, and lack of business scale to amortize the cost of software development.

The first constraint should eventually disappear as businesses go through a digital transformation and build technology capability as a core competence. The second constraint is mainly a timing and trade-off decision. Whether for a start-up business or for a new division in a large enterprise, there is sometimes not enough scale to offset the upfront development cost of a proprietary system even if it's a strategic asset. At the same time, there might be an off-the-shelf solution that does most of the job well and is readily available.

For practical reasons, it might be best to use an off-the-shelf solution early on until the business case is proven or the growth scales enough to justify investment to build a customized proprietary system. Doing it too late could stall the growth of the business due to the lack of flexibility and slow response time.

Why Internal Quality Matters for Strategic Assets

If a software system is treated as a utility, it is often compared with water and electricity. You really don't want it to break. You are not going to change it often, so the biggest risk of the system is the risk of failure or of something going wrong. The system just needs to perform with low defects, high throughput, and high availability. Unlike utility software, when software is treated as a strategic asset, the biggest risk is sometimes not what it does, but what it's not doing. The customers might be demanding new value that's not being addressed. New technology might make it possible to remove some friction and create more convenience. Competitors might be adding some new features that you thought not possible. Faster delivery cycles, responsiveness, and adaptability are becoming more and more important for strategic systems.

How can we deliver more features faster, with lower cost? Some teams can do that better than others. Their secret sauce is often a simple one—build a higher internal quality.

HIGH INTERNAL QUALITY DRIVES A LOWER TOTAL COST OF DEVELOPMENT

There seems to be a common misconception that a lower-quality software product is cheaper than a higher-quality one. It comes from a common expectation we have regarding physical consumer products—lower price means lower quality.

(It's ironic that we often simultaneously believe that lower price means more value, but that's another story about the irrational brain.) A Henckels Twin Pro S 8-inch chef's knife costs $150, whereas the knife from Mercer Culinary sells at only $15. We would generally assume that the lower-priced knife was either made with lower-quality materials or with a lower-quality design than the more expensive knife. "You get what you pay for" is a common refrain.

Counterintuitively to many, when it comes to software, it's the exact opposite. It's cheaper to build a higher-quality software product; and yes, it's more expensive to build a lower-quality one.

An important concept here is external quality versus internal quality. Like a knife, software displays certain external quality features that a user can experience and perceive. Is it fast; does it have defects; does it break down often; does it look good; is it pleasant to use? So on and so forth. For this kind of quality that is visible to the end user, it does tend to take more effort to build. But software has another aspect that is unique to the virtual world—the internal quality that leads to the ability to change and evolve.

Unlike a knife, software is not forged into a shape that remains constant. Software is built one line of code at a time. Teams spend weeks, months, or even years to continue developing the software line by line, feature by feature, release after release. Software development is a continual process to add, modify, and delete code on an ever-growing and often-complex code base. A large software system could have millions of lines of code. Microsoft Windows comprises more than 50 million lines of code. The Android operating system that powers the majority of today's mobile phones has around 15 million lines of code. To many people's surprise, the various software components embedded in a car amount to a staggering 100 million lines of code.

For a strategic system that needs to respond to ever-changing consumer demands, there is really no "end" of development. The first release going into production is just the beginning of the development for the next release cycle.

Internal quality is the measure of design and structure of a code base, which is generally not visible to an end user. But it's highly relevant to how easy or difficult it is to make changes to the code base to add new features or changing existing ones. Let's look at a couple of simple examples.

Careless developers sometimes cut and paste the code, tweaking it a little for some new use case but keeping it mostly the same. When functionality is duplicated in several places instead of being reused from a common place, the next time someone comes to change the functionality, it's easy to miss one or two places where the code has been copied, and therefore to create inconsistency and defects. With proper testing and quality control, the defect could be caught eventually, but it would cost a lot more extra effort to test it and fix it, let alone sneaking into a product and causing damage.

Software is generally composed of *modules* that are wired together in order to implement features. After you've written a "balance inquiry" function, for example, any piece of code could decide to use it rather than reimplement it from scratch. This is called a *dependency* of one piece of code on another. In a code base with hundreds and thousands of lines of code, when there are many convoluted dependencies in the code base it becomes more difficult for anyone—including the people who wrote it in the first place—to understand all the implications of making even small changes. Adding a simple feature could inadvertently create unexpected behaviors in other parts of the system that you are not even aware of. Defects will slip through the process and only be caught later by someone else.

There are many more examples like this. High internal quality means clean, well-designed, and easy-to-maintain code. Even though it's not visible to the end user, it has a huge impact on the cost of adding new features and making changes as the software continues to be developed. Just like the difference between a messy room and a clean and well-organized room, it's much easier to find stuff and be productive in a clean environment.

But many people will argue that it's quicker to cut and paste the code and to "just get it done" instead of worrying about the long-term maintainability of the code. Figure 11-1 illustrates the relationship between well-designed and poorly designed code.

Early on, taking some shortcuts and not paying attention to the internal quality of the software could give you a head start on features and functionality delivered. Looking at the diagram, you can see that the blue line starts off steeply, with developers cranking out features. As time goes by, the pace of functionality delivered on a low-quality code base will begin to slow down significantly. It soon becomes cheaper to add new functionality to a clean and well-maintained code base, as we can see in the orange line picking up speed. Eventually, the early start from messy and "quicker" approaches will be completely offset by the increased effort to develop new features.

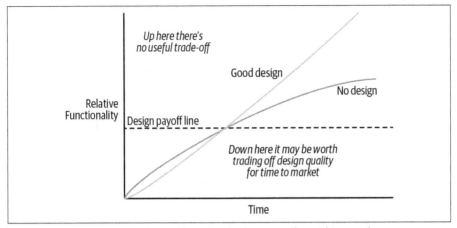

Figure 11-1. High internal quality results in less development effort within months

Unfortunately, these are not scientific measures. Software development productivity is difficult to quantify (it's certainly not lines of code). Based on years of experience from many practitioners, our estimation is that the quality payoff line is often reached in just a few months. In a recent Forrester report commissioned by ThoughtWorks, one company found that improved speed to market accounted for a gigantic 79% of the total economic benefit of the project, estimated at nearly $10.9 million over three years. It really is cheaper to build high-quality software.

TECHNICAL DEBT BUILDS UP WHEN INTERNAL QUALITY DETERIORATES

We often find "debt" a useful metaphor to consider when thinking about the internal quality of a software system.

When we choose a faster but messier solution to implement functionality instead of a cleaner approach that might take a little longer, we are delivering the functionality but also creating a small piece of technical debt. Similar to a monetary debt, if not repaid, technical debt will begin to accumulate interest. The interest is reflected in an increased cost of making changes or adding new features in the future.

As Figure 11-2 shows, the effort of developing a new feature is composed of two parts. One part is the real effort required if the code base is clean, well factored, and there is little technical debt. The other part is the extra effort, the "interest," required due to the effect of the technical debt, the "principal." The amount of interest might vary due to the relationship or coupling the new modification has with the messy parts of the code base. But as long as the principal, the technical debt, exists, the interest will need to be paid every time a new feature or a change to the system is made.

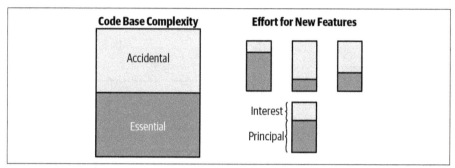

Figure 11-2. The effort to build new features always involves two parts: dealing with technical debt and actually building the feature

Of course, it's possible, and certainly logical, to pay down the technical debt in order to reduce the principal balance. This is often achieved by working on tasks that restructure the code, apply a better design, and improve the quality of the system (but not adding new features). These kinds of improvements are commonly known as *refactoring*.

If we don't keep technical debt under control and code quality high, the cost of making changes or adding new features will eventually become too expensive to justify the benefit and value of the new feature. Just like in the real financial world, that's when bankruptcy happens. The business will be forced to rip the band aids off completely, throw away the system, and rebuild a new one. This could be the equivalent of "bankruptcy" for a software system. For strategic software, the cost of building a replacement from scratch, let alone the opportunity cost due to migration, would be enormous. It is much more preferable to pay down these technology debts before reaching the point of bankruptcy.

How technical debt is created and how to mitigate it

In real-world finance, debt is usually a strategic choice. Debt is taken on by an organization to provide working capital, trading a future set of interest payments for the ability to create value immediately today using that capital. In some cases, debt can be taken on inadvertently or spiral out of control; for example, with consumer credit cards. In software, there are several reasons technical debt might accrue.

Conscious decisions to accumulate technical debt. As demand for technology solutions accelerate, investment in IT doesn't necessarily increase proportionally. With the pressure to expand margin and return on capital, the technology team is constantly being asked to do more with less. It's sometimes possible to use new technology and tools to reduce upfront investment. Other times, technology solutions just take more effort than one would hope for or would like to pay for.

When pressure mounts, the project managers or team leads will be forced to work with the business stakeholders to negotiate schedule, scope, and cost. This is the classic "project management triangle." It's not always possible to find a trade-off that all parties are willing to accept. When push comes to shove, internal quality could become the fourth tradeable variable on the table. Very often, even though there is a clean way of doing things that takes slightly longer, there is also a messy way of doing things that gets you there faster. To deliver the same scope on time and on budget, teams sometimes decide to take the shortcuts and implement the solution in a messier but (in the short term) quicker approach. This could leave behind messy, poorly structured, difficult-to-read code with less test coverage, among other things. This is done with a conscious mindset that on-time delivery of a bigger scope will create more business value than the short-term impact of technical debt.

The key phrase here is "short-term impact." Although we agree that this could be the appropriate business decision in certain circumstances, we have often seen teams significantly underestimate the negative impact of technical debt and wait too long before paying it down. Our observations indicate that it often takes weeks, not even months, for the increasing cost of development to offset any short-term gain on team velocity through taking shortcuts and dropping the internal quality. Even though it might make sense to rush to a deadline just a few weeks away and sacrifice quality, it never pays off to drop the internal quality for months in order to reach the next milestone faster. In fact, we would argue that any decision to take on technical debt for more than a few weeks will backfire, causing reduced delivery speed in just a couple of months.

An additional problem is when teams are under pressure to produce business features, they often create "tech tasks" to pay down technical debt or make architectural improvements. Product owners very often underestimate the importance of these tasks, deprioritizing them and leaving the team producing only end-user focused features, never improving the internal quality of the software. We think there's an important balance to be made here: both the customer value and the technical health of the software must be considered when balancing time spent on features versus technical improvements.

When a conscious decision is made to take on technical debt, it is critical to pay the debt back down within a few weeks' time.

Reckless messiness due to lack of coding skills. As a software developer, one aspect of the skill set is reflected in the number of languages and technology stacks one is proficient in. An experienced developer tends to be more versatile and masters a wide range of tools. The other important skill is the ability to write clean, reliable, and well-designed code. Coding skills are not necessarily correlated to years of experience. With proper mentorship and intentional practice, a developer with just a few years of experience can write clean, easy-to-read and maintain code. Without focus and deliberate improvement, you can spend a decade building software solutions and still write messy "spaghetti code."

Due to commoditization of IT over the past 20 years, there are a lot of pockets in the industry that lack emphasis on technology excellence. Productivity is defined as lines of code and features developed instead of value and long-term cost of maintenance. Everywhere we look, there are examples of messy code going into production causing defects and rising cost of maintenance. When examined and interviewed, the main reason turns out to be the lack of coding skills and the lack of appreciation of code quality in the development team.

At the same time, due to the belief that upfront architecture design is more important to ensure software quality than the coding process, many software delivery teams are structured in a model with a few highly skilled individuals doing the design thinking and an army of low skilled developers doing the "simpler" coding work. There is a myth that with proper upfront design, coding quality does not matter. Even at the lowest level of implementation, coding is still more of an art than a science. There are still many different ways of implementing a high-level design, some cleaner, some messier. With just a few shortcuts or a few spaghetti methods, a well-designed framework can quickly turn into an entangled implementation.

It's important to maintain a high-level technical skill set across the entire software coding team. There are no simple coding tasks in strategic digital assets when the software continues to evolve and extend.

Reckless messiness is a major cause of technical debt, but it is also the easiest to mitigate by assembling a team with the proper level of skill sets.

When LinkedIn's Technical Debt Came Due

From the time it was founded in 2003, LinkedIn had become what every startup founder hopes: a multibillion-dollar company with millions of users. But by the time the company went public in 2011, it had accumulated eight years' worth of "individually innocent" technical compromises that left them with a pile of technical debt and an inability to get new features into production fast enough. So, in the fast-paced world of technology startups, the company did the unthinkable: LinkedIn froze new feature development for *two months* in order to pay off their technical debt.

It wasn't an easy decision. Product managers, tasked with getting the features out the door that enable LinkedIn to be so competitive, balked at the idea. But Kevin Scott, LinkedIn's head of engineering, persuaded everyone at the company that the years of failing to make interest payments on their technical debt meant that a "balloon payment" was now due. The organization needed to, at least for a short time, quit moving fast and breaking things.

In the following two months, LinkedIn rebuilt its development architecture from the ground up. Every developer at the company spent at least some time working on the new system. When the company went live two months later—once again able to deploy new features to production—there were bugs and raw edges but everyone agreed the new system was an improvement. Six months later, it was an unquestionable success. The upgrade allowed LinkedIn to release to production multiple times *per day* instead of once per month. Over the following months and years, this capability—to experiment quickly and get fast feedback from real users—became a critical part of LinkedIn's success. You can read more about the story online (*https://oreil.ly/LhK52*).

The process of software development is really about learning. Software has always been a fast-evolving discipline. New programming languages and technology stacks have continued to emerge in the past two decades, from Java, .NET, and Ruby, to Scala, Erlang, and Kotlin. The accelerating technology changes create new computing platforms like cloud computing, mobile, and social networks. New techniques continue to be developed to enable better architecture and system integration, from DevOps and microservices, to database refactoring and evolutionary architecture. No developer in the world, no matter how brilliant, can claim to know how to use the latest tools and technology in the best possible way in an enterprise computing environment without much practice and opportunities for trial-and-error. Very often, the best way to use certain technology or a combination of languages and tools only becomes obvious after seeing it in production for a few months.

In addition to learning about specific technologies, teams working on a software system are usually learning about the problem domain itself. As they gain more experience and build more features, they will often gain insight about the best ways to think about the problem at hand and the best ways to build software abstractions to solve the problem.

It's common to see even the best team looking back at work done more than a year ago and realizing that it can be done better and differently knowing what they know now. This is the kind of technical debt that even the best developers and teams will incur.

Teams haven't done anything wrong in these cases; they simply realize that there is now a better way to use a tool or represent a problem domain in software. The act of building software is largely about learning, so we actually ought to be worried if a team says that it can't think of anything to improve! Whether we like it or not, the speed of change continues to pick up. New techniques and tools are becoming available in a matter of months instead of years. It is therefore crucial to continue work on the internal quality of the code base as new learnings expose hidden technical debt not known to the teams before.

Technology Excellence Is a Choice

This is perhaps the most important takeaway. Technology excellence is a choice that managers and leaders make. It is currently being made mostly unconsciously through small daily decisions. We think we need to change that and become more intentional.

Intentionality begins with recognizing the strategic nature of digital assets. For a system that is considered a business differentiator, technology excellence matters. The cost of developing and evolving the system closely correlates to the internal quality of the code base. High internal quality not only allows you to develop and maintain the system with lower cost, it's also crucial to providing the flexibility and speed of response needed by increasingly demanding consumers and a competitive market.

When it comes to digital technology, going faster at the cost of low internal quality is never sustainable, not even for a few months. Team leads and managers' decisions on schedule, scope, and cost have a huge impact on the internal quality of the software system. Internal quality should rarely, if ever, be the fourth tradeable factor that gets squeezed when scope or schedule is under pressure.

Coding skills are an important driver for internal quality. Leaders can set the tone by hiring people with the right attitude, allowing the team to pick the tools they deem the best fit for the task, and encouraging a culture of continuous learning and improvement. Cost should not be the only or most important factor when choosing partners to help with delivery. Technology excellence creates more value and should be the primary criterion to consider in building the partner ecosystem.

Even the best teams will incur technical debt. No matter how it's built up, no team can afford to live with the debt in the long run. Making a commitment to technology excellence requires a balance of viewpoints—the urgent, day-to-day need to deliver features and the longer-term investment in internal quality. Managers and leaders, including technical leaders and architects, need to deliver this balanced viewpoint and make deliberate efforts to build and maintain technology excellence. All too often we see business decision makers forgo technical improvements in favor of features, and teams struggling with a significant debt load. This is not to say that all technical improvements should always be made—developers do sometimes "gold plate" their work—but a healthy balance must be maintained.

It is critical for the technologist to advocate for, and for the business people to understand and support, the importance of technology excellence in building the modern digital capability.

ADOPT AGILE ENGINEERING PRACTICES, BEYOND JUST THE MANAGEMENT PRACTICES

We have mentioned Agile software delivery a few times in this book. It is a combination of techniques and tools to achieve two main goals—technology excellence and process excellence.

Frameworks like *Scrum* tend to emphasize establishing the iterative development process. Product requirements are organized into a backlog of "user stories" or "use cases" that's relatively small, independent, estimable, and testable. An Agile team could consist of half a dozen to a dozen people. The workflow is broken into a series of time-boxed efforts with a one-week to three-week duration.

Each team will pick up a few user stories or user cases to focus on during an iteration. Each iteration (or *sprint*) goes through a mini-planning session at the beginning, and a showcase and review session at the end.

At the same time, there is another set of Agile software development engineering practices that focus more on improving the coding quality. Many of these practices originally came from the *eXtreme Programming framework* (*https://oreil.ly/2yPGo*) created by Kent Beck in the late 90s. Besides the iterative development process similar to Scrum and other team management–focused frameworks, it advocates for a distinctive set of engineering practices designed to help developers write clean code that is well designed and easy to maintain. Here are a few examples of such practices:

Unit testing

Testing is an effective way to find defects in the system. The earlier that you can find defects, the easier and cheaper it is to correct them. The traditional testing approach is to run end-to-end testing of the entire system or feature sets, often manually. Unit testing is the practice to push testing into the smallest piece of code that can be logically isolated in a system and run tests automatically and continuously. This creates a "safety net" covering the code base at a granular level. Combined with continuous integration (CI), it enables effective defect detection at the earliest moment and the ability to pinpoint any issues.

Test-driven development

Test-driven development (TDD) is the practice of writing unit or functional tests before writing the code to implement the feature. TDD helps to achieve two goals. One is to use tests to express system requirements so that we know we have achieved our results when the tests pass as opposed to just guessing. The second goal is to help simplify the design. Similar to other fields and disciplines, software developers tend to overengineer their solutions from time to time. TDD allows developers to focus on getting the minimum done first to achieve the functional results—often in a rather messy way—and then using refactoring to improve the design of the code and make the code cleaner. This allows the most fit-for-purpose design to emerge out of the refactoring rather than upfront thinking.

Refactoring

Refactoring is a set of techniques and tools that allow developers to change the structure of the code without altering its functionality. Illustrated by

Martin Fowler in *Refactoring: Improving the Design of Existing Code* (Addison-Wesley), these techniques help to improve readability, extensibility, and to reduce complexity. Refactoring is focused on gradually improving the design and internal quality in an incremental and piecemeal approach as opposed to a Big-Bang rewrite. It is supposed to be done on an hourly basis in very short cycles of writing tests, implementing, and then refactoring. This is the day-to-day, hour-to-hour, and even minute-to-minute action development teams can take to reduce technical debt.

Continuous integration

Software development is a highly collaborative process. From as few as half a dozen developers to as many as a few hundred developers could be working on the same code to produce a software product. All the individual's work on their own functions and features need to be integrated at some point so that the system works well holistically. There are often many unforeseen problems or fundamental design issues exposed only during the integration phase. It is sometimes referred to as the "integration nightmare" because issues could result in large amounts of rework. Continuous integration (CI) is a set of practices and tools that run the integration process automatically every day, or even every hour. This allows detection of potential catastrophic problems downstream as early as possible so that the risk can be nipped in the bud. Combined with automated unit testing, it will also allow developers to detect their own mistakes early, often introduced inadvertently when code modification for new feature breaks old functionalities.

Pair programming

This is perhaps a more controversial practice. It's a set of practices wherein two people work together, often on a single computer, to develop software. Pair programming increases software quality. Simply put, when it comes to software programming, two heads are better than one. It's easy to spot mistakes early. Pairing helps to solve difficult problems efficiently through discussion. When you must explain to the other person the rationale behind the code, better ideas and cleaner design tend to emerge. Because two people have worked on the code, knowledge about the code base will be better spread among the team, often with less need for formal code reviews and less siloed knowledge. Some people question the productivity aspect because it appears to be an ineffective use of resources. Although it might be counterintuitive, many empirical studies have shown that two people pair programming will add as much functionality as two working separately, except that it will be much higher in quality.

As you can tell, there is a lot of synergy between these engineering practices. They are highly effective at improving the internal quality of a code base so that the cost of future development stays low in the long term while the velocity and responsiveness of the development team stays high. They have been widely adopted by software development teams around the world since the early 2000s.

That said, it takes teams longer to adopt and excel at better coding practices. For leaders and team managers, it's easier to focus on only the management practices because you can see and feel the impact of small cross-functional teams, shorter sprints, and daily team standups, showcase, and review sessions. The buzz and energy created early on in the room is visible and contagious. The impact of engineering practices, on the other hand, could be less visible initially, especially to nontechnical people, and take a longer time to have a big impact. But eventually, with higher-quality code, better design, more automated test coverage, and low technical debt, the team will be able to produce high-quality features at high velocity, with fewer defects and high flexibility. It should feel more like an efficient machine beyond the initial buzz and energy.

Many organizations have had a bad experience with frameworks such as Scrum. In our experience this is often because underlying engineering practices are neglected. Backlogs, planning, iterations, and showcases provide better visibility into software creation, but you also need technology excellence underpinning those practices. In recent years Scrum has introduced a "Certified Scrum Developer" program specifically to teach these kinds of practices and to help ensure successful Agile adoption.

Leaders and managers can be very effective at creating technology excellence by encouraging and supporting Agile teams to adopt the good engineering practices. They can also do the opposite by not recognizing or underestimating the value of engineering excellence compared against process excellence.

Key Points

Following are the key points that we hope you take away from this chapter as well as two actions for you to take to begin implementing what we've discussed:

- Business strategy determines which digital assets are utility and which ones are strategic. It's not the function, age, or the technology of the system that drives its strategic importance

- High internal quality is the foundation to achieve a fast delivery cycle, adaptiveness, and responsiveness in your strategic software systems.

Here are two actions to take:

- Build delivery teams with highly skilled technologists: Avoid mixing in too many low-skilled staff (often from low-cost vendors) for "simple coding tasks."

- Reinforce the discipline to keep the technical debt low: Most important, give teams the time to do it. Foster a collaborative relationship between business and IT such that a good balance between features delivered and internal quality can be maintained.

12

Growing and Empowering Talent

World-class digital capability requires world-class talent. In a market where everyone is seeking talent, acquiring and retaining talent are becoming some of the highest priorities in a digital transformation journey. In this chapter, we discuss the critical factors that affect the result of acquiring and retaining talent.

Build More Core Digital Capability In-House

Building technology at the core of an organization requires not just the right processes, architectures, and technology itself; it requires the right technical talent—people—to deliver them. Almost without exception, talent comes up during every conversation we have with CIOs and senior technology executives. Everywhere we look, there seems to be a shortage of technology talent. What kind of capability to recruit and retain in house and what kind of capability to borrow and rent from partners thus becomes a critical question to answer for any organization going through a digital transformation. Let's have a look at two of the key areas involved in increasing talent available to your organization.

INSOURCE VERSUS OUTSOURCE

As discussed earlier, when the majority of technical assets are viewed as a utility, the conventional management wisdom will lead to outsourcing as much as possible. As a result, many businesses outsourced the majority of their IT functions, especially software development, to third-party vendors. Some kept a few key functions internal—for example, program management, architecture, and product management—because they were deemed to be higher "value add" parts of the software development process. What we have discovered by interviewing many technology organizations is even more disheartening. If we dig a level deeper and are honest with ourselves, the skill sets of a lot of internal staff have been stripped to a very narrow array—in fact, mostly around vendor management instead of technology itself.

The head of the digital service division of a very large organization told us that when he took over the division, he did a thorough skill assessment of the four thousand staff members he inherited. It turned out that, regardless of their role, most of their responsibilities and tasks concerned procurement and vendor management. They are essentially vendor managers. Given their ratio of one internal staff member to six vendor staff members, it took 4,000 people to manage 24,000 external contractors. No wonder IT is viewed as expensive, inefficient, slow, and complex. It took quite some courage to face reality and take real actions to repurpose, reskill, and rearrange the internal staff members so that they were retrained and their skill sets were aligned with the new digital capabilities. The good news was that the majority of the four thousand people did come from a software delivery background. It was difficult, but not impossible, to get the staff's job functions back closer to technology and software development.

In this new Digital Age in which "every industrial company will become a software company" where "technology strategy is at the heart of the business strategy," technical capability is now viewed as a competitive advantage and digital solutions as a key differentiator. It makes sense that many businesses are beginning to "insource" versus "outsource," reversing the trend of the past 20 years.

It's worth pointing out that not all insourcing is driven by the need to build a digital competitive advantage internally. As the cost of vendors and contractors continues to go up, some COOs or CFOs have concluded that it might be cheaper in the long run to hire people internally than body-shop from vendors. But that mindset is still cost driven instead of value driven. A cheaper cost center internally is still a cost center. Insourcing should be about building a competitive advantage versus a utility function; it's about building a revenue center instead of a cost center.

Insourcing is a complex process—consider the facility build-out, software license transfer, asset migration, and training and transition. There are plenty of articles available online discussing the benefits and challenges of insourcing IT work. We are mainly going to focus on talent and skill sets here—the most important cornerstones of insourcing to build core digital capability.

HIRING IS EFFECTIVE ONLY WHEN YOU HAVE THE PROPER INTERNAL CULTURE

This is a trend we have observed across industries, from retail, financial services, and automobile manufacturing, to health-care, manufacturing, and business services. There is no longer a dispute as to whether this is the correct strategy; the questions we are hearing are mostly around the "how's." How do I reskill the mismatched, outdated roles I have internally? How do I hire new talent with the new digital skills—software engineering, mobile, cloud, DevOps, microservices, augmented and virtual reality, AI, machine learning, and so on? How do I deal with attrition after I build this capability given that every organization that is known for software engineering excellence carries a target on its back for poaching? Can I afford it? The list goes on.

Hiring is the most commonly asked-about topic. To bridge the gap between what's needed in the Digital Age and what's available internally, most executives are focusing on hiring new talent from the market. From Sydney to Singapore, from London to Berlin, from Beijing to Bangalore, from New York to São Paulo, everywhere we look, there is a shortage of IT talent in the market. Hiring is becoming almost like a zero-sum game, but it cannot be the only solution to the talent shortage problem for all companies.

We strongly believe that the real answer is not outside of the company, it's within the company. It's about developing your own people, including the people you just hired, and making them more productive. There are two key aspects here:

- Building a culture of learning so that your people continue to develop and become better over time

- Building an environment that empowers people so that they are more productive

For example, Kroger is an American retailing company founded in 1883 in Cincinnati, Ohio. It is the largest supermarket chain by revenue in the United States and the second-largest general retailer (behind Walmart). Traditional grocery retailers have been slow to adopt digital technology. Many are now feeling the heat as Amazon is now becoming a disrupting force in the grocery space by acquiring Whole Foods. As an example, it has recently opened a new type of semi-automated cashier-less store, Amazon Go. Being an early adopter of digital technology and an outlier in the grocery industry, Kroger has been focusing on taking advantage of technology to modernize its grocery stores for a while, giving it a head start among its peers on the digital journey. The company invested heavily in data analytics, mobile, Internet of Things (IoT), and had rolled out click-and-collect, scan-bag-go, edge-shelf-display, and other services to give consumers a more personalized shopping experience.

Kroger ran into the talent issue early on in its journey to build digital capability. Cincinnati is far from Silicon Valley; it's certainly not known as a destination for technology talent. As early as 2012, ThoughtWorks started a partnership with Kroger to help build up its digital capability. There were fewer than 25 people in Kroger Digital at the time. Some people were doubtful about the feasibility of hiring enough world-class digital talent in Cincinnati, then perceived more of a digital backwater. The team strongly believed that by building the right culture that nurtures and empowers people, they could attract good talent, make them better, build a reputation, and attract more talent. The reinforcing feedback loop worked and paid off in the long run. Kroger has been named to *ComputerWorld*'s "Top 100 Best Places to Work in IT" for 2018. It ranked 58th among large companies and is the only retailer to be recognized by the publication. In 2018, its digital sales soared by 66% compared to a year ago, making it a strong competitor to Amazon and Walmart.

One thing is for certain: the war for talent is on, and building your own technical talent will be imperative to your success.

Build a Culture of Learning

Relative age effect (RAE) is a commonly accepted concept. It describes a bias, mostly evident in academia and youth sports, that those who are born earlier in the relevant selection period tend to do better.

A well-known example, made popular by Malcolm Gladwell's bestselling book *Outliers* (Little, Brown, and Company) is the age bias in Canadian ice hockey players. According to online science journal *PLOS ONE* (https://oreil.ly/igU_k), nearly 40% of players on elite junior teams are born between January and March. The reason is that young players born in January are, on average, bigger, faster, and stronger than the kids born in December of the same year. This small head start gives players born in the first months of the year a small advantage. They are more likely to be chosen by the coaching staff on the ice during a game, especially during a time that matters. With more ice time, better coaching and more visibility, they tend to be perceived as better and sometimes more "talented" than players in the other age groups. Subsequently, they are more likely to be chosen for top-tier competitive teams. And the cycle repeats. This is evened out a bit when they arrive at the professional level, but that small head start advantage remains visible. More National Hockey League players are born between January and March than any other months.

The point is that success is due to a combination of hard work, talent, and a bit of luck. When we claim that we want to hire the "best talent" in the market, we are really saying that we want to hire people who have done the hard work to learn and gain relevant experience. It's worth pointing out that they are also lucky, to some extent, to have gained the right experience at the right time.

In this Digital Age, the ever-increasing pace of technology improvement is pushing all of us into a lifelong-learning mode. When technology is progressing at an exponential speed, technologists are required to gain new skill sets, no longer in the time frame of every few years, but every few months, every few weeks. Learning is no longer something you do once a while through some training program; it's becoming part of the everyday job.

The willingness to learn, the commitment to learn, and the ability to learn are thus more important than a head start and the current level of experience. With the appropriate learning culture and proper support, the biggest asset most companies have today—existing employees—could turn into an even more differentiating strength and an accelerating competitive advantage for the future. There are many things leaders of an organization need to do to create this type of environment. The following sections present some areas to consider.

CREATE A SAFE ENVIRONMENT TO PROVIDE FEEDBACK

Although training is a great opportunity to learn and improve, the majority of the learning for most people is done on the job. Sometimes it is through learning from the outcome of the work; sometimes it is through pairing with experienced staff. More often than not, it is done through reviews and feedback from colleagues. It is thus critical to create an environment that is safe to provide constructive and effective feedback.

There are three important principles about providing feedback—the intention is to help the other person improve; it's based on facts; it's given directly (as opposed to via someone else). Whenever there is a situation in which one person is about to provide feedback to another person, it's always a good practice to repeat and agree on these three principles first. This will greatly reduce the friction and misunderstanding often caused by assumptions of ill intentions, back channeling, toxic rumors, and so on.

Leaders have a great deal of influence on a constructive feedback culture by being a role model and helping reinforce these three principles by correcting wrong behaviors like back channeling and undermining.

ENCOURAGE CONTINUOUS FEEDBACK

Feedback should not be given or collected only during annual performance review cycles. Due to the nature of these annual performance reviews, the official feedback collection process is also run once a year in most organizations.

This tends to be interpreted as the only time to provide work-related feedback to peers and colleagues. Annual performance reviews should focus on goal setting, evaluation of achievements, and compensation review. When feedback is closely associated with performance review, the learning and development aspect tends to be overshadowed and even ignored. The feedback is given under the context of "performance management" instead of "performance enhancement."

It's worthwhile to decouple them and build separate processes and tools in order to provide feedback to each other all the time in the spirit of supporting and developing each other. In the development context, it's also easier to give constructive feedback aimed at performance enhancement instead of management.

CREATE AN ENVIRONMENT IN WHICH IT'S SAFE TO FAIL

It's well accepted that we learn from both success and failure; many would argue that perhaps we learn more from failure than success. Many organizations are committed to learning from failures, and many have processes and efforts dedicated to it—loss review, postmortem analysis, and so on. However, most of the people going into the process has a certain mindset: "It's very bad that we failed; Someone did something wrong; Let's find out who did what wrong, and make sure that we, and others, don't make the same mistake again." Very often, the lesson learned is something along these lines of "Joe didn't follow the process and skipped a critical step, we should avoid that in the future," or "We made a wrong assumption about the market conditions, we should do more research before the development of the next product." Failure is bad and there is someone or something to be blamed is often the single biggest blocker to effective learning from failures.

This is especially important in the Digital Age in which the ability to experiment fast and innovate fast will separate the winners and losers. Jeff Bezos famously said that "Our success at Amazon is a function of how many experiments we do per year, per month, per week, per day." No matter how well analyzed and designed upfront, most experiments fail instead of succeed. This is very different from the traditional operational mindset in which success is mostly driven by doing the same thing more efficiently, faster, and with less cost. Minimizing mistakes and failure is the key to productivity gains.

We found many organizations struggling to shift the mindset. It's partially due to the fear of cost of failure—sunken cost, brand impact, customer loyalty, and so on. As we have stated throughout this book, there are many ways to reduce the cost of experimentation and contain the impact of failed experiments. What leaders need to do next is to create a culture that looks at failure through a more positive lens.

There are "good" failures. An intentional experiment will start with a hypothesis, whether it's about customer behavior or market condition. The experiment is designed to validate that hypothesis with the minimum amount of cost and brand impact possible. Not all hypotheses will be proven to be correct. In fact, there are likely to be more invalid hypotheses than valid ones if we truly want to push the boundaries and be creative. A new product development process should consist of a series of such experiments, each designed and built on top of the learnings from the previous successful and failed experiments.

In this context, the failures are "good" failures, "smart" failures. It should be perfectly safe to have such failures if not encouraged already. This kind of positive attitude toward failure is the most important foundation to build an effective learning culture.

DON'T CUT THE TRAINING AND DEVELOPMENT BUDGET

Most businesses have some kind of training and development budget for their employees. Value from the training budget is difficult to measure and the return is not immediate. It's often viewed as discretionary spending. When operational pressure begins to pile up due to less-than-expected financial results, training and development budget, together with other discretionary spending, often are reduced in the current and potential future financial planning cycles. That sends the exact wrong message; that is, learning is optional and can be stopped at any time.

Not cutting the training budget even when time is difficult reinforces the important message to the company and employees—the leadership team takes training and development seriously; learning and development should be a high priority for the business and for everyone in the company.

LEARNING AND DEVELOPMENT IS AN IMPORTANT FUNCTION

To use a sports analogy, we often see some golf players continue improving by practicing, rising to the professional ranks, and still pushing the boundaries. At the same time, there are others who never stopped playing golf and trying to learn new tricks, but somehow plateaued at a certain level and struggled to progress further. Technologist and other professionals have similar situations.

Besides the motivation to learn and the effort to learn, the actual improvement can come only from *intentional* learning. An intentional learning experience requires a few key elements: a good coach, an idea on where to improve, practice designed to improve it, and an effective feedback loop.

The learning and development team (often a subfunction of the HR department) is an important function. It needs to help design a capability model for each role and its disciplines that outlines the progression/learning path to achieve mastery. There should also be coaches and mentors identified for each discipline at different maturity stages to provide help for people who are engaged in the learning activities. Training/lessons/workshops and other activities should be organized to achieve these learning goals on the learning paths, as opposed to training "benefits" randomly assigned to employees based on budget and performance reward.

Build a Culture of Empowerment

A couple of years ago, Adrian Cockcroft spoke at a ThoughtWorks conference. A lot of people in the audience were CIOs and CTOs. Given Cockcroft's well-known achievement of helping Netflix build a world-class cloud platform, many questions focused on how Netflix made the big strategic moves, from DVD to streaming, from datacenter to public cloud, from the US-only to international.

There were also questions on how to hire and retain the best digital talent. One person made a comment and asked a question from a more traditional enterprise perspective. The comment was: "A main reason that Netflix can pull off these big strategic moves is the world-class talent you have, especially around digital technology and software engineering. But it's not a fair comparison. Netflix has the brand that can attract the talent, and we don't. We are just a big traditional enterprise, world-class technologists and software engineers won't come to a traditional insurance company. How do we innovate without the talent?"

Cockcroft responded almost without a pause:

We didn't create the talent, we hired them from you—from big enterprises like yourself. The difference is that once they join our organization, we simply get out of their way, allow them to use the tools they see fit, and build software the way they see fit. Guess what, they become twice as productive and innovative right away compared to where they come from.

There was a long pause. The room went so quiet that you could almost hear a pin drop. He went on, "And you still have many of them in your organization—way more than the so-called Big Techs have. It's your job to create the right environment so that they can be productive and innovative." Many people later told us that it was one of the biggest a-ha moments for them at the conference.

Not only does empowerment make people more productive and innovative, it also better motivates them. Self-determination theory suggests that people are motivated to grow and change by innate psychological needs. A critical psychological need that is believed to be both innate and universal is the need for autonomy. Human beings need to feel that they are in control of their own behaviors and goals. It's a powerful and deeply buried reason why people choose where to work and what to work on.

The Sense of Belonging

Having a sense of belonging is possibly one of the most important intrinsic states you need for sustainable change to succeed. When people have that sense of belonging, they are more likely to be genuinely interested in the success of the business and the success of your transformation. They will be more tolerant of the inevitable mistakes you will make along the change journey, more likely to speak up when they see things not going well, and more capable of pushing forward in the face of ambiguity.

There are two challenges here. The first is maintaining a sense of belonging. This means feeding the connection to the broader company purpose and meaning through work and measures alignment, clarity, and visibility. Also making sure that people have a clear concept of their "home team," a support network that they can lean on both emotionally and for their craft. In a way, it is how people see their own personal brand in relation to the brand of the organization they are working for. "How I see myself is how others see the organization I work for."

Secondly, helping people associate belonging to the broader organization versus a smaller subsection within which they belong. In times of change, people can tend to close ranks and become overly attached to their current teams. It becomes about "my" value system instead of our value system, "my" activity instead of a correlation to purpose. Behavior can become competitive or even adversarial toward other teams in a fight for survival. Protecting the status quo becomes more important than supporting the change. Failure to maintain a broad belonging can have the unintended consequence of creating orphaned employees. Changes in team make up, even though logical and aligned to customer outcomes, can remove any sense of belonging the employee had to the organization and you can lose great talent.

Having a sense of belonging means your employees know their team, feel supported, have a shared sense of ownership of the organizational outcomes, and feel secure. They instinctively know how to contribute their talents. It is an emotionally intelligent issue rather than a logical or rational one, requiring attention and monitoring from leaders who can view change through this lens.

Getting out of the way sounds easy but it's actually really difficult—what about architecture standards, API design, and code quality; what about measurement, progress tracking, and spending control; and so on and so forth. A large enterprise inherits many processes, structures, and legacy constraints. Many stand in the way of empowering people and unleashing their creativity. Not everyone has the luxury to start from a green field or build a new company.

To that end, the following sections highlight some common practices that can help to create an empowering environment.

COMMUNICATE AND SHARE INFORMATION

One thing people working at smaller startups often cite as an attractive culture characteristic is the ability to communicate freely in the organization—almost everyone is accessible, from team leads to the CEO. It becomes more challenging when an organization becomes bigger. Layers and layers of hierarchy grow out of the need to organize and manage an increasingly complex workforce and business processes. Even though information flow and accessibility become more difficult naturally, given the bigger size, it's sometimes unintentionally stifled.

First, it's perceived that information can flow only up and down a command chain, like a pyramid. It cannot skip nodes; it cannot flow horizontally. This is a major misunderstanding and can be corrected by creating additional processes, tools, and networks to facilitate more channels for information flow. As discussed earlier in Chapter 6, big visible charts and other information radiators are great hierarchy-agnostic tools to share information creatively and broadly.

Second, probably a more difficult problem to solve, some unnecessary hurdles are created not because of the structure, but because of human nature. Consciously or unconsciously, there is a need to feel important and in control by people in the middle management. Information is power, and asymmetrical information is even more powerful. Hoarding information and using asymmetrical information to one's own advantage have become second nature to most people in today's society. Managers are not exempt from it. It's partially why we see more resistance to transparency in an organization than any other culture aspects we advocate for.

Although it's difficult, there are many things leaders can do to help break the information asymmetry: be a role model, make yourself accessible, push the boundaries, and be more open and transparent regarding your own communication. If some of the things you communicate with the broader organization haven't raised the eyebrows of your direct reports, you probably haven't pushed the envelope far enough.

Better communication and information flow is a key foundation to empowering people. This leads to the next building block: decision-making authority.

DELEGATE DECISION-MAKING AUTHORITY

The Agile Manifesto includes this principle: "The best architectures, requirements, and designs emerge from self-organizing teams." After more than a decade of practices by hundreds and thousands of teams across the industry, the community is getting better at influencing the team leader's role at decision making in a self-organizing teams.

Command-and-control style of management philosophy puts most decision-making authority into one person's hands. They are typically the middle management. More often than not, this kind of micromanagement takes away the employee's sense of ownership over their work and suffocates innovation. A CIO led the digital transformation of a company with 2,000 people in the IT division. Speaking of his own experience, he said that a key principle the organization established early on was that no manager's daily tasks should be centered on telling other people what to do and how to do it. This forced the division to repurpose and retrain almost a quarter of the people it had so that each person could focus on real value-add activities and allow teams to make their own decisions. At the end of a long journey, a staff survey showed that employee satisfaction increased from 5 to 8 on a 0 to 10 scale.

If the proper amount of information is fully accessible to everyone, more people will be in a position to make good decisions, not just a few managers. Common sense and logic are as important, if not more, than gut feeling and experience. In a self-organizing team, the leadership role of the team is to facilitate discussions about new patterns and behaviors that emerge from the work, combine the information and context everyone has, and let the best decision emerge. This is in stark contrast to a command-and-control style in which they would specify in advance what that best decision should be.

NURTURE THE SENSE OF OWNERSHIP

The decision-making authority comes with the sense of ownership. The self-organizing teams will need to take the responsibility of meeting the goals and targets set by the company while at the same time, evolve the way they work, and continuously improve. Besides having the authority to decide how things are done, a stronger sense of ownership will come from being part of the process of setting goals and targets.

Leaders' effort on communication should help to create a clear understanding of key objectives of the company and business units. The effort of further cascading key objectives down to smaller divisions and teams should involve the teams themselves so that they are engaged in setting the goals and targets for their own divisions and teams.

There is often a fear that if we let people do whatever they want to do and however they want to do it, few will have the aspiration and commitment to do more than necessary. When it comes to digital knowledge workers, we have rarely seen that fear materialize. In fact, we have mostly seen the opposite. When people and teams understand the vision, have access to the right information and the decision-making authority, they would feel a greater sense of ownership and aspire to achieve more and have a bigger impact.

As a professional, it is extremely satisfying to understand the vision and meaning of your work, help to create your own goals and targets, and, more important, be able to evolve the process that works best for your team and have access to the most effective tools and digital assets available. This kind of experience always leads to higher employee satisfaction and a better chance for the company to retain talent.

Recruit for Potential

Finally, we come to recruiting and retention. We believe if you focus on building a nurturing and empowering environment, not only does it help to unleash the untapped potential from existing employees and make them better at working with digital technology, it should also make it easier to recruit from outside of the company and retain them after they join.

A company known for developing and nurturing digital talent is more likely to attract aspirational talent than its peers. People who feel that they are learning new skills and are being empowered to make an impact are less likely to leave for a higher salary.

Our main recommendation for recruiting is to focus more on passion and potential than experience and current skill level.

Recruiting is a highly specialized and well-developed field in HR. There are plenty of best practices on the sourcing and selection processes. Most companies have a dedicated recruiting team in their HR department, always aiming to hire the best IT talent available. In the past few years, the recruiting process is taking longer and longer. According to a report by Fast Company in 2015 (*https://oreil.ly/ GSMBO*), the average length of the interview process almost doubled to 23 days in the previous four years. Nevertheless, the rate of successful hires from the large volume of applications continue to drop. To some extent, this is a reflection of the supply-and-demand mismatch in the digital talent market. If we just look for existing experience and existing skills, we will be getting into a zero-sum game with everyone competing in the same pool for the same scarce resources.

But it doesn't need to be that way. An effective learning and development culture will also direct you to recruit more for potential than just experience. It could open more channels and create more sources for excellent hires that might seem unconventional by traditional standards.

We have tried a few different approaches at ThoughtWorks and seen various levels of success in finding high-potential people from nonconventional sources.

For example, we went after college graduates who are not computer science majors, not even in science and technology fields. We provided an extended training and development program (longer than six months) for the people who don't have the technology background. Given the cognitive strength and learning capability, many of them are able to pick up the challenging skills quickly through intentional practice. Combined with their excellent problem-solving skills, emotional intelligence, and collaborative approach, which we looked for during the recruiting process, many became leaders in their teams and communities in a rather short period of time.

Scaling Digital Talent Through Digital Partners

Does the insourcing trend mean that there will eventually be no more need for vendors to provide IT services? That's unlikely to be the case in the foreseeable future. It's probably going to be the opposite. As the landscape of information technology continues to expand, as new technology continues to emerge, as the pace of change continues to speed up, no one company can build all the capability internally. Tools, infrastructure, expertise, and economy of scale will create more need to collaborate with external partners.

Perhaps most important, even in the digital space, scalability will be a big challenge facing most companies in the world. The need for this new kind of capability is growing exponentially, more than the industry can provide at the moment, and probably also in the next decade. The right kind of digital consultancy will create a different, if not necessarily better, environment of developing digital technology talent. This source of digital know-how and capacity will complement the insourcing strategy by providing capability uplift, specialized expertise, and talent scalability.

Many companies continue to evolve their sourcing strategy—which part of the capability is to be built internally, and which part to co-source, and which part to outsource. Sometimes it's driven by the corporate strategy; sometimes it's driven by the financial performance and budget; very often it's simply driven by the preference of the new CIO.

In this new Digital Age, in which technology innovation is driving more and more business model innovation, where organizations need to be a lot more responsive, where technology platform and architecture will continue to evolve, there needs to be a new way to select and collaborate with external partners. Even though there is no one-size-fits-all solution, the following section provides some guidelines that we believe to be important to consider.

THE COST-DRIVEN APPROACH IS OUTDATED

As mentioned earlier, in the late 1990s and early 2000s, the IT outsourcing trend was mostly driven by the premise that information technology is a utility, like water and electricity. Besides reliability and basis standards, there is not much difference in quality and value. Value is assumed to be fixed and the same for everyone. To maximize the value/cost ratio, the only factor worth considering is cost.

This indirectly encouraged the Waterfall software development process in which the life cycle of application development is broken into several major phases that take advantage of different skill sets. Coding, testing, and maintenance in particular are treated as almost unrelated activities that can be outsourced to volume-based vendors that can drive the lowest cost due to economies of scale. An otherwise Agile, holistic, and CD process, as the modern development methodology would require, is replaced with several handovers and long and rigid delivery cycles, which often ends with lower quality and lack of responsiveness. No wonder IT departments are often viewed as slow and unresponsive.

Sometimes, this approach is mitigated with engaging higher-caliber individuals (internal staff or consultants) to form hybrid teams—hoping that one can achieve both quality and low cost. But when a large outsourcing company's business model is to train hundreds and thousands of people on very few specialized skill sets in a wholesale approach to achieve the economies of scale, it often ends up with a rather narrow set of capabilities that can solve one problem very well, repeatedly.

As most software practitioners would argue, software development is rarely about solving the same problem again and again. It's a highly complex and unpredictable field that requires a broad set of cognitive capability, as we suggested earlier in the learning and development section. Although the theory of economy of scale based on Waterfall methodology works well on paper, it's rarely successful in reality.

As a result, we often hear CFOs and CIOs complaining about the ever-increasing need for more IT capacity, more vendor headcount, and more budget to fix old issues, while at the same time new digital capability development is starved for resources and people.

In one typical example, the new CIO of a large financial institution observed an average of 30% year-on-year increase of discretionary spending on IT over a three-year period. At the same time, there was an average of 60% year-on-year increase of nondiscretionary IT spending. Why was that the case? The organization attributed this partially to the wrong mix of a large volume of low-cost staff from external vendors and contractors. Under the pressure to deliver more, more people at lower cost was the only solution to the problems under the previous procurement constraints. While code, features, and applications were rushed in by a lot of finger tips, the amount of technical debt accumulated caused a lot of production issues and challenges for further customization. The new CIO's number-one priority was to reduce technical debt and stabilize the platforms; the number-two priority was to fix the labor mix.

It will only go so far to mitigate the issues by building a modern technology architecture and platform, by building a world-class in-house digital capability, by building a responsive internal organization. A modern digital organization requires modern digital partners to achieve talent scalability and capability uplift.

There is an argument that, just like other inherited messiness in organization structure, architecture, and process, it's not easy to switch the outsourcing paradigm completely overnight. There are still utility software systems that need to be maintained and supported (but Software-as-a-Service is reducing this need); there are still in-house datacenters that need to be managed until it's moved to the cloud; there are still dozens and even hundreds of application delivery projects in-flight that cannot pause or stop.

But a digital partner is a very different kind of partner than the large traditional outsourcing companies. In the next section, we look at what we believe to be important to consider when choosing digital partners.

WHAT TO LOOK FOR IN A DIGITAL PARTNER

Most large outsourcing companies have pivoted their strategy to focus more on modern digital capability due to the requirements in the new Digital Age, and, probably more important, mitigating the existential threat to the outdated legacy capability. Some are doing this through organic growth (hiring and training), many more are doing this through acquisition. The industry is observing an acquisition frenzy in which design agencies and digital consultancies are being acquired by large management consulting and IT services firms.

Just to name a few, between 2012 and 2015, PWC acquired BGT, a digital creative consultancy; Accenture acquired design firm Fjord; Deloitte bought Ubermind and Banyan Branch; and EY bought Seren. In 2015, Cognizant acquired Cadient, and Wipro bought DesignIT to start their own digital divisions. According to the annual report published by Clarity and Jegi on M&A trends in marketing services, the usual large agency holding companies like Dentsu and WPP have done much less acquisition relatively while big technology consulting companies like Accenture, Deloitte, and IBM led the way on their acquisition of digital agencies in 2017.

Meanwhile, many small- to medium-sized digital consultancies are seeing strong organic growth as their digital-native brand, opportunity to work with high-caliber peers, and flexible working environments are attracting more and more talent.

These are all good news for the industry. Better capability and more choices would better fit different needs from different companies. Depending on the level of internal digital maturity, capability gaps, location, and scale, companies might have different priorities when evaluating digital partners. Based on what we have learned and observed, here are some important principles to consider:

- Unless you are fairly advanced in the digital transformation journey, most large organizations still have a fair amount of legacy systems to maintain and move. The need to outsource the maintenance and support efforts won't go away immediately.

- There is also still a certain amount of software delivery work (and teams) that are not going to be modernized and transformed immediately. For this kind of outsourcing work, the traditional outsourcing vendors are still there to fill the gap. But even when many of them can claim to have a digital division, that doesn't mean that they are the best partner for digital capability.

A digital partner needs to be able to work closely with your digital team, almost seamlessly, to form a one-team environment. It is important to first examine two aspects: culture alignment and process compatibility. A digital partner is also not just a body shop that provides people to your team; the partner should bring in technology excellence and talent scalability. We would suggest examining the following aspects carefully when selecting a digital partner.

Culture alignment

As mentioned earlier, In the Digital Age, work is done iteratively and collaboratively, internal staff (from both business and technology) will work together with people from external partners at the same time. You cannot have part of the team having an empowering culture while some team members are still following a command-and-control mindset. You cannot have part of the team motivated to learn and continuously improve while other members just want to get the minimum done and advocate "good is good enough." The wrong type of mentality from the partners, when joined together with an aspirational internal team, could hinder the development of a healthy culture, or quickly offset any progress made internally.

It's important to dive deeper into the partner's organizational culture, ideally through interviewing people on the ground (rather than just listening to presentations), getting references from former employees and former clients on clearly defined culture behaviors to understand the alignment (or gaps) between the two organizational culture.

Process compatibility

It is well accepted nowadays that Agile software delivery methodology is a fundamental building block for digital capability. Although most organizations have adopted or started to adopt an Agile process, many are struggling to include the large number of external contractors and vendors to be part of the Agile and CD process. When Toyota pioneered the Lean Manufacturing disciplines and started to pull ahead in its productivity and creativity, it quickly recognized that the suppliers became the new bottleneck. Given that they were the pioneers themselves, they had to develop programs to train their suppliers to follow the same Toyota Production System.

The good news in the software development world is that Agile software delivery has been around for almost two decades. It's well known and well accepted by most practitioners. But many large-scale, volume-based vendors have generally fallen behind in adopting the Agile disciplines given the symbiosis of large outsourcing deals and traditional Waterfall methodology. Although many would claim to be Agile already by demonstrating their certifications, doing Agile institutionally is very different.

Technical excellence

In the digital space, software excellence is generally associated with the ability to deliver customer value early, fast, with excellent UX and lower product maintenance and evolution costs. A lot of the recent improvement of these capabilities in the IT industry benefited from better architecture, tools, and process. However, there has been a tendency to downplay the importance of coding skills, as if coding were the lowest value-add part of the software delivery process. Some development methodology tried to create enough upfront design and guardrails so that coding can be done by low-skilled workers who can be trained to specialize in a few simple tasks. This is the right mindset to scale and low-cost in a twentieth-century industrial and manufacturing environment, but this does not work in the modern software development environment.

Because of the fast-changing technical landscape, the fast-changing business requirements, and consumer demands, software development requires a broad range of technical knowledge, conceptual thinking, and problem-solving skills. Despite the various efforts to simplify it, it remains more like a craft than an engineering practice.

As discussed earlier in Chapter 11, it is important for the organization to focus on coding skills and coding quality, and maintaining a high standard in the software developer community. All practitioners in the organization should aspire to become masters in their own fields as well as proficient in adjacent fields. Everyone should aim to be a specialist and generalist at the same time—being able to demonstrate world-class depth in one or two fields, but also learning and grasping enough in other software development areas to become better general problem solvers.

This applies to the digital technology partners, too. When looking for a digital technology partner, it's important to examine the technology excellence aspect across the organization, especially the majority of the practitioner community, rather than focusing only on quality control and the senior layer of the delivery capacity (or just a few superstars).

If you focus on culture alignment, process compatibility, and technology excellence, and select the right partners to work with during the digital transformation, these partners could form a smart ecosystem that becomes an extension of your digital organization.

The digital partner ecosystem could help to provide the necessary skills set that you don't have internally; it could help to provide training and development opportunities for internal staff to close the internal capability gap. When new technology emerges, the digital partner ecosystem can be a source of technology radar and provide early adopter experience. Working together in a co-sourced environment with a one-team mindset, you can achieve a high level of productivity and creativity you internal team aspire to achieve. The right kind of digital partners can be a true source of talent scalability and become a competitive advantage your digital organization will have over the other competition.

So, it's not just about hiring the best talent available in the market. It's about hiring motivated and passionate people, and developing them continuously.

If you run a responsive and modern technology organization, your vendors need to keep up the pace, too. The single-skill-set, low-cost body shopping model will not meet your future digital needs. You need to ask a question: what is your vendor's talent management philosophy and is that compatible with your own culture on talent management?

Key Points

Following are the key points that we hope you take away from this chapter as well as two actions for you to take to begin implementing what we've discussed:

- The true secret in the ability to hire and retain top digital talent is the learning and empowering culture a company should build internally

- There is a lot of untapped talent within most organizations. Learning, development, and a sense of empowerment can be very effective at unleashing their employees' potential to deliver better digital solutions.

- Recruit for passion and potential over current skill sets. This can also unlock new sources of talent that would be ignored otherwise.

- When you're looking for digital partners for scaling, don't just focus on cost; conduct in-depth examination of culture, process, and technology excellence to make sure that a partner is compatible with the digital culture you are building.

Here are two actions to take:

- Assess your current level of digital talent: Take a long, hard look at your real capabilities. Do you have top-class teams capable of delivering modern solutions?

- Create a strategic plan to insource critical areas: Be aware that the technical landscape is now incredibly broad—you will likely need to find partners for specialist areas given that it's almost impossible to cover everything within one organization.

13

Continuous Delivery and DevOps

As discussed in Chapters 2 and 3, digital transformation is about finding a new way of working such that the organization can handle rapid changes with more effectiveness and less fatigue. The entire organization will be realigned to the purpose of delivering more value to customers, faster. Business and technology teams need to work together to complete the build-test-learn cycle end to end.

From a technology perspective, one of the key enablers over the past decade has been the cloud. Amazon launched the Amazon Web Services (AWS) cloud platform in 2006, making it possible to create a server in seconds just by clicking a button on a web management console. Faced with slow-moving internal IT, many organizations jumped on AWS as a way to move faster. But simply using AWS as a way to "get servers faster" was only a small part of the benefit—by applying automation and scripting, you could, for example, also create testing environments to remove bottlenecks or scale your infrastructure to handle Black Friday traffic spikes. Automation, of course, is at the heart of Agile engineering practices, and it is a key part of CD and DevOps culture, as we describe in this chapter. Together these technologies and techniques reinforce each other, delivering massive productivity and faster creation of business value. We examine each of these in turn in this chapter.

First let's look at CD. This is the key enabler to change the software delivery process from slow and long release cycles to a faster and iterative approach.

Release Software Features Early and Continuously

With CD, teams ensure that every feature that has been developed can be released to production at any time, and that the decision to deploy rests in the hands of the business. Changes can be released at the push of a button with no need to wait for a long testing and release cycle.

At the beginning of this section, we intentionally focused more on the engineering best practices in Agile. Here, we elaborate a bit more on the process and management practices that support the ability to release features early and continuously:

Break requirements into user stories

Unlike formal, detailed system requirements or use cases, a "user story" is a simple, informal description of a feature. It's often in the format of "As a [a type of user], I would like to [do something], so that [to achieve some value]." A user story is not intended to be a precise documentation of a system requirement; rather, it's a vehicle for verbal communications between the business user and the technology team at the time of the development of that story. A user story at a high level can be broken down into many smaller, lower-level stories. The list of user stories is the backlog of work to be prioritized, picked up and worked on.

Small cross-functional teams

In Chapter 5, we discussed the benefits of cross-functional teams. In the Agile software development context, an Agile team often consists of 6 to 10 people who own analysis, development, testing, and deployment of the user stories. Such a team size has proven to provide the best balance between communication and ability to stay aligned with the least overhead and broad enough skill sets to own the development end to end.

Work in iterations, or sprints

When broken down into the lowest level, user stories should be at the size of a few days of work at most, not weeks of work. With some practice and experience, they can be more easily estimated than large, complex use cases. The team will work in small cycles of one to four weeks, often called *iterations* or *sprints*. In each iteration, the team will follow a similar process: iteration planning (picking stories from the backlog to work on); daily delivery; daily standup meetings (half an hour); showcase of the feature after a story is finished; retrospective at the end of the iteration; and, finally, preparation for the next iteration (estimation, prioritization). This cadence allows the team to focus on a smaller chunk of a feature at a time, work out the detailed requirement in real time with the business users, code the feature, and showcase it to immediately gather feedback.

Planning/standup/showcase/retrospective

These are some of the common practices Agile teams use to organize and facilitate collaboration in an iteration. Planning is done at the very beginning of the iteration. The team will get together to discuss the goals of the iteration based on business priority, feedback from users, and the current state of the product backlog. It picks the user stories to work on based on the goals and estimated effort of the user stories. For a team of eight starting a two-week iteration, it might take two hours to get through. In a daily standup meeting, team members get together to coordinate their efforts or raise issues. Standing up, as opposed to sitting down, can help to keep the meeting short (ideally less than 30 minutes) so that it doesn't become a drawn-out theoretical debate. Hence the name (and lack of chairs...). A showcase can be done when each story is completed or batched at the end of the iteration to demonstrate the features to stakeholders for suggestions or acceptance. It's also an opportunity to get feedback on priorities and future directions. A retrospective is a meeting to reflect on the "how's" (not the "what's") of the iteration so that the team can continue to improve.

Many organizations have struggled to adopt Agile practices. In particular, we see a lot of focus on iterations, backlogs, and standups, but much less on the more difficult practices such as breaking requirements down into small stories and doing pair programming and automated testing.

Scrum has been a hugely popular flavor of Agile, but many Scrum projects failed because developers didn't know the important engineering practices that underlie the project management approaches of Agile. Martin Fowler coined the term "flaccid Scrum" (*https://oreil.ly/oDGBs*) to describe this problem. Realizing this gap, the Scrum Alliance now offers a "Professional Scrum Developer" certification, which emphasizes these important engineering skills.

As mentioned in Chapter 12, CI is an important concept to enable iterative development. This technique began to come into prominence in the late '90s. The following Focus section relates our own experience of how ThoughtWorks practiced CI in a large delivery team and built the tools to enable large-scale adoption.

A Story About Continuous Integration and the Birth of CI Tools

In 1999 at ThoughtWorks, one of the authors of this book, Guo Xiao, was part of a team of more than one hundred people building a rather complex leasing application using the *eXtreme Programming* (XP) method (later part of Agile methodology). Before that attempt, XP was mostly used on small-sized teams between half a dozen and a dozen people. This experiment was probably the first attempt to scale the XP process to a team as large as one hundred people. We broke the large requirement documentations into smaller "user stories." The hundred-plus members of the team were grouped into a few subteams, each focusing on a different functional area and consisting of business analysts, developers, and quality analysts. In the early days, we hadn't pushed the iterations to shorter cycles, and decided to run four-week iterations. At the beginning of each iteration, the business stakeholders and technologists spent half a day together picking which user stories to focus on, prioritizing them and flushing out the high-level goals and success criteria for each.

The large scale presented some interesting challenges, one of which was how to continuously integrate the code written by so many people at the same time.

Even when the teams were working on different functional areas from the business user's perspective, there were many shared components and architectural infrastructures everyone depended on. Microservices, event-driven architecture, and other modern architecture techniques were still yet to be formulated and adopted. There was certainly an attempt to decouple the code base as much as possible so that there were fewer dependencies between the components. But the components were still in the form of libraries that were to be reused between teams. There were also small central teams building the functional infrastructure and reusable components of the database layer, business logic layer, and the frontend user interface (UI) layer.

All of this code had to be downloaded from the source control system, compiled, and built together to be able to test the application end to end. Ideally, this was done every time a small piece of functionality was programmed and code is checked into the source control system. For a small team, this could be done manually within a few minutes. It's a tolerable overhead even if it needs to be done a few times each day. For the hundred-person team, this quickly became impractical. First, the manual process to compile and combine everything together took more than half an hour; second, many people and subteams needed to add code to the source control system throughout the day, dozens of times. The integration could not be done frequently enough and many sub-teams decided to branch out from the central code base for weeks to avoid the need to integrate with everyone else every day. Many errors, issues, and conflicts were discovered much later resulting in a lot of delays, rework, and wasted efforts. The integration process was essentially broken.

To resolve this, we decided to write some scripts to batch together the commands that downloads, compiles, and builds the application so that it could be done easier and faster. Piece by piece, the tasks were automated through the scripts until there was one "master script" that did the entire integration. Finally, anyone who wanted to integrate and deploy the whole application could do this with one single command. Instead of half an hour, it took just a minute or two to complete.

Why stop there? The testing framework offered command-line tools, too. We batched all the unit tests together with another script and incorporated it into the master script so that compilation and testing were done together. It converted another tedious manual process to an automated task. The result? Developers and teams were much more willing to compile, build, and run the tests for the entire application, not just their own part of the system, after they had done some work during the day. There were no more branches and everyone was working on the same code base most of the time. Potential integration errors, broken features, or architecture conflicts were discovered a lot earlier, almost as soon as any new code was added or a change was made.

The source control system also had a useful feature: it would fire off a notification as soon as someone checked some code into it. It became obvious to us that besides asking every developer and team to run the integration and testing themselves, we could have a dedicated computer in standby mode and run the entire integration as soon as the notification was triggered. We even set up a small website hosted by the computer to display the results of each run. This was the birth of the idea and the prototype of the first *CI tool*. It was later developed and released in

2001 as an open source application called *Cruise Control*, to support the broader community. There are now a variety of CI tools available in the market—Jenkins, TeamCity, Bamboo, and many more. It all started from these small steps to automate a few manual tasks.

This humble origin of Cruise Control also represented two important principles in the Agile software development movement, especially the development of the CD concept. First, if it's painful, do it early and frequently. Second, computers are good at automating mundane, tedious tasks to free up humans to solve difficult problems.

CI is a foundational technique that can help you on the road to achieving your goal: to release functionality early and often to create value for the business. First, though, we want to examine *why* releasing software is so fraught.

DOING THE HARD AND PAINFUL THINGS EARLY AND MORE FREQUENTLY

First of all, the longer you wait to tackle a difficult problem, the more painful it becomes. Integrating different pieces of a code base together to build the final software product is full of potential errors and problems. It gives many teams heartburn when it's time to compile and combine the various components and build the entire application. In more modern systems, the integration work might not be about simply collecting and compiling code, it might mean the integration of components such as those in a microservices ecosystem, or integration between one system and another.

There is a strong correlation between the amount of pain and work of integration and the time lapse between each successful integration. The longer the span between integrations, the more effort it takes to resolve issues and errors. Similar to the technical debt concept, there is also *integration debt*, which will accrue interest and cost more to fix over time.

Integrating more frequently also offers you the opportunity to practice and improve at it. In the earlier anecdote about the birth of CI, the scripts to automate tasks were not built at the outset. They were written piece by piece, task by task, and added up to make the integration process faster, smoother, and less painful over time. This allowed our team to discover potential problems, refine the scripts, and improve the automated process. After running this automated integration process hundreds, if not thousands, of times during a release cycle, the high-risk integration activity eventually became painless, low-risk, and sometimes even a rather dull moment. We had achieved success when no one was making a fuss about compiling the entire application any more.

Of course, a key building block here is using computers to automate manual tasks as much as possible to reduce the effort of doing the painful tasks more frequently. There are two types of pain here: the tedious and time-consuming manual tasks to perform, and the problem-solving effort after an issue is discovered. Even when it often means additional effort to write scripts or tools to automate tasks, the effort will be well justified when it can free up technologists to focus on the more difficult and valuable problem solving.

After the initial success of applying the "if it's painful, do it early and frequently" principle to the compilation and testing of a software product, we began pushing it further, beyond just integrating code. Another high-risk and painful step in the software delivery life cycle (SDLC) is the actual deployment and go-live stage. This is the final step of taking a well-developed build, deploying it to a staging environment, running end-to-end tests with production data and, if all goes well, deploying to the live production environment so that end users can begin using it. Many things could still go wrong in this step. For example, the staging and production environment could be different from the development environment (hardware, operating system, security constraints, and so on) causing defects or breaking functionality, and production data could be different from testing data, exposing issues not faced in the development stage.

There are also many repetitive and tedious activities that are traditionally done manually—different hardware and security environments need to be configured manually; testing data needs to be prepared and managed; functional tests are often run through a graphical user interface (GUI); so on and so forth.

The technology community came up with several techniques to automate deployment tasks and perform them faster, more repeatedly and with a higher success rate. Here are two of the most important techniques:

Infrastructure as Code (IaC)

Using a high-level declarative or templating language to manage configurations and automate provisioning and maintenance of infrastructure (the servers, networking, load balancers, firewalls, etc.). Infrastructure configuration is treated like code itself using version control, testing, incremental deployment, and often code pipelines. Infrastructure configuration is tested and maintained just like software code itself, making it easy to track and change and to provision infrastructure automatically. IaC gives development teams the ability to create and re-create environments on-demand as well as to remove "snowflake server" problems that are the result of each production server being unique and hand crafted (and often contains bugs waiting to bite us!). IaC techniques are usually a prerequisite to creating highly scalable cloud environments

Functional test automation

Unlike unit tests written by developers to maintain the integrity of the system, functional tests are end-to-end tests performed from the end-user's perspective. These often involve clicking buttons, entering text, and doing other things via a GUI. In the pre-Agile world, these tests were performed manually by QAs as part of a regression-testing stage. A test "script" was a series of manual steps written in an Excel sheet that a human would perform to test the software. Selenium, an open source application developed by ThoughtWorks, and other similar tools can now automatically run these graphical tests by driving the UI or a web browser, at machine speed without any human involvement.

These advances allowed further automation of infrastructure provisioning and configuration, functional testing and test data management, and other critical steps in the software "last mile" to production. Again, at ThoughtWorks, we began building a tool to expand the CI concept to include these end-to-end testing and deployment stages. Initially released in 2007 and named Cruise (highlighted in the earlier Focus section), the tool later became GoCD. CD, of course, being the abbreviation of CD, the concept that highlights the end-to-end cycle of delivering software into production as opposed to just integration in the development phase. In 2010, Jez Humble and David Farley of ThoughtWorks published *Continuous Delivery* to detail the methods and techniques (it was around that time that Jez Humble was on the GoCD team).

Since then, the CD approach, shown in Figure 13-1, has been widely adopted by technology communities around the world. It became the foundation for software teams to deliver value to customers early, more frequently, with high quality and reliability. The 2018 State of DevOps report found that "Elite" performers (those with exceptional CD and DevOps maturity) are able to deploy on-demand multiple times per day and have a lead time for changes from development to production of less than an hour.

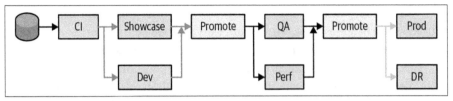

Figure 13-1. A CD pipeline from development to production

DevOps Further Extends the Cross-Functional Team Concept

Starting in 2009, around the same time when CD became the standard practice for Agile teams, another idea, called DevOps, started to catch up in the software development community.

In most technology organizations, building the software and running it are viewed as two entirely different types of activities with different skill sets required. As a result, there is generally a different team operating the software system after it goes into production. This team will be managing and maintaining the production environment, configuration of the software, monitoring performance, and escalating any production issues or user complaints.

The success of Agile methodology and CD is pushing more organizations to want to release software faster and more frequently. This puts more constraints on the release management, production environment management and the monitoring and escalation processes. Although separating the building and running of the software provides the benefit of scalability and efficiency like most separation of labor does, accelerating changes and shorter release cycles are creating more communication issues and knowledge management inefficiency. The community often found developers and system administrators at odds, even pointing fingers at each other when things went wrong in production.

Few strategic software systems can stay static for long. Most of them now need to be frequently updated and forever evolved to cater for the fast-changing market and customer expectations. There is no longer a stable or so-called run stage after the initial few releases. The software system was becoming a platform that new features and functionalities continue to get built and released to business users and consumers. The development and operation teams are forced to work side by side in close collaboration.

With the rise of cloud infrastructure—especially AWS, which was at the forefront of the cloud revolution—it became possible to manage infrastructure automatically at machine speed. Even traditional IT organizations came under pressure to move faster, to do what more nimble startups were able to do.

Because we had the ability to push software into production continuously with less effort and less risk, why couldn't we consolidate the effort of developing and operating the software into the same team—the true end-to-end ownership?

The idea was initially practiced at Flickr, where John Allspaw and Paul Hammond decided to hire "ops who think like devs" and "devs who think like ops" to resolve this issue. The two articulated this concept at an O'Reilly conference in 2009. Around the same time, an engineer named Patrick Debois from Belgium decided to organize a small conference concerning "Agile system administration," a similar idea, and coined the term "DevOps" to represent it. DevOps quickly becomes the name for this movement to combine the development and operation effort.

Like CD, this approach is based on the same Agile principles to deliver incremental changes frequently into production, provide value to end users, and gather feedback as early as possible. DevOps' emphasis is that the system administration and operation of the software should not be a separate effort; it should be included in the same team that build the software.

This expands the cross-functional team concept even further to include system administrators. The production system administration skill set and responsibility allows the team to have more visibility into the end-to-end software life cycle, collecting and analyzing real-time user feedback more efficiently and closing the build-test-learn cycle within the same team.

The advantage of this new way of working quickly caught the community's attention and has been widely adopted since then. New companies were established to build tools supporting the DevOps movement, notably Splunk and Puppet. These two companies also publish the aforementioned annual "State of DevOps Report" (check out the 2018 edition (*https://oreil.ly/Yj4bW*)) that is widely used and referenced to improve the practices.

DEVOPS IS A CULTURE CHANGE, NOT A NEW JOB TITLE

Similar to Agile and CD, DevOps is a culture that emphasizes the collaboration and communication of both software developers and other IT professionals. However, maybe since the very first well-known attempt to hire "ops who think like devs" and "devs who think like ops," there was a strong tendency to create a DevOps role in a team, and it even became a new job title: "DevOps engineers."

We have mixed feelings about this new job title. On one hand, we are glad that it's an indicator the movement is catching on and more people are intentionally broadening their skills. On the other hand, we are worried that a separate role in a team dedicated to DevOps is missing the broader culture change this movement is supposed to bring and possibly creating yet another silo.

Making developers think like Ops is a more important change than adding one developer dedicated to operation in a cross-functional team. If there is indeed such a job title as DevOps engineer, this person's role in a team should be more about helping the rest of the team think like Ops than just owning the system administration responsibility.

Even if a small delivery team with a DevOps engineer should be able to own the end-to-end development and operation responsibility for a software product, the team still doesn't really own everything related to system operation. The system monitoring tools provide fast feedback cycles allowing the team to identify issues early. Resolving these issues in code requires a better understanding of the operational aspects of production systems. Ward Cunningham, the inventor of wiki, once told us that the best way to make a developer better at writing high-quality software was to spend a year doing system support and maintenance. System administration is an important perspective that any software team needs to have to build high-quality products.

Many organizations are building a DevOps culture at the same time as building an internal platform. In many cases, "DevOps" is used to refer to the team building such a platform or to part of the platform team responsible for evangelizing the platform and promoting adoption within the organization. While we support the trend toward platform building, it's important to make sure delivery teams don't abdicate responsibility to a DevOps or platform team. DevOps culture is all about developers thinking a bit more like ops, and ops being more empathetic to the needs of developers. We believe that all teams need to have a proper appreciation of the platform and infrastructure on which their software is deployed; DevOps culture does not negate the need for this understanding.

Four Key Metrics for Success

In their seminal book *Accelerate* (O'Reilly), Nicole Forsgren et al. show that there is a direct link between organizational performance and software delivery performance. Their research showed that just four key metrics differentiate between low, medium, high, and elite performers:

Lead time

The time taken for code changes to make it from development through to production

Deployment frequency
How often an organization deploys code

Mean time to restore (MTTR)
How long it takes to recover from a failure

Change failure rate (CFR)
How often changes going into production cause a failure

An organization that improves on these metrics will be more successful at getting working software into production. It's a surprising result that just these four numbers can be used to predict IT performance in an organization.

Another important point about the research in Accelerate is that these metrics are valid regardless of technology stack. Legacy systems are traditionally difficult to manage and difficult to change, with organizations reluctant to pursue faster approaches and maintenance teams often making excuses for why they can't move faster. But the research shows that even teams working with legacy technology can improve their performance as measured by these metrics.

We have always contended that CD and a positive DevOps culture are a direct way to improve your IT performance. Accelerate backs up this experience with hard data and peer-reviewed research.

Summary

We have come a long way from simply realizing when someone forgot to add a file to source control, to systems that are capable of continuous, rapid, reliable deployment into production. We've also come a long way from the "throw it over the wall" mentality to a true partnership between developers and system operators. In return, we have achieved the ability to deliver software products into production sooner and with higher quality and to respond to changes from the market faster and more reliably.

The key concept is to break software development from a multistage, long planning cycle to an iterative and incremental approach. This leads to the principle to bring painful or risky steps in the software delivery cycle forward and do them more frequently, whether the pain is integration, end-to-end testing, or deployment.

To lower the cost of doing-it-early-and-frequently, the community has been developing more and more tools to automate repetitive manual tasks throughout the development cycle. The amount of automation has crossed the threshold to make CD economically viable in most development environments. There is really no reason to not engage this approach in most industries and organizations.

DevOps pushes the cross-functional team boundary further "downstream" from product development to product and system maintenance. It represents another common philosophy shared by the Agile, CD, and DevOps community.

Successful adoption of Agile principles creates a new "superpower" for IT— it can deliver faster and with higher quality to keep its business partners happy. But what about the business? How should an organization wield its newfound abilities? At the end of the day, delivering the wrong thing into production faster doesn't really help us create more business value. We need to make sure we deliver the *right* things into production faster. A focus on customer value, thin slices, and measures will help ensure that now that IT can move faster, it actually generates a meaningful business benefit.

Key Points

Following are the key points that we hope you take away from this chapter as well as two actions for you to take to begin implementing what we've discussed:

- Releasing products early and frequently to shorten the feedback loop relies on adopting the best practices in Agile software delivery, especially the CD practices.

- Besides the actual practices, learn from the two important principles in the CD approach: if it's painful, do it earlier and do it frequently, and automate the repetitive tasks as much as possible.

- DevOps calls for expanding the cross-functional team further to combine software development and system operation. It's also a rallying call to develop more polyskilled generalists in development teams.

Here are two actions to take:

- Start measuring the "four key metrics": Measure lead time, deployment frequency, mean time to restore, and change failure. Rate your IT teams and see whether you observe a correlation between the metrics and good delivery performance.

- Begin using CD's principles: Use the principles as a litmus test for your IT organization—can the business deploy changes at will to production with high reliability and no bottlenecks?

14

Digital Platforms

Digital transformation is often associated with a goal to become a digitally enabled platform business. The concept of platform business has captured the interests of many business executives across different industries. Some of the most successful companies in the Digital Age are platform businesses (or API business): Apple's iTunes, Alibaba, Amazon's Marketplace, Salesforce, Uber, and Airbnb, just to name a few. A platform business is a nonlinear business model connecting ecosystem participants.

The platform could be a marketplace that connects the supplier and consumers to each other like Amazon, Uber, and Airbnb. Or, it could be a community that allows users to interact with one another socially like Facebook, Twitter, and Google so that advertisers can benefit from reaching a large audience. The platforms create value through the network effect wherein benefits to all sides increase exponentially as the number of participants increases. It can also provide a foundation for other participants in the ecosystem to go faster; for example; Salesforce and Amazon providing client relationship management and fulfillment capability for small- and medium-sized businesses to quickly get up to speed and focus on their core value creation.

Connecting ecosystem participants is not a new concept. Marketplaces have existed throughout human history, from ancient bazaars to modern shopping malls, where merchants and shoppers meet and trade. Newspapers have also existed for a few hundred years, from which advertisers get the benefits of a large, captured audience.

What's common about these modern platform businesses is the digital and online infrastructure enabled by the development of information technology. Built on top of perhaps the biggest platform of all, the internet, digital technology makes connecting people a lot easier and cheaper. The increasing amount of data captured by the platform allows more value creation opportunities to all parties through new analytical tools, generating more and more insights.

There are a lot of recent studies analyzing the platform business model and recommending the thinking process, a framework and tools to build your own platform model. *Platform Revolution: How Networked Markets Are Transforming the Economy—and How to Make Them Work for You* (W.W. Norton & Company) by Geoffrey G. Parker et al. is one of the good books to gain more insights on how it works.

The digital platform we are going to discuss here is not the platform business itself. Rather, it's the digital technology platform that serves as a prelude to the business model revolution.

Although necessary, the use of a digital technology platform doesn't need to always lead to a platform business. In fact, we don't think the majority of large enterprises in various industries need to become the so-called platform business to differentiate themselves. A platform business accelerates growth, but these businesses are still going to be a small part of the overall economic landscape.

Regardless of whether you are going to expand your ecosystem to become a platform business in the long run, a digital technology platform is always going to be a crucial step to take now for any modern business to be able to deliver new value to customers faster, with higher quality and at a lower cost.

We believe there are three important pillars supporting a digital platform:

- Modular, API-enabled architecture
- Self-service data
- Delivery infrastructure

We cover each of these in this chapter, beginning by examining the importance of a modular, API-enabled architecture and how it's different from the traditional monolithic architecture.

Modular, API-Enabled Architecture Instead of Monolithic Architecture

In the United States, ecommerce represented 13% of total retail sales in 2017, increased from 11.6% in 2016. It also represented roughly 49.4% of all retail sales growth in 2017 (versus 41.6% in 2016). That said, this remarkable growth of online shopping does not mean that physical stores and malls will soon be closed to leave ecommerce the only way for people to shop. Physical retail continues to grow, albeit at a far slower rate than online shopping. Customers still want the ability to touch and feel the product and sometimes enjoy the pleasure of window shopping.

Nevertheless, the digital convenience and experience is driving a different kind of consumer behavior in the physical world. Even in the physical store, consumers often want to check on their phone for additional information about the product and to do online pricing comparisons. Some even want to make the payment on the phone instead of having to check out at a kiosk. When shopping online, some people would prefer to reserve the product in a store nearby so that they can pick it up themselves and receive it sooner, or simply to save the shipping fee. This is the so-called *omnichannel* retail experience.

Given the monolithic nature of many retail enterprise software systems, the simple feature to reserve online and pick up in store might not be that easy to achieve. The ecommerce system is often built as a standalone system with its own catalog, customer management, and inventory management logic embedded. The store also has its own catalog, customer management, and inventory management logic, all entangled in its own software systems. First, we need to build a new capability, "Find in Store," that connects the ecommerce system to the in-store systems to confirm the availability of the product.

When the store's inventory management system was built, it was one monolithic system with all the business logic embedded in the software. It was not separated into various independent building blocks designed to be accessed or even controlled by other systems. There is no need to blame the software product team; who would have thought that the world was so quickly going to move to such a new place that consumers now suddenly want this new feature?

But that's the world we are living in today. New value streams are being created constantly to deliver products through new channels, or new value-add digital services to consumers. The concept of a digital platform is to build an internal marketplace to connect providers and consumers of digital capability not so differently from an external marketplace connecting buyers and sellers. The platform is an ecosystem in which technology and business capabilities are not just built to meet the immediate needs, they are also exposed as potential building blocks for new products and services with a different value stream.

IS THIS SIMPLY SOFTWARE REUSE?

Building digital capabilities as services is certainly related to the concept of software reusability, but it's also more than that. Reusability itself is perhaps the "holy grail" of software engineering. Started in the early days of computing, programmers have been searching for various ways to reuse software code.

Subroutines and functions are the simplest ways of reuse. These consist of a series of program instructions performing a very specific task, packed into a unit that can be invoked again and again in a software application. Take "array" as an example. In any programming language, there is likely a function or a structure that deals with a series of elements (numbers or characters). It manages the list, adds or removes items, counts or searches them. This little reusable function is probably invoked millions of times every day on your laptop, phone, or your smart watch. Software is essentially built on top of layers and layers of reusable components (functions and subroutines). Many of these reusable components are packaged into the so-called "libraries" that are available for any software programmer to reuse.

This kind of code reusability generally stops at the programming language boundary. You need to take the code you've written as well as all the libraries referenced and compile them to form a "deployable" package that can be installed on a computer to start running. Then, there are common infrastructure-level software applications installed and run on the same computer, often called *processes*, that most software products will rely on to perform properly.

Software developers put a lot of effort into writing code to build their products. But compared with the number of reusable components they depend on, these efforts are only the tip of the iceberg. Reusability not only reduces the effort required to build new products, it also reduces potential duplication that can cause defects and inconsistency in the future if one dependency is upgraded but others missed.

When a team designs and develops a software product, they often consider the reusability of their own code in future scenarios, too. This is built into the culture of most software development communities. But code reuse outside of a single project or use-case tends to be difficult. This is especially the case in the enterprise context. Here, an enterprise will often try to create reusable software packages that implement a "known good" business function or process, that can be used across different companies or even industries. That's different from reusing technology solutions in the same organization to create new value or solve slightly different problems. Here are some reasons as to why this kind of reusability is difficult:

- Programming languages and tools continue to evolve. Computing as a discipline is still in its early age compared with other scientific or engineering disciplines. The most popular programming languages around 1996 were C++, Java, PHP, and Python. Fast forward to 2016, when besides those four languages, the most commonly used languages included C#, Scala, F#, Clojure, Go, Swift, and Kotlin. On average, one new programming language was widely adopted every two or three years. Even though one language can be used to build solutions for almost all problems, we are continuing to discover new languages that can solve a particular set of problems more efficiently and effectively than others. Over time, business functionality built in one language might not be able to be reused when a team found a language to build solutions for the set of problems in that business area.

- Reusability is not free; it takes effort to continue to maintain and evolve the reusable components. When a new reusable situation occurs, the "source" might need to be updated and changed accordingly to fit the new purpose. At the same time, all the other places that depend on this code need to be recompiled, tested, and verified. This often conflicts with the way enterprises are organized and funding is allocated. Often, the easiest way is to copy the code and change it locally, as opposed to doing it properly in all places. This again could result in duplication and fragmentation. It's not uncommon to see three or four different customer login pages across different business units in a large enterprise grown organically over time.

- Merger and acquisition. For a large organization, this could be the single biggest disruption to an otherwise well-designed and integrated enterprise architecture. Migrating and merging data and functionalities across two different business not only involves a tremendous amount of effort, it also stretches system and integration design to cope with too many edge cases. Very often, leaving some systems duplicated and running in parallel is even a lesser evil compared with the cost and disruption of a full migration.

MICROSERVICES

There have been many attempts to create modular and API-driven architecture in the short history of information technology, most notably service-oriented architecture (SOA). Around the early 2000s, the concept of SOA became very promising and popular at the time. Due to the fragmentation of enterprise application integration (EAI) software vendors and the lack of community support, the API-enabled architecture vision was never successfully implemented. Fast forward to 2014, the rise of *microservices* was perhaps the first real massive adoption of modular and API-enabled architecture across the entire industry (Figure 14-1).

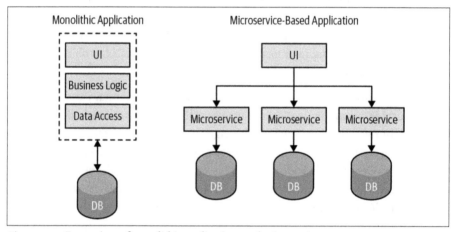

Figure 14-1. Comparison of monolithic applications and microservices

Written in a widely referenced article in 2014, here is how our colleagues Martin Fowler and James Lewis described microservices:

> In short, the microservice architectural style is an approach to developing a single application as a suite of small services, each running in its own process and communicating with lightweight mechanisms, often an HTTP resource API. These services are built around business capabilities and independently deployable by fully automated deployment machinery. There is a bare minimum of centralized management of these services, which may be written in different programming languages and use different data storage technologies.

Since 2014, we have seen the adoption of microservices skyrocketing in the enterprise computing world. At first, we were a little skeptical. Was the community ready for another round of SOA, just with a new skin? What was going to be different this time? After working and gaining experience on this new architecture style in various enterprise contexts, we noticed a few promising characteristics:

It was community led, not vendor led

The open source movement has been slowly but steadily reshaping the software development tools landscape. With Google, Microsoft, Amazon and other major technology companies offering more and more development tools as open source software, large organizations are more comfortable moving away from large, expensive, and heavyweight packaged software development tools to lightweight, fit-for-purpose, and free open source tools. The tools market itself was becoming a less lucrative market for the traditional vendors, who had been losing their clout over the tools selection decisions. This indirectly helped the adoption of microservices.

Most of the well-adopted tools to support the deployment, management, scheduling, and monitoring of these independently deployable small services are available as open source. Some of them offer basic functionality as open source software and higher-value-add features as paid components or services. The communication and coordination are also based on simple lightweight open standards like REST. Although the field is becoming more mature with more frameworks and tools supporting it, the microservices concept has largely remained an architecture style as opposed to one software product from any specific vendor. It did not inherit the EAI middleware baggage SOA once experienced.

Organized around business capabilities

Microservices is intended to map to the more fine-grained business capabilities as opposed to an end-to-end value chain that traditionally sits in one department or a line of business. Hence the notion of "micro."

In the "reserve online and pick it up offline" example mentioned earlier, the end-to-end value chain would require access to business capabilities like "store management" and "inventory management" that traditionally belongs to the offline value chain. Building microservices around those business capabilities will make it easier to build new services like "find in store" and "reserve in store." These new services are new business capabilities extending off the previous offline capabilities that can now be available to online channels. The microservices movement is helping enterprises to reshape the structure of existing monolithic software products, allowing them to be modularized around finer-grained business capabilities as well as building new software products with a similar mindset.

You build it, you run it

One of the key motivations of centralized standards and top-down management of all software development efforts was the division of labor, which unfortunately also introduced a handover process, and increased coordination overhead. The Agile methodology, CD, and DevOps movements have created the ability for smaller cross-functional teams to own end-to-end responsibility for building and running a technology solution. By taking away the standardization constraints, a small cross-functional team building services can now choose the best technology and tools to build the business capabilities they are responsible for. Due to the fast-evolving nature of the technology world, it shouldn't be a surprise that there are often very different technologies, programming languages, and tools best suited for different business problems. By mapping services and teams to business capabilities, the two critical central functions of the previous generation of EAI tools are less relevant—defining the granularity of services, and managing the search and discovery process. How a company defines and finds business capabilities is the answer to how a technology team defines and finds technology services and solutions.

An iterative approach

Unlike the top-down, hierarchical approach, microservices architecture is bottom up and evolutionary. You don't need to design all the microservices at the most granular level across the entire organization before start building the first service. Instead, you can, and probably should always start with one independently deployable and upgradeable service to achieve a business capability.

Again, take the "reserve in store" service as an example. The team might not recognize that "find in store" is a business capability that could be modularized and reused in another situation beyond the "buy online and pick up in store" scenario. They might decide to build the "find in store" functionality embedded in the "reserve in store" service. A new team engaged in another customer outcome might discover that they need the "find in store" functionality, too. The two teams could work together to recognize "find in store" as a first-class business capability; hence, a separate service. In a well-designed, high-quality code base, it shouldn't be too much effort to split this logical component into a separate service. The two teams could work together to achieve this with a lower overall cost than one team having to repeat the effort to build the same functionality embedded in another service. They can also then decide the ownership of the "find in store" service to be with the first team or the second team. The technology architect's community or the central architect group should play an important role to facilitate these communications and collaborations to let the precise service granularity and architecture design emerge out of necessity.

As these services continue to develop and are shared across the organization, some of them could be curated into APIs that can be used by external parties outside the organization. A retailer could tap into other channels and digital ecosystems to allow a broader range of customers to shop through other portals and find in their store or inventory by using the APIs. These external-facing APIs will allow the business to innovate with new business models that could lead to a platform business model or API business model, as we described at the beginning of this chapter.

Of course, the microservice movement is still in its early stage. We have seen great success with microservices when done well in companies like Amazon and Netflix. They have been applying these principles and pushing the boundaries on system design and architecture for quite a few years. Traditional large organizations are facing more challenges with legacy systems and skill set gaps when trying to adopt this new architecture style (later in this chapter, we further discuss our learnings on the modernization approach for legacy systems).

Nevertheless, the guiding principles behind microservices architecture are highly aligned to what we have been advocating for throughout the book. It will not be the end of the road for modular and API-enabled architecture. There will surely be new development of the microservices architectural style itself, new tools to support it, and maybe even new architecture patterns beyond microservices. What's important is the concept of modular and API-enabled architecture, the first critical pillar supporting the platform thinking. Next, we discuss the second pillar: self-service data.

Self-Service Data

In Chapter 9, we talked about the need to "let data decide" rather than relying on the HIPPO. Although most people would agree with this approach, in practice it can be quite difficult to actually put the relevant data together in order to really let the data speak for itself.

Organizations typically have data scattered among disparate silos, often caused by a legacy of heavyweight systems that performed useful tasks but also hoarded data and didn't play nice with others. Key assets like customer information, purchase history and inventory information are often spread throughout the organization. This makes it very difficult to get a single view of these assets, which is needed to create new offerings and drive cross-sales and upsales to existing customers.

In the age of apps, wearables, and push-notifications, customers expect real-time experiences driven by their latest interactions with an organization, not dragged down by slow batch data integrations. For advanced machine learning to be useful, it typically requires near-real-time access to integrated data sources.

When we talk about "self-service" data, we don't mean handing a bunch of users a big database and a copy of Tableau so that they can build their own queries (although that might be a valid part of an overall data strategy). We're really talking about self-service for disparate teams across the organization. Typically, accessing data involves a huge amount of bureaucracy, red tape, and friction. In some cases, this is appropriate, especially for consumer data that must be controlled and protected, but in many cases teams within an organization find it difficult to access and understand data that would be useful for them to build customer value. The data is locked up in another system or controlled by another team. "Self-service" in this context means that teams across an organization can access appropriate data easily and with low friction.

The specific techniques to enable self-service can vary. Addressing this need is a key part of a good enterprise-wide data strategy. Here are two common approaches:

- Building a data lake as a centralized storage of "raw" data for all systems, with lakeside "data marts" that bring together business-meaningful collections of data and allow consumers to understand and access that data in a coherent way.

- Using event-stream technology to wire up a constant stream of small updates between systems. Teams can choose to tap in to the event streams, listening to updates that are relevant to their needs and ignoring updates that are not.

Most organizations will create an explicit data strategy that includes elements of a "data platform." Whether you are using a data lake, event streams, or a combination of technologies, the self-service aspect is critical in allowing teams to be effective. Uber's Michelangelo (*https://eng.uber.com/michelangelo*) is an example of a self-service data platform that gives the organization considerable competitive advantage. Data science is a core foundation of Uber's business, with dozens of teams building, training, and deploying machine learning models against petabytes of data. Michelangelo allows Uber's teams to find the datasets they need, use entire datacenters of compute power to analyze data, train machine learning models, and deploy into production serving predictions for some of the highest-loaded online services at the company.

Delivery Infrastructure

With business capabilities available as services and enterprise data accessible in real time, the enterprise computing environment is becoming a platform ready to be applied to develop new products and services at lighting speed with one last technology roadblock to remove: the infrastructure bottleneck. It's yet another silo in most large enterprises and a barrier in the development team's path to run experiments faster and shorten the feedback cycles.

We all know the importance of customer experience in this Digital Age and most organizations are focusing on building a differentiating user experience as part of their core strategy. But we often deprioritized how our employees feel, especially the developers who must deal with software development kits (SDKs), frameworks, tools, and development environments all day long. Why? Because the customer has a choice (to use your product or others), and developers don't, because they work for the company, and the company can tell the developers what tools to use. Even though the consumer's emotions and attitudes about using a particular product is highly critical for an enterprise, the developers' experience of working with technology is always a lower priority.

Developers do complain about a poor experience when they feel it, but it doesn't always get a broad audience within the company. It attracted an audience in one case, though, and it led to one of the most important business models in the digital industry today: cloud computing. Around early 2000, Amazon hired a lot of developers to meet the growing need for new products and platforms. However, despite throwing a lot of people at the problems, the project delivery was not any faster. It took many months for any projects, no matter how small, to complete and go to production. Andy Jassy was the chief of staff for Jeff Bezos (CEO of Amazon). When Jassy focused on this problem, he heard a recurring complaint from the developer community: it took too long to build a working development and production environment from scratch every time a new project was kicked off. Teams had to install a development environment for the language they chose to use, set up a database, set up a source code management system, create a build environment that assembles the application, request a staging environment to test their applications, and so on and so forth. It often took weeks, even months, to have all this set up and running before a single line of application code could be written. By the way, we are still seeing this symptom in some traditional enterprise environments today—in 2019!

Jassy and the internal team decided to tackle this problem head on and build a set of common infrastructure services that every project team could easily access upon request. It's a long way from here to the Infrastructure-as-a-Service (IaaS) concept, to the launch of the external facing AWS, to the adoption of cloud computing across the IT industry. Many people stare in awe at the wild success of AWS today but miss the humble original intention of removing friction experienced by developers.

Even when companies are adopting cloud computing at scale today in the mainstream, many mainly focus on the cost benefit, that it's cheaper to run your applications in the cloud than owning your own infrastructure. Companies often overlook the other more significant impact it brings to developers: the flexibility and freedom that comes with a cloud-based self-servicing platform.

REMOVING FRICTION

The third pillar of platform thinking is focused on improving delivery infrastructure to remove the friction technology teams experience when trying to develop products in fast, iterative cycles. Fast, self-service access to computing environments is just one of many areas to improve on:

Elastic scaling of compute resources
Take advantage of virtualization and the cloud platform to reduce provisioning time of computing resources like servers and storage from hours

or even days down to minutes. Provide the ability to scale computing capacity on demand.

Provisioning and setting up environments
Automate the installation of operating systems, databases, and other common programming platforms like Java to quickly and reliably set up development environments.

CD tools
Automated and standardized provisioning of CD tools. As discussed in the previous chapter, these tools are becoming table stakes for Agile teams to continuously and incrementally build and release software

Deployment runtime provisioning
Easily and efficiently launch runtime environments. For microservices, this could mean launching containers like Docker and using tools like Kubernetes to automate deployment, scaling, and management of services.

Monitoring
Provide easy-to-use and efficient monitoring tools for infrastructure, applications, data, and security at a fine-grained level that can be used by small teams to monitor the health of their own services with the end-to-end responsibility.

It's a nontrivial effort to build such a delivery infrastructure across a large organization similar to Amazon, Netflix, and Google. The good news is that, given the benefit of efficiency gains for developer time and productivity increases, a lot more open source tools are being developed and becoming mature for wide adoption. However, it also means that this is a fast-changing field; new techniques and tools continue to emerge as we speak. A state-of-the-art delivery infrastructure could soon be outdated in two- or three-years' time.

Given the fast-changing nature of this area, building modern delivery infrastructure is never a one-time effort. It also means that it needs to be taken more seriously than just cloud computing subscription and some additional scripts. We advocate for the mindset of taking Delivery Infrastructure-as-a-Product (DIaaP) with developers as consumers. Chapter 15 introduces the "product thinking" approach in more detail, and explains how you can consider even internal infrastructure to be a product with customers.

Successful delivery of such a product requires real product ownership over the road map and development of the backlog. It doesn't need to be done overnight, or with a Big-Bang approach. It could easily begin with a single-delivery infrastructure product team with responsibility for the life of these capabilities, but focusing on solving one particular problem for the customers: the developers in the organization. Over time, the breadth of the capabilities of the product will favor creating additional teams; each focused on delivering a specific capability within the larger (DIaaP). This would allow these dedicated capability teams to develop the enterprise-wide knowledge around their product to deliver value at scale to the larger organization.

Digital platforms and modern infrastructure allow an organization to move faster, but much of the creation of customer value will need to use existing technology assets and systems. Typically, these assets are older, difficult to change, and are frustrating for an organization to deal with. The next section discusses how to effectively modernize while also delivering value.

Legacy System Modernization

Any organization, no matter the size, bears a legacy burden; some developers even joke that something is "legacy" as soon as it has been released into production. Although this legacy has enabled businesses to compete up until today, it won't help in the future: legacy estate reduces profits, eats up operational budget and stifles your ability to innovate fast—your innovation cycle time is measured in months, if not years. What's more, it impedes your ability to build in-house expertise: in the competition for tech talent, nobody wants to work for a digital dinosaur.

Application modernization is fundamental to your ability to transform, your ability to deploy innovations in customer engagement or supply chain management, and to deliver automated and flexible operations. But getting it right isn't easy. Mature organizations must consider a large "estate" of interconnected systems, featuring a wide array from old to new, from custom code to shrink-wrapped packages, created in-house or outsourced or acquired from a vendor.

From an IT perspective, legacy burden exerts itself across five horizontal forces:

Data

Siloed infrastructure hinders your efforts to view data holistically. Legacy systems will prevent you from becoming a data-driven business and stymie your attempts to get closer to your customers.

Architecture and infrastructure

The world today demands constant availability, turnkey scalability, and quick responsiveness to customer needs. But legacy systems are often the antithesis of these characteristics, compromising customer experience. Legacy systems are often afflicted by escalating costs and long lead times—even for menial tasks—causing business frustration.

Legacy processes and governance

The organization of tomorrow understands that rapid feedback cycles and the breaking down of silos are critical to deliver a holistic customer experience at speed. Legacy organizational structures and procedures often work on slow annual cycles and are reactive instead of proactive, forcing a business to guess where the market will be months or even years ahead.

Cloud

It's been clear for a long time that cloud—whether public, private, or hybrid—is the best modern hosting platform. Legacy applications are rarely cloud-ready, and a simplistic "lift and shift" approach can create headaches because the cloud typically trades high reliability of individual servers for high reliability of the platform as a whole. To work, legacy applications must be updated using "12-Factor" techniques that account for this trade-off.

Security

Every week we read a news story about a breach or data loss, and consumers are ever-more attuned to the security stance of companies they buy from. Although legacy systems are not inherently less secure, applications that are difficult or costly to administer can fall behind in security fixes and patches and presents a large attack surface to the outside world.

Technology, people, and business aren't separate. Improving a legacy technology situation forces you to reexamine business processes and organizational structures as well as technical systems. In fact, trying to solve technical problems on their own is one of the main stumbling blocks for organizations that seek to modernize.

While making the journey toward modernization, remember these critical principles:

- Break down silos and barriers and align your organizational structure toward common goals. Every handoff is a potential for miscommunication, slowdown, and frustration, and every misalignment is an opportunity for someone at your organization to "win," whereas another "loses." Ensure that your organizational structure sets everyone up to win together, which is a win for you all as a whole.

- Shorten feedback cycles, whether they are technical, organizational, or business. Developers love to use automated tests to see whether their code works and they are making progress—the amount of time from deciding to change something to getting feedback on whether the change was a success is called *cycle time*. Apply this thinking to your business strategy as well as IT—how soon can we see whether our strategy is a success? How can IT systems help us to reduce our cycle times?

- Empower local decision making by those with the closest connection to customer need. Whether a customer is an internal team using an API or platform or a consumer choosing your company's products, people who work closest with the customers are best placed to understand and fulfill their needs. Push decision making "down" to those closest to the customer.

SEVEN STEPS TO MODERNIZATION

Even though every modernization scenario is different, it's important to focus your efforts on systems that are most critical to supporting delivery of customer value. If a legacy system is impeding efforts to create thin slices of value or stopping you from organizing your teams around the appropriate measures and giving them real autonomy to create outcomes, that system is a high priority for modernization.

Broadly speaking, we think a modernization effort should follow these seven steps:

1. Approach modernization as a road map exercise, not as a plan to be cast into stone. As you make progress on the modernization journey, new priorities will emerge. The business landscape will change, competitive threats and opportunities will emerge, and technology will change, too.

When the next Docker arrives or machine learning explosion occurs, your plans will need to shift to accommodate the new advance.

2. Own the seams between systems and components. Any enterprise estate will contain a variety of technologies, in-house custom-developed systems, vendor-maintained systems, and packages. Your enterprise integration strategy must be firm and opinionated as to how these components should communicate with one another, share data, and collaborate.

3. Prioritize action by evaluating each of your systems based on the following characteristics:

   a. Actual pace of change of the system as well as desired pace of change

   b. Cost of change as well as time taken.

   c. Business impact/importance/revenue opportunity loss of not transforming.

   d. Risks of not transforming versus the risks of transforming, along the dimensions of severity of effect on products and processes, occurrence, detection during design and delivery, and operational risks.

      Systems that you want to change quickly but cannot and that have high business importance are a good candidate for immediate action. Systems that take a long time to change but actually aren't touched that much are probably lower priority. Remember, choosing what *not* to upgrade or replace is as important as choosing where to make big investments in changes.

4. Consider downstream impacts and knock-on effects for changes. In recent years, an explosion of "digital" technology has improved customer connectivity and increased touch points. But these enhanced frontends often put significant stress on downstream systems that can fail under the load. What used to be a simple linear flow has become disrupted by new use cases—for example "buy online, pick up in store"—and has now become a complex graph with many potential entry and exit points. Your modernization plan must account for likely interactions *between* systems, not just consider components in isolation.

5. Apply a legacy modernization pattern for each system. Although there are a large number of techniques at your disposal, modernization patterns fall into three buckets:

   a. *Replacement,* either by custom code, a new package, or SaaS. We recommend incremental replacement using strategies such as dividing the system by business process or functional area, or using the *Strangler* pattern to overlay and kill an old system, but nonincremental, Big-Bang migrations can work in some cases.

   b. *Augmentation,* by adding a new system alongside an old one and mediating requests between the two, adding a service interface that all new integrations should use.

   c. *Continuation,* where we keep an older system running but make some improvements to make it a bit more modern; for example, adding better testing, build automation, or APIs. Remediation is not a dirty word; some systems are going to live a long time. Create a baseline of "acceptable" characteristics for a system (automation, deployability, etc.) and improve systems that fail to meet that bar.

   An important idea to consider is *evolutionary architecture*—described in more detail in the next section—which allows us to incrementally improve a system over time. With this approach, we define architectural fitness functions that encapsulate what "good" looks like for the system and then make incremental changes improving the architecture and its adherence to the fitness functions.

6. Include existing staff in the success of new systems. Any modernization journey will cause major changes for your current people. Many IT staff are fearful of efforts to update legacy systems—after all, a large part of their job is to take care of that older piece of technology, and they might be concerned that their skills won't map to newer systems. Legacy IT staff will continually create political obstacles to the success of a new system and in some cases will outright sabotage your efforts. To get around this, it's important to include existing staff, making them at least partially responsible for the success of the new system and to engage their exper-

tise in creating a replacement. After all, that staff has years of knowledge about how your business works: use that to your advantage!

7. Reevaluate your plan periodically, taking into account changes in the business and technology landscapes. But remember not to "over plan"—your plan should be a guide rather than a rigid structure. After all, you never know when the next big technology shift will occur and you will need to adapt to account for it.

Legacy Modernization at a Global Telecom

We worked with a telecom company that found itself in a highly competitive, saturated market. It needed to enhance its customer offerings for new handsets and services bundles. These bundles were the cornerstone of its new customer experiences and deployed on a brand-new digital platform.

But the new customer experience systems were planned to be updated much more frequently than legacy assets, creating a kind of "impedance mismatch" between old and new. We used technologies such as facades, gateways or adapters that acted as a shock absorber between systems advancing at different paces. The customer experience applications used a lightweight API wrapper to integrate with backend legacy fulfillment systems. This approach enabled our client to respond quickly to consumer demand and reduce call-center costs while allowing the business to operate as usual.

In a second phase, we protected and reinforced the API facades, applying an "industrialization" approach to both the facades and the underlying legacy systems. In this case, industrialization means ensuring that the systems are stable and scalable and a good foundation on which to build further. Because both old and new systems were going to coexist for some time (realistically at least several years), we established patterns to ensure that it was clear whether one system or another was the master for any particular data, whether data would be written to both systems, or whether some kind of synchronization mechanism would align the two. Whichever solution we picked, we made sure to use the new API facade to mediate access, so consuming systems would not need to be updated if our strategy or the underlying systems changed.

In a final third phase, we were able to take on the larger battle to consolidate and replatform costly legacy systems, without accruing technical or architectural debt within the new customer experience systems. As far as those new systems were concerned, they got their data via a well-defined API, and the teams managing legacy systems *underneath* that API were free to remediate, augment, or replace that legacy system without disturbing other parts of the systems estate.

In some organizations, a well-enforced barrier between a digital platform and legacy systems can be a good solution for several years. The digital platform can be used for ongoing experimentation, to support new user experiences and enable new channels while the enterprise continues to adapt to the changes.

For more details on this transition, visit ThoughtWorks (*https:// oreil.ly/Wmjbp*).

EVOLUTIONARY ARCHITECTURE

The state of the art in technology moves at a rapid pace, and so does the business context in which tech plays a supporting (or sometimes defining) role. It's virtually impossible to predict what disruptive new technologies will be available two years from now, just as it is difficult to predict how a company's business strategy might evolve or how the competitive or regulatory landscape will change in the future. It's therefore more important than ever to build systems that can accommodate *change* as a first-class requirement. One approach that has come to the forefront over the past few years is that of evolutionary architecture, which is detailed more completely in the book *Building Evolutionary Architectures: Support Constant Change* (O'Reilly) by Neal Ford et al.

Admitting that the future is unknowable is difficult for many software architects. Over the years, "architecture" has often come to mean "expensive stuff that's difficult to change later." Architects often spend many months analyzing requirements to create systems that will support some version of a likely future state, but end up guessing wrong or having external circumstances (such as a change in business strategy) invalidate their assumptions. Meanwhile, building systems with lots of flexibility comes at a price—each piece of speculative future extensibility costs money to implement, test, and maintain, and generally increases overall system complexity.

Architects already design systems with various "ilities" in mind. Availability, efficiency, reliability, interoperability, scalability, security, and usability are common "ilities" for modern systems. Evolutionary architecture adds a new characteristic to this list: evolvability.

Rather than guessing at how the technology and business landscapes will change, architects who create evolvable systems admit that they can't predict the future. They build systems to support today's requirements but use specific techniques to ensure that those systems will be easily adapted to support tomorrow's requirements. We begin our examination of evolutionary architecture with a definition and then break down its component parts:

An evolutionary architecture supports guided, incremental change across multiple dimensions.

Each part of this definition is important:

- *Guided change* means that architects can judge how close a given design is to achieving a set of design aims. Here we borrow a term from evolutionary computing: the fitness function. A fitness function is an objective integrity assessment of some architectural characteristic (here, "objective" means that if two people make the assessment, they will agree on the result—technologists arguing about subjective measures don't help us!).

- *Incremental change* means an evolutionary architecture can inform us as to whether a proposed change will make the system better or worse at achieving its goals, and the architecture allows us to make small steps toward improvement. Using fitness functions, we can be sure that our incremental changes have not made the overall system worse by some important measures.

- *Multiple dimensions* means that evolution is supported across more than one type of "ility" and that improving one dimension will not hurt another. For example, security is often at odds with performance—an evolutionary architecture approach will help ensure that while you improve security you are not making performance worse or, if you are, that you realize right away and can make an informed decision about the trade-off.

The foundation of an evolutionary architecture is the fitness function. Because these need to be objective measures, they require architects to be very specific about their design goals. Instead of an architect saying "the system should be scalable," a fitness function might specify "if we double the number of servers in our infrastructure, our overall throughput doubles." Instead of an architect saying "we should keep up with security patches for the libraries we use," a fitness function might specify "the system updates to new library versions within two weeks of their release." Fitness functions should be expressed as executable tests that can be run against the system itself, either at build time or at some point in the CD path to production. If recent changes have degraded our architecture—for example, if the throughput does not improve when we double the number of servers—we can fail the build immediately and get feedback to whoever made those changes. This rapid feedback loop is critical. Architectural "ilities" become concrete numbers and a pass/fail score for the overall system, as shown in Figure 14-2.

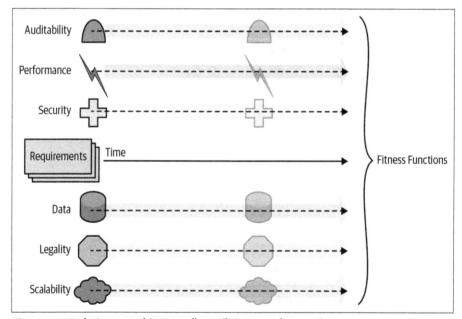

Figure 14-2. Evolutionary architecture allows "ilities" to evolve over time

With evolutionary architecture, we can codify the design goals for a system, ensure that we achieve those goals, and then make incremental improvements over time, safe in the knowledge that the overall system health and performance is where we want it to be.

Key Points

Following are the key points that we hope you take away from this chapter as well as two actions for you to take to begin implementing what we've discussed:

- Modern successful digital business runs on digital platforms featuring the following:

  — Modular, API-enabled architecture

  — Self-service data

  — Infrastructure modernization

- Mature organizations must consider a large "estate" of interconnected systems, featuring a wide array from old to new, from custom code to shrink-wrapped packages. They need to become part of the digital platform, too.

- To successfully modernize, apply this seven-point plan:

  — Approach modernization as a road map exercise.

  — Own the seams between systems and components.

  — Prioritize action by evaluating each of your systems.

  — Consider downstream impacts and knock-on effects for changes.

  — Apply a legacy modernization pattern for each system: replacement, augmentation or continuation.

  — Include existing staff in the success of new systems.

  — Reevaluate your plan periodically.

Here are two actions to take:

- Review your organization's platform strategy: Is there a clear difference between an infrastructure platform, an internal business platform, and a "platform business" that creates value through a connected ecosystem of participants? Is it clear how your underlying platform strategy supports the wider business strategy?

- Make it clear who the platform customer is: For each of the platforms (of all types) within your organization, is it clear who the customer is for that platform? What is the platform team doing to keep its customers happy? Does the customer have other options if they are unhappy with the service?

15

Products over Projects

In the IT industry today, there is a significant movement toward thinking about (and managing) software assets as though they were products. A typical product has customers who derive value from the product; long-lived teams that envision, create, evolve, and market the product; and a life cycle that includes retiring products when they cease to be market worthy. You might already have heard the advice to "think about products instead of projects." This chapter dives into greater detail on this concept, how you can apply it to alter the way you think about and fund software assets, and how all of this relates to a focus on customer value and delivering via thin slices.

Defining Product Thinking

Throughout this book we've used the word "product" with various different nuances. At the time of this writing (toward the end of the book production process) there are several hundred instances of "product" in our manuscript and many references to "product teams." Clearly, something about the word *product* is important to our story; this chapter goes into depth on what we mean when we say "product" and what we mean by *product thinking*.

Product thinking comes from the hyperactive Silicon Valley startup world in which everyone has a money-making idea. The process of taking an idea, shaping it into a business, and shooting for a billion-dollar valuation has been honed and refined over the past two decades. The Valley's success has been imitated around the world with countries setting up technology parks and competing to be the "Silicon Valley of <X>," where X is usually a country or geographic reference (but sometimes something more interesting such as "crypto" or "cannabis"). For a startup, the product they are building and selling—whether it's traditional goods or services or a social media company for which the product is actually users' eyeballs—is front and center of everything they do. There's an entire ecosystem around product management, market research, product-market fit, and so on. In the startup world, a focus on products is as natural as breathing.

A focus on products is natural for traditional companies, too, but only for those things that they sell to customers, and only in some parts of the organization. For the majority of an organization that is further away from things actually sold to consumers, such as supporting functions or departments that might only indirectly contribute to a customer's experience, products are hardly thought about at all. The product-thinking movement seeks to change this: what if everything that everyone throughout an organization created was treated as a product?

Let's look at some key characteristics of a product:

- Products solve a problem or satisfy a need. The best products solve a need that people didn't even know they had (remember the iPod? Who knew consumers needed a thousand songs in their pocket?)

- Products uniquely differentiate against other, competing products. The best products might solve the same need as other products, but distinguish themselves through feature set, speed, ease of use, or cost.

- Products are built with a clear customer (or set of customers) in mind. Feature set, build quality, and price are all tuned to appeal to a particular target customer. Often, a product team will do significant market research as well as create prototypes to ensure that a product will be desirable with the intended customer.

Product thinking applies these same principles much more widely and is not limited to organizations that sell products to consumers. Cloud infrastructure providers such as Amazon (AWS), Google (Google Cloud Platform), and Microsoft (Azure) consider their cloud services to be products, with developers and IT departments as their customer. Business-to-business (B2B) services are treated as products with the customer being another organization. Internal capabilities within an organization, such as an internal cloud platform or an internal API or business capability, are also treated as products.

The Difference Between Products and Projects

Product thinking contrasts heavily with the traditional IT notion of a "project." In the project world, after a project is complete, it's finished, and we can move onto the next piece of work. But a product can have a long lifespan, and many products are never truly finished. In modern IT, there is now a notion of "products, not projects," and it highlights the differences between the two on many dimensions:

Timescale

Projects are of limited duration with a defined completion date. Products live for as long as the product is valuable.

Team structure

Projects bring people together for the duration of the project, with the specific skills needed to complete the project. After they're complete, a project team is reassigned to other parts of the business. Products are built by product teams comprising the skills needed to design, build, support, and evolve the product. Typically, a product team will be stable; members stay together working on the product for the long term.

Funding

Projects usually are funded by estimating effort, adding a large contingency, and then managing to the overall budget. The majority of the budget will be directed toward building a solution, and a small amount toward ongoing support. Products are generally funded by estimating the size of the team you'll need to build a useful, valuable product and then funding that size of that team for the long term. The majority of funding is spent enhancing the product rather than on the initial build-out.

Success measures

Projects are oriented toward *completing the project* over anything else. Usually projects are kicked off in order to contribute to some larger strategy of value creation, but after they're running, most projects focus on hitting their deadlines and scope. "On time and on budget" is usually the measure of project success. Products are laser focused on creating value for their customers, and as long as a product is valuable, more effort can be put into enhancing it. In many situations, a product team will opt to release a less-complete version of its product into production and create value sooner rather than waiting for a more complete, more desirable version to be finished.

Although it's simple to state the difference between these two modes of operation, the changes across all of these dimensions have a deep and profound effect on the way an organization operates. The way success is measured, the way funding is secured—even the way the staff is managed and evaluated—will change radically when you apply product thinking across an organization.

The Benefits of Product Thinking

This book is about refocusing organizations toward creation of customer value. We believe that an organization that excels in creating values *for* its customers, not just getting business value *from* its customers, will be much more successful commercially. We discussed the different ways customers derive value from an organization in Chapter 2, and the ways in which organizations must shift their mindset to deliver on heightened customer expectations. Products, by definition, focus on the value that they deliver to customers. Products survive only if customers find them valuable; otherwise, we stop investing in a product and will eventually retire it. Product thinking is a natural way to align the things that an organization creates with the overall philosophy of the importance of value creation.

REA's Journey in Product Thinking

REA is an Australian online real estate company that, like many, grew from a humble garage to be a global company, expanding its global footprint through brands like Realtor.com. REA earns nearly a billion dollars in revenue every year and has a market cap of more than AUD$10 billion.

Describing itself as a "product company," REA's goal is to create compelling experiences for its home-buying users and rental seekers, in turn creating value for customers who use REA to reach those audiences. As more home buyers use the site and apps, and more sellers create listings, the value to both increases, creating a positive reinforcing system. REA considers its story to be one of platform-enabled growth with its underlying technology platform as an accelerator.

The philosophy at REA is that "product development is a team sport," and it builds small, empowered teams that can get the job done.

This requires multidisciplinary teams that have all the skills to get the job done. Teams are given a mission and set out to achieve it. REA puts teams close to the customer. Some teams don't report up through traditional IT reporting lines: they are embedded in lines of business in which they can work most closely with *their* customer (the business). The primary job of a team is to deliver value to its customers, usually by building a product or delivering a feature.

Tom Varsavsky, chief engineer at REA, told us the company thinks about technology delivery at three levels: infrastructure, APIs and data, and UX. He explains:

> *As a growing startup, when you're small you just work as a multidisciplinary team directly with your customer. When you get a little bigger, maybe you have several teams, but you basically still focus on the customer. But as you get larger, the teams can't all sit in the same room anymore, maybe even the same building, and the cost of solving similar problems for each team, or of having divergent solutions, starts to rise.*

At this point, a common strategy is for organizations to factor out commonality. The intent is to reduce the amount of duplicated work or divergent solutions to similar problems. Many organizations come to the same conclusion. But the key is to extract commonality in a way that doesn't detract from customer proximity or team autonomy.

A traditional solution would be to create a common (say) infrastructure team, solve the problem once, have all the teams use that. But Varsavsky cautions that this approach "reduces autonomy, creates distance from the customer, and creates a mismatch in goals." This is because centralized infrastructure teams are generally tasked with keeping costs low and uptime high, which translates to resisting changes. On the flip side, product teams are trying to provide customer value and need to keep getting their changes pushed through into production. The two goals are at odds with each other and create friction.

At this point in their journey, REA was stuck. They felt that as they scaled out, they spent more on technology but they weren't getting any faster. Products took too long to get out. Engineers felt they were reinventing the wheel when they didn't need to. The CEO asked whether they were gaining productivity and getting a good return on their technology investments.

Varsavsky's approach was to do a platform assessment, to try to understand their own maturity. They broke things down using their three-level model—Infrastructure, APIs and data, and UX—and found that although they had reasonable platform maturity and reuse at the infrastructure level, they had very little at the UX level. They had no "UX platform." This was counterintuitive because most of their teams were deployed at the UX layer, they had significant investment there, but were getting the least leverage.

REA looked at why reuse is so hard. It turns out that when you have squads close to the customer, solving customer problems, the teams are not really incentivized to solve global problems. As Varsavsky puts it, "The teams have good *intentions* around reuse, but when the pressure comes on or when the project slips, those good intentions go out the window." An example would be a team intending to create a reusable API for some capability but then skipping that step when faced with schedule pressures. It seems odd that a well-intentioned team would do something like that, but as Varsavsky points out, "The cost of *not* creating a reusable thing is not borne by the team that fails to create the reusable thing. They still deliver, but they inadvertently make it harder for other teams." Worst of all, it's difficult to measure the cost of not having something such as an API because that cost is distributed across the organization.

Tom's team did find examples in which they had very good leverage. One of these is Shipper, a deployment tool that over the course of two years grew to support deployment of more than six hundred systems. Why was it a success? Shipper solved a real problem that almost all teams have. It was easy to use and teams wanted to use it. It had strong vision around what it should do (and not do) as a tool. It had ongoing investment. It had a dedicated product person who was the product manager on the team. The team provided internal training for its product, and it had a destination on Slack and its intranet so that users could learn more about it and get support.

REA realized that these success factors are in fact about product management: Shipper delighted customers and used product management techniques to succeed. The organization went on to make a key insight: products, even internal ones, need a brand. As the company invested further in its internal platform, it created an associated "Colab" brand for it, including a logo, product hierarchy, marketing and go-to-market strategies, merchandise, and so on. The idea was to create an internal platform brand that teams would want to be a part of. They defined the requirements to be considered part of the brand. An REA Colab product has the following:

- A *product manager* who is responsible for product vision, defines road maps, audiences, metrics, business cases, adoption strategies, and communication plans

- A *custodian* who keeps quality by trimming the backlog, advancing technology, providing support for users, maintaining documentation, and upholding SLAs

- A *destination* where teams can find out about the product, read documentation, make contributions, see examples, learn, request features, and provide feedback

In addition to a strong brand, internal products at REA have a specific product life cycle, taken from the book *Lean Enterprise* and covered in more detail in Chapter 9:

Explore
At this stage, we are not sure what the answer is, so we test the usefulness of a concept, starting small and experimenting, trying multiple things and learning.

Exploit
We begin to consolidate, put in place a centralized team, a product manager, and a team to develop the product.

Sustain
We ensure enough capacity to continue to evolve the product, to do "business as usual" evolution of it.

Retire
If we find a better way of doing something, we help users upgrade to the new thing and retire the old one.

Use of internal products is optional at REA—they are intended to provide an easy way for teams to get a benefit, so teams will *want* to adopt them. Internal products need to offer a compelling value and work to earn adoption. This is in contrast to some organizations that build an internal product and then *mandate* its use, essentially providing a monopoly to the team that creates the product. As we all know, monopolies tend to stifle innovation, and this kind of mandatory use often breeds substandard internal products. For teams creating such products their competition might actually be external products, which should give rise to either very high-quality internal products or teams actually deciding to use an external product (both of which are a win—if the external product is better, skip the effort of building an internal one!).

REA tracks customer metrics for both of its types of teams: those that create consumer-facing products, and those that create products for use by teams within the organization. Product teams with an external customer use *revenue* as a primary driver, whereas those with an internal customer use *leverage* as a primary driver. But all teams use identical success metrics: adoption (number of customers, consumption by customer, consumption by product), service (issues raised, time to close issues), customer satisfaction (NPS, customer feedback), performance (uptime, throughput, response time), and delivery efficiency (velocity, cycle time, road map delivery).

On its journey toward product orientation, REA realized the needed new roles within the company. Key roles for REA included the following:

- Technical product owners who manage the underlying technology's long-term needs and balance business features with technical quality and determine what customers really need from the product
- Technical writers who can produce really great documentation so that other teams can effectively consume an internal product
- Developer advocates who create excitement about Colab products and help teams to quickly see the value in using them

REA is very happy with the outcomes that it's achieved through the product-thinking mindset. Across the company, people are using the platform and products to communicate their strategy and intentions and to organize and make investments. Varsavsky says that internal brands and product thinking have really helped people focus on internal products and efficiency. "The conversation is changing at all levels, from product managers to the executive table, and even for technology teams who are now excited about things like product and customer service," he says. Critically, REA has improved its efficiency through product thinking without eroding customer proximity or team autonomy.

Product thinking gives an organization a number of distinct benefits:

- Ability to reorient quickly because each product has a team ready to implement new features and respond to customer demand. A traditional project-based organization might need to wait for a project planning and budget cycle in order to move in a new direction.

- Reduction in Big-Bang releases because products naturally live in production with a continuous stream of small new features constantly being added. Project mentality often leads to a single big release, which significantly increases risk.

- Shorter end-to-end cycle times because product teams are given the autonomy to manage their software through to production and take full advantage of the DevOps movement, ensuring that they can deploy at-will.

- Ability to iterate long-term: a product team is stable, funded for the long term, and with a direct incentive to ensure that their product has a long useful life span. Because the product is the key outcome, product owners (especially when paired with a technical product owner) can make long-term decisions for the good of the product. This encourages evolution and directly combats software rot. Project-based teams often need to make short-term decisions to get things over the line in time for the project end date.

- Better knowledge retention because team members work on a product for the long term, building relationships and knowledge within the team. At the end of a typical project, all the people who have been brought together to achieve the outcome are reassigned elsewhere, with all of their accumulated knowledge dissipating.

- Ability to harness IT as a competitive advantage rather than considering it a cost center for which efficiency is the most important goal. Products are designed to create customer value, and technology teams naturally become viewed as valuable business partners.

Large organizations, not just startups, are succeeding with product thinking. We've already hinted at some of the ways we can achieve product orientation through the description and benefits so far, the next section provides a more detailed approach that you can apply yourself.

How to Enable Product Orientation

Being truly product oriented is a revolutionary change across an organization. As you saw in the REA example, product thinking affects everyone from development teams through to executive leadership teams. Here are some steps to introduce product thinking into your organization:

Determine what constitutes a "product" for your organization.
Throughout this chapter, we have used examples in which an existing *thing* could be considered a product. Every organization will be different, but it's important to identify all potential products and their customers. This will be more natural for existing things that are consumed externally to your organization—and especially those that are paid offerings—but even nontraditional items should be considered products. Your corporate website could be considered a product, with the various readers of the site its customers. A dataset that you share with a partner organization could be considered a product. An internal infrastructure platform used by your teams could be considered a product. A security team's vulnerability and risk assessments could be considered products. An internal API or data feed could be considered a product, and so on.

Connect product teams with your thin-slicing approach.
In Chapter 3, we discussed the importance of the thin slice. Big programs tend to fail, and thin slicing gives us a way to drive a specific outcome while exposing constraints such as funding and organizational structure. There is no one-size-fits-all product strategy, which means that there is a variable correlation between products and thin slicing. In some cases, a thin slice can be encapsulated in a single product that delivers value to customers. In other cases, a thin slice will require multiple products orchestrated

together. A product is a solid lens to choose as a thin slice; other options include outcome, customer journey, or value stream. The key is to be clear on how products in your organization will relate to the thin-slice approach.

Create long-term funding for your products.
Many of the benefits of product orientation lie in the ability to get away from short-term projects and the associated antipatterns. In Chapter 8, we discussed functional constraints that hold back organizations that are trying to make the leap to digital. We said that a key change is to fund capacity rather than projects, and to measure value delivered rather than completion of work in order to determine success and ROI. To set up product-oriented teams, estimate the funding that a stable team will require to create the product and deliver a steady stream of valuable features. If that funding proves insufficient, there are a number of levers you can pull to alter the outcomes:

- For a short-term increase in capacity, consider adding "flex" on top of "core" team members. We recommend something on the order of three to six months of flex capacity; with less than three months working on a product, team members are unlikely to contribute very much. If you need to flex for more than six months, it's probable you should simply increase the funding and permanently increase the size of the team.

- If it seems like you've underestimated the team needed to deliver the product or you're happy with the team but want features faster, simply increase the funding for the product and permanently increase the size of the team.

- It's possible that the product is correctly funded, but the team is not moving as fast as they'd like to. Consider running a retrospective to ask the team how it would move faster. It's possible that aspects outside of the control of the team are slowing them down, such as dependencies on other teams or a lack of autonomy.

Create empowered, cross-functional product teams.
Successful products are built by teams comprising all of the skills needed to design, build, and ship the product. A critical role is that of product

owner, and it needs a significantly different skill set to that of a project manager. Increasingly, it is also important to have a technical product owner, who will help to balance the technical direction of the product with the more features that a product might have. Product teams should be empowered, long lived, and cross-functional:

- Empowered teams are in control of their own destiny. They have a clear mission, vision or goal—often expressed as a metric or KPI—and they are empowered to "move the needle" on that metric. In concrete terms, you should create "you build it, you run it" teams that both build and operate the product. Team members should be the ones carrying the pager and ensuring their product meets its SLAs, and it should not run into roadblocks such as a hand off to a separate operations team in order to get the product into production or make changes to it.

- Long-lived teams have a consistent makeup, with people moving occasionally in and out of teams. This encourages strong depth of knowledge of the product, knowledge retention, and expertise, as well as good team interactions.

- Cross-functional teams contain all of the differing expertise required to build the product. As technology evolves, teams will need to incorporate a wider range of skills. A recent example is the rise in the importance of data: all product teams now need to be data-literate and, depending on the product they are building, might even need advanced analytics or machine learning skills directly on the team.

Challenges when Moving to a Product-Centric World

Many of the steps we've described in this chapter come with obvious challenges. Switching from project-based funding to long-term product funding is often an area in which organizations become stuck, and we hope that the advice in Chapter 8 will help prepare you for the switch to a more flexible funding model. Here are a few more stumbling blocks along with some solutions:

The role of product owner is extremely difficult.
In our experience, having a good product owner is absolutely critical for the success of this approach. But you can't simply rebrand a project manager, who is adept at managing a series of tasks and driving to an end date, as a product owner responsible for driving a product's vision and balancing its evolution over time. Similarly, it's not simple for a business analyst who is adept at breaking down business requirements into an actionable development backlog to "graduate" to the bigger picture job of a product owner. We've found that finding and hiring competent product owners is very difficult; a good product owner is in high demand. There's no real silver bullet to help with this; just ensure that you recognize the difficulty of the role and work to support any existing staff who are moving into the role.

Teams and product backlogs must be "right sized" to maintain good utilization.
With a stable, long-term team and funding, it's possible that the team will either have too much work to do or not enough. Product owners will work to ensure that their team has a good backlog of work, but it's possible that either the backlog will run dry or that the team will end up working on less-valuable features while waiting for higher-value features to be identified and added to the road map. If either of these conditions occur—too much or too little work—it can be a sign that adding flex capacity or changing the team capacity permanently is the answer. But keep in mind that as long as the team is responsive and able to deliver value quickly, that might be more valuable to the organization overall than a theoretical "high utilization" target. Beware of returning to the bad-old days of IT as a cost center, with efficiency as the most important metric.

"Backlog coupling" can impede overall throughput.
Our colleague Evan Bottcher coined the term "backlog coupling" to refer to the situation where when one team adds an item to their backlog, another team must add a corresponding item to its backlog. The first team is typically dependent on the second team to complete its item before the first team can proceed. This obviously leads to a large impact: teams slow down as they wait for downstream teams to complete work, and productivity takes a nosedive. If you encounter this kind of problem, the first thing is to ask *why* such coupling is occurring. Is it because two apparently separate teams are actually interwoven in some way? Is there a layer of abstraction missing or a platform that might enable your teams to avoid the coupling?

Are the teams sufficiently empowered through self-service access to infrastructure and data?

Summary

Applying product thinking to how we build software and services in an organization isn't just a Silicon Valley fad. A "products over projects" strategy can create significant value even within a traditional enterprise. The simple act of asking "if this were a product, what would deliver most value to our customers?" can be revolutionary and provide teams much better insight into the best decisions.

Switching to real product centricity isn't easy. It requires restructuring teams and the organization, finding elusive product managers, and switching to a product-centric funding model (often the biggest issue for many organizations). Getting a product approach correct can provide significant benefits across the organization with more responsive delivery of value to customers, teams that are more invested and knowledgeable, and even some gains from retiring weak assets that aren't generating enough value.

It's definitely possible to make an incremental switch to a product-centric world, starting with assets that already have some kind of clear customer and then branching out into products such as data assets and more amorphous "services." Organizations should start small and gain some experience and confidence before making larger bets on product centricity.

Key Points

Following are the key points that we hope you take away from this chapter as well as two actions for you to take to begin implementing what we've discussed:

- This entire book is about refocusing organizations on creation of customer value. Products, by definition, focus on value that they deliver to customers. This is a natural way to align the things that we create with this philosophy of the importance of value creation.

- Organizations have been extremely successful by switching to this model. REA is a billion-dollar company reaping the benefits of product thinking.

- Switching to a product mindset enables teams to reorient quickly, reduces Big-Bang releases, shortens end-to-end cycle times, allows teams to iterate in the long term and evolve software, directly combats software rot, allows an organization to retain knowledge better, and positions IT as a competitive advantage rather than an order-taking cost center.

- To move to a product-centric operating model, organizations should define products, create long-term funding for them, build empowered, cross-functional teams, and connect the products and teams with a holistic, thin-slice approach.

- Product-orientation isn't easy. Finding good product owners and technical product owners is critical. Teams must be right-sized to the vision of their product, and you must take care not to introduce accidental backlog coupling between teams.

Here are two actions to take:

- Identify your products: Look through your organization for things that you can identify as successful products. What makes them a success? Is it clarity of purpose, branding, a great product owner, a great team, or other factors?

- Form a product team: Select one or two internal capabilities or services and form a product team to steward the development of that product.

16

The Future Shape of the IT Department

Redirecting an organization to center on customer value requires significant shifts at all levels. The IT department has for decades been seen as a cost center, with decisions made to optimize efficiency that often resulted in reduced costs but also reduced speed, increased time-to-market, and a reliance on third parties for technical expertise. Today's world is full of ambiguity and rapidly emerging technology; the IT department must reshape itself to become a valued partner in fulfilling heightened customer expectations.

Better Alignment Between Business and IT

Over the past 30 years, IT organizations have always been evolving. In many cases, IT became bigger, more centralized, more outsourced, and also more complex. The Global Financial Crisis in 2008 put a lot of pressure on most business functions, IT departments included. With the rising demand for more and more software applications and technology solutions, and the pressure to reduce costs, IT often ended up with more outsourcing than it would have liked, with increased complexity. The department also runs almost like a business unit by itself—it offers products and services to internal business users and consumers; it manages a large number of suppliers; it employs a large pool of IT staff that engage in a wide range of activities. It also starts to build more and more Center of Excellence (CoE) and other equivalent units within the IT department based on skill sets specialization in the hope of taking advantage of the economy of scale as the organization grows bigger and bigger.

Although the skill set–based model should increase efficiency and reduce cost at executing the same tasks again and again, it is not ideal for fast-paced innovation and product evolution. According to a 2017 study by the Hackett

Group, based on a survey of 160 executives in companies with annual revenue of $1 billion or more, 64% of respondents lacked confidence in their IT organization's capability to support digital transformation execution. At the same time, the study found an increasing demand for IT capability, which will likely increase by more than the number of full-time employees in IT. The Hackett Group suggested this would mean that IT would need a 2% productivity boost, on average, just to keep pace. However, it said the largest percentage increases in workload (5%) and IT staff (4.2%) are happening outside corporate IT. Business groups appear to be investing in their own IT capabilities.

Sometimes, a business unit will engage directly with a SaaS provider for a specific service because the procurement and implementation process seems to be simpler and faster. It's also common to see a "digital" division formed within a business unit tasked with building customer engagement solutions using the division's own technology staff and partners. In other times, an R&D department will expand its own information technology team to build solutions that connect to the broad digital ecosystem outside of the company. Very often, we end up finding a complicated and fragmented technology capability landscape in large organizations. Information and data lives in disconnected silos. There is often duplication, inconsistency and inefficiency in such a complex system. How a digital division fits in or overlaps with the IT department is still an evolving situation.

These are all opportunities for the IT department to add more value. With better structural alignment, the IT department and the business should be able to work together more collaboratively and more effectively to maximize the value delivered to customers while reducing complexity, duplication, and, ultimately, cost.

This is where we would want to bring us back to the thin-slice approach discussed in Chapter 3. Transforming team structure and alignment is highly disruptive to an organization. To make it worse, we often don't know the answers at the outset due to the complexity of the business and the complexity of human relationships. The thin-slice approach allows us to iteratively evolve teams and structure to be more aligned with business outcomes (defined by customer value) instead of with functional budget or skill set specialization dimensions.

What does the future state look like? Although we don't think we can define a one-size-fits-all structure, there are some common themes to think about.

Create an Explicit Strategy to Handle Growing Tech Complexity

There is a seemingly inevitable growth in technological complexity of modern systems. A few years ago, most applications ran on a simple web server and database, probably using some kind of HTML and JavaScript combination for the frontend. Nowadays, it's common to see systems that need to support mobile phones, tablets, and web browsers, as well as integrating with third parties via APIs. Instead of a single backend business logic server, logic might be distributed among dozens of microservices or even executed within a cloud provider's Functions-as-a-Service (FaaS) offering. The explosion of data and its use to create valuable, compelling customer experiences has caused a corresponding explosion in the number of data-related components in a typical system architecture. Figure 16-1 shows a comparison between a possible 2005 system architecture and a 2019 architecture.

The point here isn't to baffle you with tech buzzwords or claim that any particular systems architecture is the correct one: the point is to make it clear just how broad the modern technology landscape is. Most organizations are unlikely to have the resources to acquire deep expertise across the entire landscape, so you will need to borrow or buy capabilities from vendors and partners. Chapter 12 discusses in detail on how to select a partner; the key factors are skills and cultural alignment, not cost.

Your strategy must be clear on what capabilities your organization is going to build strongly in-house versus those you will not. It's inefficient (and possibly even foolhardy) to try to cover the full breadth of the landscape yourself. It might be that certain technology capabilities are extremely strategic for you and should be grown in-house. For other specific capabilities, perhaps you already have a trusted third party with whom you are happy. The key is to be strategic and explicitly determine which capabilities you *will* and, more important, *will not* create in-house.

For capabilities that you decide to obtain outside your organization, you must still have the expertise to manage a vendor delivering those capabilities. Many organizations are in trouble due to decades of low-cost outsourcing, an inability to manage those vendors, and not being able to determine whether the vendor is doing a good job: avoid repeating this mistake in the Digital Age and ensure that you have enough expertise within your organization that you can effectively manage third parties.

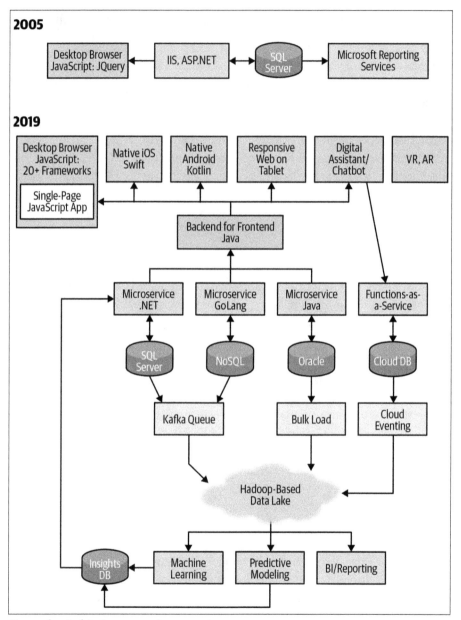

Figure 16-1. Architecture comparison, 2005 to 2019

Align Teams with Customer Outcomes, Not Functional Systems

Chapter 5 examines the concept of cross-functional teams that can break silos and deliver value, and Chapter 7 emphasizes the need to create stable teams. Both of these concepts alter how organizations approach the concept of "team," and these changes need to also extend to our approach to IT.

Commercial airlines have used information technology systems in creative ways ahead of many other industries. In the late 1960s, the first "online" reservation system was built to keep inventory correct in real time, accessible to agents around the world. This is way before the time of the internet. A series of large mainframe computers were deployed to coordinate the message flow. Teleprinter machines located all around the world fed information into the system, which then sent orders back out to all the teleprinters. It was one of the first online systems.

It is therefore not a surprise that many airlines have built and inherited a large variety of IT systems to run their operations. The functionality ranged from flight scheduling, aircraft maintenance, reservation booking, crew dispatching, passenger boarding, and all the other crucial areas. The IT department was also commonly organized around these critical systems. As demands for new features and services grew, systems became more complicated and teams began to become isolated silos.

In the Digital Age, with heightened customer expectations, more and more systems need to coordinate to deliver the desired services and experience to customers. In the delayed flight scenario mentioned earlier in the book, different systems such as flight operations, aircraft routing, airport operations, crew scheduling, baggage tracking, customer care, loyalty, and even hotel booking must work together to deliver the optimal solutions for passengers. Real-time information from these systems will need to be dispatched to flight crews and passengers to reduce anxiety and allow preparation, often through multiple channels including the web, messages, mobile app, and phone calls. Getting the systems to integrate with one another is both a technology challenge and a people/organization challenge.

We have seen many airlines moving away from this siloed technology–oriented structure to a business capability–oriented alignment. For example, teams will be built around specific business capability to support different parts of customer journeys—booking, trip preparation, airport experience, boarding, in-flight experience, arrival, and so on. In any particular part of the journey, multiple IT systems will work together to deliver the value and the best experience to the passengers. On the business side, cross-functional skill sets will be required to understand the customer value and experience; on the technology side, cross-system skill sets will also be required to deliver the technology solution.

Although this does not completely remove the need to have a core development team around a particular IT system at various times, the knowledge and skills of developing and integrating these systems are spread much more broadly across the organization than concentrated in one place.

Building alignment between business and IT is only just the first step. If, as Jack Welch said, "every industrial company will become a software company," eventually, there shouldn't be an IT department. Yes, in a software company, there are still specialized teams that maintain the utility assets like email systems, networks, and laptop and mobile phone management. But the majority of the technology team working on strategic digital assets should be embedded in cross-functional teams that are accountable for customers outcomes. They might no longer call the traditional IT department their home. Just like a software company or a native digital business, information technology is the business; there is no separate IT department in the traditional sense.

There Shouldn't Be Two Speeds

The Agile movement was mainly driven by software developers frustrated at the document-driven, heavyweight development process known as Waterfall. It's a rigid, slow, and often wasteful process because the market and user expectations change at a faster pace than Waterfall can handle. Because Agile was seeking an alternative to the then mainstream methodology, it was often branded as "extreme" (not surprising due to its name at the time: *eXtreme Programming, or XP*), risky, and unsafe. In the early days, the adoption of Agile also mainly started with small teams that had some autonomy or startups with less legacy process. We can clearly recall the disbelief and pushback we got while going around in the early 2000s advocating Agile software development in larger teams and enterprise environments.

Around early 2010, with more failures from the Waterfall process piling up and more evidence of success from Agile accumulating, many IT departments in large enterprises were pressured to adopt the more iterative, exploratory, and experimental delivery techniques. Still, there were all kinds of excuses as to why the new techniques could not be applied to the mission-critical core legacy systems for which safety, stability, and accuracy were deemed more important, even at the cost of speed and adaptability. Facing this dilemma, some IT executives embraced the concept of "Two-Speed IT" or "Bimodal IT," in which systems are categorized as "systems of record" that store authoritative data and tend to change more slowly, and "systems of differentiation" that interact with customers and tend to change more quickly. Two-Speed IT explicitly separates these types of systems and creates different management processes around them.

Although we welcome a strategy that explicitly caters to very different kinds of systems, we disagreed with a risk-averse approach that keeps the status quo for systems of record. This was basically a way of delaying the inevitability of a better development approach to avoid the disruption and pain that might come along with the change. We accepted the fact that it might be a necessary compromise at certain times in certain situations dealing with major changes in a large enterprise. We also believe that now is the time to move on from the Two-Speed or Bimodal IT concept.

The glaring issue facing most businesses is that systems are more and more interconnected with one another in the digital world where consumers expect to engage with the business anytime, anywhere. Most of the frontend "customer engagement" software depends on several core backend systems to deliver value to customers end to end. For a consumer to order on their mobile phone and pick up goods in store, a mobile app and ecommerce, store inventory management, forecast and replenishment, customer service and loyalty systems all need to be updated to enable the transaction.

We think that simplistic classifications of systems as "slow" or "fast" are wrong, and in the worst cases extremely damaging. Legacy systems can be extremely strategic when creating customer value. We see a lot of organizations using Two-Speed IT as an excuse for not properly remediating their legacy systems and simply living with slow, difficult-to-change systems. But to create customer value, we need systems of record *and* systems of differentiation to be created and changed, not just systems of engagement. The two-speed organization ends up moving at only the speed of the slowest common denominator. Even though it's true that mainframe technology probably can't move as fast as a mobile app, it still needs to keep a reasonable pace. Everything must work together to deliver end-to-end value to customers at a faster pace. Systems can move at different speeds within an organization—that's reasonable—but interactions between different speed components are like gears in a car's transmission: the gearbox is under stress to adapt between the different speeds. IT systems are similar, and if the speeds are mismatched too much, the gearbox will burn out.

Mismatched IT Systems Lead to Business Disaster

In the world of mobile phones, the ability to quickly get new products to customers is critical. If a new phone is released—particularly a popular model such as the Apple iPhone—a vendor needs to be able to get the phone in stock, advertise it on the web, and allow customers to easily purchase the phone. Customers have little loyalty, so if the phone they want isn't available, they will simply find another company to provide it.

One UK phone vendor with online, in-store, and business-to-business channels wanted to revamp its systems. A multiyear program costing tens of millions of pounds was launched to replace the majority of the company's systems using a Two-Speed strategy. It developed a dynamic, content-managed system for the frontend so it could quickly get new phones onto its website, but the organization did not focus on speed of update for its in-store and backend warehouse and logistics systems. In addition, they outsourced the management of the majority of their systems in an effort to reduce costs.

Unfortunately, this strategy led to serious business problems. Even though this vendor able to quickly get new phones onto its website, it was unable to actually make them available in stores. Uploading new images and content to the web was fast, but making a "change request" for the store or backend systems took up to five days. Each change request went to the outsourcing company that actually managed the systems.

The key fallacy the company had made was assuming that the back-end systems would not need to change very quickly. But new phones have new attributes and features and *did* require changes to more than just the website. The company had sliced its systems horizontally rather than vertically in chunks that would actually deliver value to customers. Incredibly, company leaders had been convinced that it was only the website (not even store systems!) that needed to be updated at a fast pace.

A five-day delay might not seem like much of a problem, but in the fast-paced world of cell phone sales, it's an eternity. Revenue from phone sales is extremely spiky—a seller must capture revenue from phone launches over a short two- to three-day window. To compound the problem, Apple regularly changed the embargo and release dates for its new phones. It wasn't uncommon for the release date for a new iPhone to be moved forward by one or two weeks. If the UK phone vendor was unable to update its systems in time, customers would simply buy the new iPhone elsewhere. The lost revenue would never be recovered—a new iPhone is a once-a-year event and missing out on that revenue was a serious problem.

As time went on, it became clear that the company was in major trouble. Dwindling profit margins, expensive retail locations, fierce competition, and missed revenue from new phone launches eventually drove the company into bankruptcy. In the end, competitors acquired hundreds of its prime stores at a discount, and thousands of jobs were lost. Had the vendor used a thin-slice approach and asked "what do we need to do to get a new phone into the hands of customers?" and structured their systems around quickly delivering end-to-end value, it might still be in business today.

We believe there is a common misunderstanding that legacy systems can't embrace faster delivery cycles due to the age or complexity of the system. In fact, neither is the case. There is plenty of clean code written a long time ago that is easily integrated into an Agile development process. As we noted in Chapter 13, the authors of the book *Accelerate* find that the four key metrics of cycle time, deployment frequency, CFR, and MTTR are predictors of IT performance *regardless of technology platform*. This is good news: even legacy systems can be made to reliably and frequently deliver value into production. Chapter 14 demonstrates that there are patterns to follow to modernize legacy systems so that they can become part of a modern digital platform, and you can modernize iteratively without the need to rewrite the entire system through a multiyear, Big-Bang approach.

Another reason that Two-Speed or Bimodal IT struggles is the talent aspect. If you are working on the "slow" part of IT, all the CD and DevOps tools and API-enabled architecture and platform thinking will not be available to you. There is hardly any tolerable trade-off an ambitious technologist is willing to make to become stuck in the "old and slow" part of an organization. Not being able to learn and practice new technology and techniques is a career death sentence in the Digital Age in which everything is changing so rapidly. Even though passion and creativity are being unleashed in the faster part of the organization, morale and commitment will continue to drop for people stuck in the old and traditional areas.

It's OK to sequence the transformation in the near term to better take advantage of resources and change capacity, but there shouldn't be a formal Two-Speed or Bimodal mindset as a long-term strategy. There will be only one speed in the future: fast.

Focus on Building Teams

Division of labor increases productivity. From Adam Smith to Henry Ford, there are plenty of theories and case studies supporting this argument. The entire history of industrialization, all the way until mass production, was a history of increased specialization and further division of labor.

Adam Smith visited a pin factory employing 10 people who produced 48,000 pins per day. The process was broken down into 18 distinct steps, including packaging the pins. Each worker specialized in one or two of these steps. The pins flowed through these steps, passed from one worker to another until it became the finished product. Smith said that if these 10 workers did every step themselves, they could each produce 10 or 20 pins per day. Through specialization and division of labor, the increase in labor productivity (output per person per day) is as high as 50 times that of individual pin makers.

Fast forward from pin making to software development: we have also now separated software development into distinct steps performed by specialized roles—business analyst, developer, tester, deployer, and maintainer (system operators).

In a *Labor and Monopoly Capital* (Monthly Review Press), published in 1974, author Harry Braverman vividly described the economic reasons to separate the programming activity from analysis activity. It's so insightful, it's worth quoting the entire passage here:

> *The upper level of the computer hierarchy is occupied by the systems analyst and the programmer. The systems analyst is the office equivalent of the industrial engineer, and it is his or her job to develop a comprehensive view of the processing of data in the office and to work out a machine system which will satisfy the processing requirements. The programmer converts this system into a set of instructions for the computer. In early computer installations, the programmer was generally a systems analyst as well, and combined the two functions of devising and writing the*

system. But with the encroachment of the division of labor, these functions were increasingly separated as it became clear that a great deal of the work of programming was routine and could be delegated to cheaper employees. Thus the designation of "programmer" has by this time become somewhat ambiguous, and can be applied to expert program analysts who grasp the rationale of the systems they work on, as well as to program coders who take as their materials the pre-digested instructions for the system or subsystem and simply translate them mechanically into specialized terminology. The training for this latter work occupies no more than a few months, and peak performance is realized within a one- to two-year period. In accordance with the logic of the capitalist division of labor, most programmers have been reduced to this level of work.

That was still the early days in computing. From there on, further division of labor separated testing, deployment, and system operation into distinct steps performed by specialized roles. The Waterfall project management methodology is closely related to this division of labor and specialization driven by economic reasons. Work artifacts (documentation, code, specifications) flow through the steps and passed on from person to person, team to team. However, digital technology is a highly complex and fast-changing field, it's also a cognitively intense process that cannot be easily separated into repetitive and mundane tasks.

Growing up in the industrial specialization age, many people in large organizations struggle to think beyond their departments, cubicles, and immediate tasks. Many of us are too focused on completing the distinct tasks at hand to think holistically about the end-to-end value and goals. Separating software product development—a cognitively intense effort—into too many siloed steps reinforces the tunnel vision we are conditioned with and reduces our ability to do systems thinking, which is a key perspective for innovation.

Here is a simple story from 1999: the first large-scale Agile project mentioned earlier in this chapter. The team did not embrace Agile from the get go. The project was running the same traditional Waterfall approach before it decided to adopt Agile out of frustration. A lot of requirement documents were already produced and ended up being used to come up with the first set of high-level user stories. One of the stories was to print out an invoice for certain charges. It turned out that the print out was passed to another department only to be manually entered into another system for further processing. A dialogue between the software developer and the business user about the value of this story discovered a better solution: we could just send the information to the other system electronically without bothering with the print out at all. Without adopting the Agile way of working, that requirement would have been implemented through a lot of effort to create a nice-looking print out to be passed on, a success for both departments, but little value for the whole.

Even Adam Smith himself acknowledged the perils of overspecialization at the same time recognizing its benefit on productivity. In the book *Wealth of Nations*, he also wrote:

The man whose whole life is spent in performing a few simple operations, of which the effects are perhaps always the same, or very nearly the same, has no occasion to exert his understanding or to exercise his invention in finding out expedients for removing difficulties which never occur. He naturally loses, therefore, the habit of such exertion, and generally becomes as stupid and ignorant as it is possible for a human creature to become.

It's a little extreme to say the same thing for modern knowledge workers in the Digital Age. But the essence is the same; we lose our problem-solving capability and creativity if we are too focused on optimizing the siloed task and not thinking about the whole problem space end to end. A lot can be gained from simply developing a broader perspective, with a better awareness of the whole, and of how the parts within those wholes interrelate. Cross-functional teams in the Agile and DevOps movements are all trying to reequip teams with this broad perspective through adding more end-to-end responsibility and more skill sets and knowledge.

The "T-Shaped" Professional

The DevOps engineer role still begs the question: should everyone on an Agile team become generalist and be able to do everything, or is there still room for specialization? Although we will always favor generalists when possible, there is certainly plenty of room for specialists on a cross-functional team. For example, database administration is a highly specialized role. There is a long list of skills and capabilities that takes years to acquire and hone—database capacity planning, database design, installation and configuration, data migration, performance monitoring, security, backup and data recovery, let alone the new emerging technologies like NoSQL database, data lake, streaming data processing, and more. Depending on the workload, it sometimes makes sense for a small cross-functional team to have such specialists as full time members; other times, specialists can be shared across small feature teams or even bigger product teams.

That said, polyskilled members are more productive (making it easier to balance work on the team) and tend to be more creative and better problem solvers. For some other common roles—for example, analyst, programmer, tester, and system administration—we have seen benefits with respect to blurring the lines between them.

Each role has its own depth and special skills required to be the expert that can deal with the most difficult problems in that area. But there are also enough simple skills that can be acquired with some training and learning. Acquiring such skills and knowledge not only allows the team members to share a broader common set of tasks to load balance and be more productive, it also gives them a more holistic view of the entire problem space and able to come up with more innovative solutions. To be fair, different roles working together on the same team can already give you the benefits of improving communication and coordination, reducing handover and rework, and becoming more innovative. Sharing the knowledge and skill sets to create more generalists on the team will further advance that. How far can a team push the generalist boundary depends on the depth required for each role on the project and the skill level team members already have in each area.

It is important to keep in mind that in a cross-functional team and an Agile team, we should not organize the work by role. It should be dynamically organized by task or process, and allow team members to apply themselves to the workflow in the most efficient way based on their own skill sets. What matters most is that the work is done in the proper order by the best resource available at the time, not who does what. There should be regular reviews and adjustments based on the progress and feedback; for example, during the iteration planning meetings or daily standups. It's a rather soft and dynamic division of labor. Overtime, more team members should become familiar with one another's area and able to perform a broader set of tasks.

As an individual technologist, there is also the tension between specialization and generalization from a personal development and career perspective. An often-referenced metaphor is the "I"-shaped professional versus the "T"-shaped professional, introduced by David Guest in 1991.

Through the industrialization age, division of labor and specialization have created more and more I-shaped professionals. That is, professionals are becoming deeper but narrower after spending years and years drilling down into a specific field and honing their skills around it. As technology becomes more complicated, it takes a lot of learning and practice just to keep up with the latest techniques, let alone branching out to other fields or disciplines. The reality is that we have more and more "I"-shaped professionals in organizations than ever before.

A T-shaped professional also has deep specialized expertise in one field, represented by the vertical stroke of the T. The horizontal stroke of the "T" represents a broad set of interdisciplinary knowledge and skills. More and more executives are recognizing that they are better at fostering the diverse connections and conversations that bring exceptional ideas to the surface. They make a key difference on cross-functional teams.

When you bring a lot of I-shaped professionals into the same team working on the same problem, they don't automatically collaborate smoothly from the beginning. What could happen is that each individual discipline brings its own point of view to the table. Without the interdisciplinary understanding, it could become a negotiation at the table as to whose point of view wins, and you get the lowest common denominator between all points of view. Empathy, an often-underestimated skill, can mitigate this issue to a great extent. What we found is that T-shaped professionals tend to be more empathetic due to their experience across disciplines and the exposure from a broader context.

Another character the T-shaped professionals bring to the table is their insatiable interest to learn more about other people's disciplines and to practice them if possible. This is likely the most important factor giving them the "T" shape after a lot of exposure and practice across many fields. This is also the biggest benefit a T-shaped person brings to the table to a cross-functional team—the genuine enthusiasm to learn about one another's disciplines.

Thomas Edison was one of the most famous inventors of all time. He was deeply interested in world history and English literature. He was especially fond of Shakespeare, often saying, "Ah, Shakespeare. That's where you get the ideas!"[1] His point was that general reading was often the best reading, general knowledge was often the best knowledge. By the early 1920s, he had become increasingly frustrated by the fact that college graduates applying to work for him didn't have the breadth of knowledge he needed. To better test their mental model, he created written tests of 150 questions for the positions they were applying for. Some were specific to the discipline; many others were broad and general.

---

1 *Harvard Magazine*, April 1977.

To some extent, the DevOps movement in the twenty-first century is also an echo of the sentiment expressed by Thomas Edison in the 1920s.

Kent Beck took this notion even further. A T-shaped professional is a "general specialist," a person who can do many things, and is really good at one thing. In the digital world, when technology changes so fast, it's more difficult to predict which field is going to be more important to master. There are also too many intercorrelations that even a specialist in one area needs to be good enough at several related fields to be productive. He came up with a new metaphor: the *Paint Drip People*:

- You draw a brush across the top of the canvas.

- Sometimes enough paint accumulates that a drip starts to roll.

- Once a drip starts to roll, it's not clear how far it will go.

- You keep drawing the brush across the canvas, regardless.

It's a model to develop more generalists than just general specialists. It also allows professionals to follow their interests and curiosity to explore the possibilities than limit themselves to the role definition or a prescriptive career path.

The Blurring Boundary Between Business and IT

We've been talking about business and IT alignment for a while. In Part I, we focused on the shift to customer value being the most important metric and the need to align work and organizational structures to match. In Part II, we covered common organizational constraints that get in the way of this alignment and some patterns to tackle the constraints. The structure of the IT department can certainly be a constraint on achieving a customer-value focus and thin-slice approach.

It makes sense to build cross-functional teams involving both business and IT to achieve goals defined by customer outcomes. These are teams formed around these goals based on the skill sets needed. Is it a far stretch to consider these teams as the primary organizational structure in the future where IT and business merges? We don't think so. If we look at technology companies, there is no separate IT department. There are teams that manages the hardware infrastructure like phones, network, laptops, and the utility software systems like email, video-conferencing, accounting, and others. With the rise of cloud computing and SaaS, it's becoming cheaper and easier to rent, manage, and maintain them as services. The majority of the IT department will be more focused on strategic digital assets that enable the business to compete and differentiate.

At the same time, not all IT spending is charged to the IT department or even executed by the IT department. It's also becoming typical to see a new digital division created outside of the IT department.

In some cases, the digital division is created to attract talent and form a new breed of technology teams just for the new digital business without the influence of the traditional IT departmental mindset. In other cases, it is created to spearhead the digital transformation journey leading to the eventual modernization of the entire IT department. According to Harvey Nash (*https://oreil.ly/__cgr*), a quarter of organizations (25%) now employ a chief digital officer; in 2017, it was 25%; 2016, 18%; 2015, 17%; 2014, 7%; three times as many as just three years ago.

There is a clear overlap between the digital division and the IT department, between the chief digital officer and the chief information officer. We have sometimes seen duplicated functions and systems built in this context, leading to even more fragmentation and inconsistency. This separation can be only a temporary solution. It's possible that in some scenarios, the IT department will become fully transformed and modernized, capable of delivering "all things digital." In other scenarios, the IT department's scope and responsibility will be reduced to a narrow focus on infrastructure and utility systems, whereas all the strategic technology assets will be managed directly by the business through a digital division.

Regardless of how it evolves, we believe that there will be three patterns of how the technology capability will be organized in a digital business in the future:

- Teams managing the physical technology infrastructure (phones, laptops) and utility systems (emails, accounting systems, etc.). This will remain a separate centralized division.

- Teams building and running the delivery infrastructure (as a product), data infrastructure, and commonly shared services in the context of platform thinking. This could remain a separate centralized division working closely and aligned with the business teams.

- Teams building and running the digital products will converge with the customer outcome–based teams driven by the business divisions. The long-term development of these technologists will be supported by a learning and development culture and a central learning and development organization instead of a technology division.

When it comes to the capability of building innovative digital solutions and constantly delivering value to customers, the line between business and IT will begin to blur. When the time is right, it makes sense to combine the business capability and technology capability into the same function or division. That's what most technology companies do when technology is the business.

In the short term, the definition and scope of the IT department, the responsibility and title of CIO and CDO, will continue to evolve in different ways in different organizations due to their specific corporate culture, context and priority.

Business Leaders Will Be More Involved in Technology Decisions

There is generally a perceived risk to having business experts leading technology teams. They might not only influence what features to build and what customer value to focus on, but also want to decide how the work is done.

The most commonly seen issue is the lack of understanding of technology excellence and the lack of appreciation of software internal quality. As mentioned earlier in Chapter 11, internal quality often becomes the first to lose when business pressures mount up. It happened so often that strong influence from the business was often met with skepticism and concerns by the technology teams. This could be caused by the lack of communication or the lack of ability from technologists to communicate the value of quality. But it could be caused by the lack of understanding and appreciation of these technology principles by the business leaders.

By taking the thin-slice approach and building outcome-based cross-functional teams, business leaders and technology leaders are jointly accountable for the long-term outcomes of the whole team's work. Business leaders cannot ignore advice from technologists, whether it's the impact of technical debt, quality, or the need to build platforms.

We have seen an increase in business leaders understanding "enough" about technology and technology leaders understanding "enough" about business. If we push the generalist over specialist principle further, we believe that a new breed of business technologists or technical business people will emerge and become better leaders of such modern digital business.

Finally, we have some old suggestions for the CEOs. CEOs have a great deal of influence on the effectiveness of IT departments, both in the old world and the new digital world. As early as 1994, there was a well-researched study done by *MIT Sloan Management Review* on how CIOs could add more value, be a strategic partner to the business, and "create competitive advantage and enable business transformation." When it comes to advice to the CEOs, the following were highlighted in the study:

1. Position IT and the CIO as agents of change.

2. Focus on achieving effectiveness, not efficiency, from IT.

3. Institutionalize business values for IT.

4. Build an executive team that includes the CIO.

5. Manage IT as integral, not as an adjunct to, the business.

This was true 30 years ago, and it's still true today.

In technology companies, everyone should be working together solving problems collaboratively and iteratively. Instead of functional silos, modern digital organizations have cross-functional teams: from business stakeholders, marketing, product, operations, designers and engineers—all working together focused on a single market objective or a product vision. Teams are aligned to achieve customer outcomes, not functional optimizations. Generalists are better at connecting diverse thoughts and experiences to allow innovative solutions to surface, and making cross-functional teams more productive and collaborative.

The entire technology organization will be modernized to deliver innovative digital solutions from the backend to the frontend. There will be no more Two-Speed IT; there should be just one Fast-Speed IT. The formation of a digital division is often just the starting point of the transformation process. This would lead to the blurred boundary between the IT department and business departments, between technologists and business people. Eventually, we should see the rise of a new type of leader who understands both business and technology.

Key Points

Following are the key points that we hope you take away from this chapter as well as two actions for you to take to begin implementing what we've discussed:

- The technology landscape is impossibly broad, so organizations should decide which expertise they will create and, most important, not create in-house.
- Align teams with customer outcomes, not functional systems.
- There shouldn't be a Two-Speed IT. The entire IT organization needs to be transformed to move at a fast speed.
- With customer outcome–based teams, the boundary between business and IT will become blurred.
- Business leaders need to understand technology better.

Here are two actions to take:

- Start merging business and IT: Add an item to business strategy that reflects the desired future state of your IT department.
- Take technology to the board room: Ensure key members of IT are present at key business meetings. Invite them to provide technology narratives linked to the business strategy.

Final Reflection: The Importance of Leadership

Having now read the book, it's really important that you think through your role as a leader in this digital transformation.

There are many threats and opportunities facing businesses in the Digital Age: industry disruption from nimble startups, economic pressure from massive digital platforms, evolving security threats, and emerging technologies.

At the beginning of this book, we called out the three main challenges:

- Heightened customer expectations.

- Speed and ambiguity, which forces companies to come up with new competitive advantages more frequently.

- A plethora of emergent technology choices that could create competitive advantage.

It's clear that dealing with these challenges will require a new type of leadership. There has never been a time when executives have been under as much pressure as today to let go of what they have thought to be true and explore new possibilities.

This revolution in what leadership means is particularly critical for organizations during digital transformation. Unpacking legacy systems, legacy thinking, and legacy behavior while truly focusing on the customer will likely require rewiring culture, talent, and technology. Organizations must break down barriers and remove blockers across the organization—like thawing the frozen middle-management layer—to establish new ways of working. This means being humble about what you don't know and embracing the need to constantly learn and change. A willingness to embrace and integrate technology into everyday life will be integral to providing the work environments and customer interactions now expected.

The Frozen Middle

Middle managers are the gatekeepers or conduits between employees and senior leaders. They are a critical component of transformation because they have a large influence base and can therefore enable or quash change movements. It requires constant and deliberate nudging to ensure they do not form a *frozen middle*, incapable of change themselves and restrictive when others attempt to.

It is important to recognize that "frozen" does not necessarily mean stubborn, adversarial, or obstinate. On the contrary many middle managers can be frozen because they are placed in no-win situations in which doing nothing is better than the consequences of the change they are being asked to make. The "big freeze" can come from multiple conflicting asks:

Stuck in the middle
> Being stuck between leaders trying to inspire change with bold aspirational North Stars and employees who are forming a ground swell of a movement for change, while the day-to-day work still needs to be done. This can be very distressing for middle managers as the chants of change often exceed the current possible reality and so employees become frustrated and are not able to do what senior leaders ask. Additionally, senior leaders do not necessarily understand the consequences of the North Star they are setting. They are often out of tough with the detail of the work and unaware of the workarounds that are needed today to get work done, workarounds that will be busted by the changes. A simple *lack of know-how* in how to operate and behave in a new way. For example, not all leaders are capable of leading without commanding. As a result, they will often create the facade of change to make it look like they are doing what is expected without actually changing anything, avoiding being called out.

Fear of exposing a lack of skills
> Middle managers are typically leaders who have risen through the ranks based on expertise in a craft. The craft becomes outdated or its methodology changes, leaving their craft skills obsolete. A technical manager with a developer background who does not understand CD, as an example, could find it challenging to lead their team down this path.

Measurement conflict

Often, we see a gap between what middle managers are being asked to do and the measures they are being judged on. They hear the chant of change coming from senior leaders, but those same senior leaders continue to ask for the same old measures, the same activities and reporting. This misalignment between the change and what is being measured makes it difficult for middle managers to know which way to turn. They will often quash ideas, innovation, and change suggestions simply because they don't contribute to the short-term numbers they are being held accountable for, and failure might reflect badly on them. A simple example is an ask for responsiveness, test and learn, and experimentation, with measures still referencing milestones, completion, and revenue ROI.

Empire protection

Hitting at the heart of Maslow's Hierarchy, some middle managers fall into protection mode. Rather than being open to change and helping empower their teams to build new skills, they defend their patch in order to keep staff or work they are responsible for. Often, this feeling is that the value of the middle manager will come into question if their work is deemed no longer necessary or if some of their direct reports are determined to better fit under someone else. The trap can go even more granular in some organizations where managers need to have a certain number of direct reports to keep their managerial status, so they will fight to keep that magic number regardless of what makes the best result. It is a lot easier to maintain your stature in the organization from within the "known" than in times of ambiguity.

The risk of the frozen middle is that they will *manage the message*, cherry picking the points that advantage them and avoiding the ones that don't. They will quell the fear of change by playing it down and reducing the impetus that senior leaders are trying to create. Conversely, they will oversell their or their team's contribution to the change to be seen as doing the right thing. In the end, you end up with a lot of words and posturing but not a lot of change. If senior leaders are not paying attention and measuring appropriately, they will end up with a false sense of success.

But this does not mean wholesale change or "gutting" middle management layers (although we have seen that approach work), but certainly it requires attention. Middle managers typically have a lot of legacy knowledge, nuanced understanding about how to get things done in the organization, and a degree of influence born out of their position within their craft or leadership. The preference is to thaw those who are frozen and retain the intellectual property from these traditionally long-term employees who have formed the fabric of the past success of the organization.

This requires senior leaders to engage middle managers early and often, to coach them through the change, and to create that sense of safety for learning (getting it wrong here and there) that will allow them to adapt without fear. It needs to be OK that middle managers will not necessarily have a natural inclination to work or lead this way. They need to be shown through example and mentoring and have the definition and measures of success strongly aligned to new behaviors and attributes. You can't just push the change onto them; they will need the same amount of support as staff do when acquiring new competencies and changing behavioral norms. Ensure that they are not overworked or trapped with trying to sustain the old while in parallel being asked to adopt the new. Be clear about which areas of the new you want straight away, which you would like to see exploration in, and which you are happy to be left until later. The same goes for current norms: which do you want let go immediately, which do you want phased out, and which need to be maintained until later?

At the same time there is an imperative on senior leaders to stay involved in the transformation and make sure they are holding middle managers to account for the changes that will achieve your outcomes. You must lead them through and make sure that the new ways of working are actually being adopted and followed, and is all not just theater. In the end, what you want is transparency and honesty in feedback from middle managers that allows you to make the correct decisions at the proper time for maximum impact.

Leaders need to own this technology-driven transformation. Delegating it leads to an implementation mindset, not a learning one. The implementation mindset tends to overcommit resources based on a false sense of certainty and disjointed measures of success. The leaders are in the best position to help the team resist this overcommitting to allow the organization time to test and learn its way to the correct decisions, acting on knowledge and placing accuracy above the falsehood of future certainty through a culture of experimentation. Being able to walk the fine line to balance between autonomy and control, learning and doing, small and large. As Gary Hamel famously wrote, "Right now, your company has twenty-first-century, internet-enabled business processes, mid-twentieth-century management processes, all built atop nineteenth-century management principles."[1] This is likely true for many organizations today. We need leaders to own the reshaping of work and the way value flows through the organization. This includes changing the very traits of leadership itself.

Let's explore these concepts a bit more.

Driving Technology Transformation

Leaders must be able to talk about technology in a way that has resonance with the business, and engage with technology in a way that hasn't happened in the past.

Stewart Holmes, while Managing Director of Cards, Barclaycard

As discussed in Part III, when it comes to digital transformation, leaders have no option than to straddle the line between technology and business. The impact that technology is having on operating models, customer interactions, and new products is such that you cannot afford to be out of the loop. As time passes, the gap between those with the ability to adopt emerging technology and those without is growing, and those holding on to traditional mindsets fall further behind.

To successfully drive transformation, leaders must possess both business and technology acumen. They need a relentless curiosity for technology, adopting and using it to provide more innovative customer experiences, employee engagement, and ways to bring ideas to market quickly. Technology acumen means:

- Knowing how to adopt technology for strategic advantage

- Knowing which technology trends—and, more important, which *combinations* of technology trends—are most relevant to your organization's success; for example, augmented reality, machine learning, platforms, and security

- Knowing the impact of technology excellence, modern development methodology, and their impact on high-performing technology teams

---

2 Gary Hamel and Bill Green, *Future of Management* (HBR Press, 2007).

- Knowing how to wield a high-performing technology team as a competitive business advantage

- Helping to position technology as a differentiating capability, focusing on quality and outcome, not just cost

- Using technology to create new opportunities

- Fighting the war on talent by attracting top talent with the best physical and technology environment

Leaders must own the vision. This means staying involved and breaking down the silos between business and technology so that everyone works together to iteratively and collaboratively problem solve through the transformation. At some point in all digital transformations, you will reach a critical inflection point at which the original intent of the transformation and the execution of it collide. It is identifiable when responsibility and accountability for change get delegated downward. This new owner then uses execution language to the next level below them, without passing on the original measures of the intent. Over time, the implementation imperative consumes the organization, which can become caught measuring whether they are implementing the changes, ceremonies, and structures that they decided on rather than measuring whether the change is actually working.

Sharing a couple of examples in which we have seen this happen might shed more light on the problem. In the first example, a company wanted to adopt Agile practices into around 160 delivery teams. Agile adoption is about iterative delivery of value and supporting teams to feel empowered to work together so that they can find ways to improve and create a way of working that is both in line with the organization's goals and best suits its ability to deliver value. As this imperative trickled down the line, the measure of success became "how many teams have gone through Agile training?" Teams were lined up and rammed through a week-long training course regardless of their Agile experience and credentials. It came to a head when their exemplar Agile pilot was called on to drop what they were doing and go on this training for a week. The team argued that it was already a high-performing Agile team and the "101" training was unnecessary for them and in fact had elements that would bust their high-performing norms. But the leaders' measures meant that they wanted all teams pumped through.

In a broader, more organization-wide example, a company had a goal to create autonomous squads aligned to the work. A program of transformation rolled out following a predetermined pattern for forming teams, a pattern from another organization that was untested in this one. Unfortunately, the design became the success criteria, so middle managers were being assessed on their ability to form teams in line with the predetermined roles and skills. As time passed, it became obvious that the middle managers were also biased toward maximizing their direct reports and keeping the current work going. Teams ended up either looking no different or, worse, new teams were formed and handed existing work that none of them had been involved in to that point. It's not difficult to imagine that while the implementation of the design looked like it was going well, very few of the teams were meeting the original intent of being autonomous or designed to complete work holistically. The end result was far more dependencies and handoffs then they had before and the flow of work and time to value delivery was increased rather than decreased.

We believe the future leader is one who can empathize with and better understand technology and its use in achieving the organization's strategic outcomes. They can unleash the technologists and their interrelationship with business knowledge to unlock business potential. Success requires that you must hold yourself to account for the transformative state you are moving to, keeping a keen eye on the measures of the original intent rather than the transformation "plan."

Creating Cultures of Experimentation

Traditional organizations would struggle to support the more experimental mindset needed to become more responsive because the existing culture was built on the expectation of future certainty, planning, and structure. Leaders must now help navigate the organization through ambiguity and deal with decisions that have no precedent. We need to encourage employees to think and act creatively, to explore new ideas, test them, and scale the ones that work, trading off future certainty for more short-term accuracy, better decision making, and nimbleness.

The leader's role is to stand in the face of the pressures of the current culture and support experimentation, making sure that it is not viewed as a crazy, risky solution that is underbaked and poor quality, but as a robust way to collect knowledge that reduces risk and makes decisions more obvious, saving large investments only for the things we know to be true.

Think in reverse: we want to act based on knowledge and data, the things we want to invest in are those that we know will work, therefore good ideas need to be explored before we invest. We want many good ideas, so everyone needs to be able to test. The culture of the organization must provide the encouragement to try, the safety to fail, and the recognition to act on the results not on the opinions of leaders. For their part leaders need to give the tools, resources, and permission for people to experiment. They must support the thirst for learning and be comfortable with the fact that they might not be right and therefore have the humility to change when the data says to.

A lot of the culture shift begins with the thought patterns discussed in Part I such as setting the vision anchor and mental models of what "good" looks like. In addition to this, the leadership team must make sure they are behaving and talking in ways that validate the culture. Here are a few examples of what we have seen as supporting action:

Set the guardrails for safety

This means that you are still responsible for risk mitigation and ensuring that experimentation is still toward the achievement of the outcomes that the organization is trying to achieve. Experimentation does not mean anarchy; it does not mean free reign to try absolutely anything. You do not want an organization chock full of random experiments, everyone using the name of experimentation to justify doing whatever they please. Understand intimately what proper experimentation is and demand the rigor of it; for example, which stage they are they up to, what results are they seeing, when is it time to decide?

Celebrate learning and winning equally

This is a small mindset shift and the true meaning of being "safe to fail" within an organization. If an experiment is not showing good results, it's not bad news; it means that we saved ourselves from making a large investment in something that was not going to work. It also means that we have learned new information, which could lead to another experiment that takes us down a path to a unique differentiator we were not considering. We should celebrate this! When you think of a CIO, for example, they spend a lot of their time fixing outages and firefighting. Their interactions are largely negative in nature and their accountabilities include uptime and error rates. Without a shift in culture and expectation, it would be difficult for a CIO to admit failures, seek learnings, and try new things.

Make sure everyone can do it

Having an experimental mindset cannot be the realm of special people or creatives. For the cultural change to stick, it must be something everyone builds capabilities in. When we talk of the need for stable teams, that means every team needs to be able to identify the category of the work, and if it is in explore or exploit, they need to be able to take action accordingly. This means that they need access to test and learn skills, collaboration tools, testing tools, data and data analytics, visibility, and, of course, the safety to say it didn't work and then change without repercussion.

Ask the right questions

Leaders standing on a soap box presenting the vision of transformation are wasting a lot of breath if, when it comes to the day-to-day operations, they ask the same questions around project completion, timeline, budgets, and so on. A new way of working needs new questions from leaders so that they can gather insights that will actually be useful. For example, instead of asking "are we finished yet?" leaders should instead ask "are we delivering the expected value?" For many leaders, this can be as simple as not knowing what else to ask for or not knowing how to find the "right" information in the "new world."

Leaders need to build muscle in seeing where work is in relation to moving the outcome needle and to react to that rather than asking when it will be finished. They need to be talking about how the work is designed in small chunks to ensure that we are delivering value often and call when enough is enough rather than talk timelines. And, of course, they need to understand customer value being delivered versus money spent rather than talking about budgets, reading walls, and big visible charts rather than asking for reports and quarterly reviews. This way leaders are far better informed with more accurate information, more frequent updates, and the ability to sense changes more readily to make better decisions.

Here are some example questions:

- What is the hypothesis?
- How will we know? What are we measuring to find out?
- What is the one metric that matters?
- What have we learned?

- What can we do to test this?

- What knowledge or data do we have?

- How can we get more knowledge?

- Should we stop or pivot?

- What is the smallest thing we could do to find out?

- How can I help; what blockers do you need me to move?

Experiment yourself—practice

Empathy is a great trigger for learning the right supporting behaviors. What better way to build empathy than to practice the techniques yourself and really see the benefits of working this way, yes you yourself need to live and breathe this culture.

In *The Attacker's Advantage* (*https://oreil.ly/BfXMb*) (PublicAffairs) Ram Charan introduced the concept of perceptual acuity, the ability to see around corners, analyzing things around you to look for trends that will provide opportunity. In the November 2013 issue of the *Harvard Business Review*, he said, "Getting to the right answer is tougher these days. It's not just the greater number of variables to consider; executives also need to make subjective judgments about highly ambiguous factors that are moving targets. The usual competitive analysis doesn't work well when technology keeps erasing industry boundaries and the pace of change is so fast that you can't wait for things to stabilize."

He suggests a very valuable practice technique in which at the start of any staff meeting you allocate 10 minutes to learn about and discuss anomalies in the external landscape. Team members can introduce a current trend and how it might affect an industry or reflect on a recent disruption and trace it back to an event. This way, the team becomes attuned to market forces and possible defense or attack action that the organization needs to take. The "practice" heightens the sense of ambiguity and gives people permission to suggest changes. From this, leaders can form their own hypotheses about what might happen or the action to take and work with their teams on the opportunity, experimenting your way to the precise trend to jump on.

A word of caution: when changing the culture to one of ambiguity, opportunity, and empowerment you must understand that not everyone will be ready to buy in at the same time. There are those who dive in and pick up the new ways very quickly. They will be the trailblazers setting their own path and will create early momentum. They are also the highest flight risk if you don't deliver on the promise of change or remove roadblocks in the way of their path. There are those who are optimistic and curious about the change but perhaps unsure of how to move forward. This is your critical mass that you need to provide the appropriate level of direction without hindering growth and learning that comes from them working out their own path. Then there are the pessimistic. Pessimism can mean they are inhibitors who can turn into a change virus if not dealt with. Not everyone is built to work in a way that is more ambiguous, fast paced, and less defined. Whether they are leaders or staff, some are not made for autonomy and the freedom to work collaboratively toward a common outcome. A time might come to move certain people into different roles to clear the path for transformation. When that time comes, leaders must make courageous decisions. Inaction could convert the believers and optimists into nonbelievers and pessimists, too. Be careful here because sometimes pessimism comes from those who are in the first category of trailblazer and are full of knowledge and ideas that you want to harness. Don't react too quickly to shut down pessimism in case it contains a trailblazer's nugget.

As leaders remain instinctive, passionate, and a little impulsive, go after the groundbreaking idea, the new market opportunity, the crazy idea. Just do it in a culture of experimentation in which ideas that are not created through absolute knowledge are tested first, evolved, and scaled to ensure that you are always working on the highest value to customer items that you know to be true. Then, enable everyone else to do the same.

Shaping the Future of Work

Jacob Morgan, in his book *The Future of Work* (Wiley), eloquently described five trends that are affecting how work will change. He categorized them as the expectations that millennials will have, the impact of social media, emerging technology, globalization, and mobility. This provides a great platform for thinking about the discussions in previous chapters and how the role of the leaders needs to be shaped for them.

HOW THE WORK IS DONE

Work will be done very differently. A more test-and-learn approach to exploring opportunities or defending your ground means that the work will need to be thought of in smaller chunks. It will need to be surrounded by data points and analysis that teams can use to make decisions for changing direction or stopping completely. This data will need to be visible and always available in real time, rolled up into big visible charts, so that leaders can instinctively lean in where they are needed most and make changes directly linked to customer outcome measures.

All of this means that the organization needs to be better prepared for more frequent changes, something for which leaders need to be at the forefront. Technology will massively affect how the work is done, either through new and emerging techniques, tools, and software, or in its impact on how we interact with customers. Regardless of new trends, this will need to be understood by business leaders and issues like security will need to be top of mind. Expect to have to participate in hackathons, experiments, inceptions, and so on as the pace of the organization increases and work practices become more dynamic in the name of rapid responsiveness. Smaller work, new technology, and frequent changes will challenge many policies and processes that exist in your organization today and you will need to shepherd the reshaping of these.

WHERE THE WORK IS DONE

Where the work is done might also become more complex to manage. Globalization and mobility mean that we are moving to a more borderless society, and this includes borders within organizations. Whether it's as simple as the walls between functional units coming down to form cross-functional teams, the distribution of work across country borders, or partnerships that blur the very lines of where your organization starts and ends, managing the flow of work has already changed.

For leaders, it adds complexity to accountabilities and role management, it adds expectations to the collaboration or cocreation capabilities and infrastructure from the organization and it will place pressure on traditional contract management with vendors and employees. Vendor contracts will need to be more in line with the new way or working, ready to handle change and not be locked in scope and penalties, they need to be far more collaborative and outcome based, yet you will need to find ways to ensure the qualities and standards of your organization are protected. Employees will expect more flexibility in work hours and work location, again looking to be managed based more on outcomes than hours in the office.

In Australia, tours of REA have almost become a must-do for organizations going through digital transformation in order to understand the impacts of the physical working environment. Within a purpose-built building you can find teams in "streets," "suburbs," and "neighborhoods," each with its own guardrails of autonomy. The office space encourages collaboration and communication but what sets it apart is the "always-on-audio-and-video" communications with teams in China. A lot of effort has gone into making remote team members look and feel part of the team, almost looking as if they were sitting right there. It is a consideration about which leaders now need to think long and hard. A complete reboot of the workplace environment might be required to support the work style and expectations.

WHO DOES THE WORK

Last, who does the work will need to be reshaped because the future of work is cross-functional, creating a challenge of how to build the best team. Identifying and bringing together the skills and knowledge needed to complete outcomes that will not fit neatly within a functional unit will be paramount for adaptability.

The new leader is a conductor in our earlier orchestra metaphor. They stand where they can hear the orchestra as it should be heard; if they stood next to percussion section, all they would hear is drums. Thus, a leader must participate in a way that allows them to make decisions that work for the entire organization. If all they see is their functional unit, that is how decisions will be made. In the orchestra the second violinist sits where they can see the first violinist so that they can communicate and understand what to play, and the first violinist follows the lead of the conductor looking for signals for how to play, the pace to play, even the style to play. In your organization, this placement is equally important. Those who need to work together or have interrelated work need to be placed within sight of one another so they can microplan and adapt based on the signals of the organization and the customer.

We believe the future of work will involve fluid roles and structures intertwined with AI and other technology efficiencies and value-adds that amplify talents over roles. Rather than being constrained by the description of their roles, teams will self-organize around a clear outcome and design a learning environment that is focused on customer success over annual performance measures. Patagonia, the outdoor and clothing store, hires only outdoorsy types. Why? Because that way their employees have a more empathetic connection with customers and can also provide immediate feedback on products. The company encourages employees to be their authentic selves, which includes promoting activism for the environment. Their employees get up every morning with a clear understanding of the purpose and direction of the organization and a deep connection with it. Patagonia has an astonishingly low employee turnover rate to show for it. What is your Patagonia moment?

Evolving as a leader to drive this will take courage. You must stare down the gravitational pull toward functional transformation and avoid decision making that simply validates the current constraints of organizational structures and funding models.

New Leadership Traits

The success of leadership in supporting and exemplifying the correct behaviors will go a long way toward creating and sustaining the impetus for change. Leaders need to adopt a new set of traits that will provide the motivation for moving and the reinforcement that will make the digital transformation sustainable. You will need strong leaders who understand what it means to work in these new ways. The digital leader has a unique style that returns problems unsolved; they mentor and have a talent for building communities. Giving "orders with minimum constraints" is a military concept that applies in digital transformation; the pace of change is too great to have teams constantly waiting for permission to act. A September 2018 iTWire interview with Evan Leybourn of Business Agility Institute and Vered Netzer, a transformation leader at ThoughtWorks, gave great insight into this concept:

> The army trains people to be ready for anything. So, when demand comes —for example, an operation or event—you can trust that your people have the skills to figure out what needs to be done. At that point, you set the course, say what needs to happen, and let your team figure out how to get there. In a military operation, the situation changes so fast that there is no point in planning. There is no plan A, B, or C. It doesn't work like that. Whatever you plan for the reality will be completely different. We invest a lot in teaching people how to accept reality and adapt fast.

Leaders must now be able to help teams to feel empowered, teaching them to learn how to figure things out for themselves. Rather than instructing what to deliver, leaders need to describe the outcome and the constraints that need to be applied in achieving it, be that time, money, or certain attributes. Embedding new muscle for teams to know how to work through issues, how to deal with and learn from failures and in identifying the appropriate response in a given situation based on the guardrails set.

For teams and individuals to feel empowered to initiate change, leaders need to be able to do the following:

- Own the vision

- Build communities (create the movement)

- Deal with ambiguity

- Listen, steward, mentor

- Focus on the growth and well-being of others

- Be outcome focused

- Nudge teams to avoid functional thinking

In an interview with Jeff McDonald, legendary NBA basketball coach Gregg Popovich talked about his philosophy for building a great team that can respond to change and adapt on its feet. The parallels are very relevant when you think about the changing paradigm of leadership in business and works as an analogy for digital leadership.

On managing a high-performing team Popovich refers to the continued need to *nudge the team* so that complacency doesn't set in. Even high-performing teams can get caught simply executing the cadence or the ceremony, at times losing sight of the purpose or outcomes you are trying to achieve:

> Popovich: ...Even though our core has been together so long, I still have to remind them, run a drill every now and then or have an emphasis in a scrimmage in a practice where we're talking about. Maybe we're holding the ball too long, and it's not moving, and we're not going good to great with our shots.

On getting from good to great, Popovich talks about the selflessness of high-performing teams and the need to *stay focused on the outcome* rather than the means. When we look at organizational designs and leadership, we often see the results of individuals over teams. Not looking end to end at the value you are trying to deliver to customers will often result in a "contested shot":

Popovich: There are a lot of good shots, but if you can turn that into a great shot, percentages go through the roof. Contested shots are really bad shots. People's percentage goes down almost by 20, almost without exception...It takes time to get everybody to the point where they all buy in and understand how it's good for the group to do things. You want to penetrate not just for you, but for a teammate. Penetrating because I want to make things happen. It could be for me. It could be for a teammate. It could be for the pass after the pass I make. As people start to realize that, then you get a flow and people start playing basketball rather than just running the play that's called or making up their minds ahead of time.

Contested shots in business include misaligned KPIs, hierarchical lines, siloed work efforts, and functional structures. As a result, decision making is not about customer and value but numbers and targets. Processes are followed because they exist rather than seeking out continuous improvement.

Last, Popovich speaks about *empowerment* and the role of the leader. This is really about letting decision making sit with those closest to the customer, those with the knowledge to react and adapt instantaneously. Good companies grind to a halt when leaders feel compelled to make all of the decisions, the top-down approach of the '80s school of management cannot react with the timeliness and accuracy required the Digital Age.

Popovich: ...A lot depends on the competitiveness and the character of the player. Often times, I'll appeal to that. Like, I can't make every decision for you. I don't have 14 timeouts. You guys got to get together and talk. You guys might see a mismatch that I don't see. You guys need to communicate constantly—talk, talk, talk to each other about what's going on the court. I think that communication thing really helps them. It engenders a feeling that they can actually be in charge. I think competitive character people don't want to be manipulated constantly to do what one individual wants them to do. It's a great feeling when players get together and do things as a group. Whatever can be done to empower those people...

Sometimes in timeouts I'll say, "I've got nothing for you. What do you want me to do? We just turned it over six times. Everybody's holding the ball. What else do you want me to do here? Figure it out." And I'll get up and walk away. Because it's true. There's nothing else I can do for them. I can give them some bull—and act like I'm a coach or something, but it's on them...Then you interject here or there. You call a play during the game at some point or make a substitution, that kind of thing that helps the team win. But they basically have to take charge or you never get to the top of the mountain.

A great leader needs to set direction, make the constraints transparent and visible, and then allow those in the work to innovate and react to deliver value to the customer. Just like the players on a basketball team, employees are hired to be great and use their skill and knowledge, leaders must get out of the way or risk stymieing agility.

Although it's important to recognize that your own leadership style and approaches need to evolve, don't lose confidence or mistake the learning journey for lack of inherent ability to lead in this new way. A client shared with us her personal reflection on such journeys:

This type of transformation will bring the leader copious amounts of emotional highs and lows—the highs coming from the excitement and momentum on the ground among teams already working this way that now realize their efforts will be recognized and rewarded, and from the successes, including more frequent releases of value to customers; the lows coming from the resistance (intentional or systemic) that you and your team will feel and the personal risk you'll be continually placing on your own leadership brand by challenging long-held structures beliefs and practices.

Know that the most critical leadership skills in this type of transformation naturally align to authentic leadership skills that many leaders already have and exhibit—setting a clear mission while giving people autonomy to accomplish the mission based on their own skills, knowledge and decision making in the moment; removing obstacles (including providing significant air cover); holding the team accountable and recognizing success; displaying empathy and EQ to help people on what can be a very ambiguous learning journey.

Find yourself one or two mentors or advocates, ideally those in powerful positions to provide support to you personally and to your team, and to courageously advocate for your work by pushing through the resistance—it gets harder/more painful the closer you are to the top of the mountain...

If you take anything away from this chapter, let it be this: it is essential to the success of digital transformation that leaders own the intent, not the answers. The point of transformation is not an end state but a state of constant change. For this to occur, the entire organization needs to learn how to learn, to be introspective, and make decisions in the moment. The leader's role is to own the vision of change and enable it through reimagining how work flows through the organization and how technology can be used to create new value for customers. They must remove the blockers to the culture of experimentation so ideas can be validated and medium-term commitment of money and people reserved for work you know will move the needle of the outcome.

Key Points

Following are the key points that we hope you take away from this final reflection as well as two actions for you to take to begin implementing what we've discussed:

- As leaders don't delegate the vision of transformation; your involvement plays a critical role in its success.

- Leaders need to stay in touch with key technology trends and be able to enable the adoption of emergent technology as a way of unlocking value for customers and the organization.

- Digital leaders must learn new traits of leadership and understand how to reshape the way work flows through the organization.

Here are two actions to take:

- Create the impetus for change: As a leadership team, regularly discuss and practice delivering the message that describes the need for change and what your expectation is of the way work is done.

- Create your leadership development program: Help leaders build new capabilities around the new traits and expectations of digital leaders.

Conclusion:
Getting Started

The word "transformation" is fast becoming one of the most clichéd terms in the business world. It's a word used to signal to a company that there's an intent to make a change. Often predicated on a new executive hire or a poor performance year, it's the war cry for, "We have to do something different, and fast." The next step is usually to call in your favorite premium consultancy firm and sit back as they roll out the kit-bag of recommendations that inevitably never get completed or don't fit with the culture of the company. All strategy, no execution.

The rise of digital has made transformation a far more strategic imperative. The issues of speed and responsiveness, customer engagement, leadership, and the exponential growth in technology make it unavoidable.

The problem is that change doesn't come solely from a strategy, a method, a process adjustment, or from change-management propaganda. Truly impactful and sustainable change comes from the passion of people at all levels. Passion for what they do and how they work; passion for what your business does and stands for; passion to achieve the outcome to drive the business forward successfully. You cannot shoehorn a traditional organization's leadership, structures, processes, and thinking into a time of ambiguity, fast pace, and customer centricity. Something has to change, and organizations have no choice but to deal with the following:

Tech at the core
> Technology is here to stay as the strategic differentiator for the business.

There is no perfect end state
> Introspectiveness, experimentation, incremental, test-and-learn are the new muscles to capture signals for adaptation and responsiveness.

Authenticity
> The courage to be prepared to act on the knowledge you get from data regardless of the implications of the golden calf of the organization.

Simplified business models
> Optimize and align the business to deliver value to customers, not organizational structures and functions.

The ability to adopt technology
> A delivery approach that can respond to change, take advantage of emerging technology, and cope with smaller workloads and more frequent change.

New leadership styles
> Enable great culture to thrive.

Remember: if there were a silver bullet model that would profoundly transform companies, everyone would be using it. Your organization must learn how to learn, how to identify what works for you, and how to scale those things. Hopefully, this book has given you tools, tips, and strategies that will help you formulate your game plan. But it's up to you to implement that plan—and to do so not with the intent of implementing one particular technique or method, but to move the measure of customer outcomes. Get rid of budgets and job titles; work small, learn often; gather people around a clear outcome; measure success as something your customers get; and watch what happens.

The 34 Tenets of Digital Transformation

1. **Form your team to design your simplified business model—your "road map":** Discuss the five areas of a "simplified business model" in Chapter 1 and what these might look like for your organization.

2. **Advocate for customer value:** Build your business strategy around customer value and using customer language. (Chapter 1)

3. **Learn what value means for your customers:** Using some of the example techniques in Chapter 2, describe what value means to your customers.

4. **Let customer value define your outcomes:** Rewrite your strategy as outcomes written in customer language. Apply a clear, single measure of achieving the outcome. (Chapter 2)

5. **Nominate an outcome to be your first thin slice:** Make it a substantial enough one that will expose the core constraints of the organization. (Chapter 3)

6. **Form your outcome team:** Make visible the hypothesis you have about your digital transformation, and use these to identify the cross-functional team needed to capture maximum learning. (Chapter 3)

7. **Create measures to tell you what work to do and whether you are improving:** Redesign your organization's current measures into their categories of "intent" and by the leading/lagging nature of them, separating them from the measures that determine what work to do. (Chapter 4)

8. **Learn how to measure your return on value delivered:** Practice the cost versus value delivered graphs by trying to build some for your current key programs. (Chapter 4)

9. **Create your backlog:** Cascade your measures to decide the work to achieve your outcome, build and visualize a mental model of this cascade from your strategy to "the work." (Chapter 5)

10. **Realign current work to the backlog:** Assess work in progress to see which of these fit the new way of working and will help achieve the outcomes. Assign those aligned to your first thin slice into that team, along with those working on it. (Chapter 5)

11. **Design a vision anchor:** An image and language that is a way to consistently describe and explain your desired future state, creating an echo for change in the organization. This connects your vision and change road map. (Chapter 6)

12. **Create your visual system:** Identify spaces and visuals to best reflect the key elements outlined in Chapter 6, start your tours.

13. **Use trade-off sliders to help plan and manage "transformation debt":** Create your trade-off sliders for your digital transformation; discuss the implications of this and how you will transparently manage compromises and shortcuts. (Chapter 7)

14. **Identity the culture constraint:** Understand the culture blockers and articulate and spell out how the culture should evolve. (Chapter 7)

15. **Plan your approach for functional inclusion:** Using the double-triangle or other methods, avoid policy and process constraints by ensuring functions

are a part of the broader transformation and are transforming themselves. (Chapter 8)

16. **Identify the skills needed:** You now have a full backlog of new and existing work that you "want" to do to deliver customer value. Use this to create a skills map of what you need and the skills gap against what you currently have in the organization. (Chapter 8)

17. **Use data as a strategic decision-making asset:** Rethink your data strategy to include the use of data to speed up decision making and drive your digital transformation road map, knowing which levers to pull and when to pivot. (Chapter 9)

18. **Invest in work that you know will succeed:** Categorize your current portfolio/backlog into explore, exploit, and sustain. Balancing your investments and priorities based on the amount of knowledge you have that it will move the needle. (Chapter 9)

19. **Set up tech sessions for leaders:** Give your leaders a baseline in key technology concepts, and add these to the vision anchor of how they discuss the need for change and what success looks like. Include regular interaction between leaders and technology teams so that leaders can learn and help support the adoption of new disciplines firsthand. (Chapter 10)

20. **Build internal technical capability:** Develop internal technical talent through capability uplift and recruitment. Be an advocate for enforcing delivery disciplines that ensure quality of output. (Chapter 10)

21. **Build delivery teams with highly skilled technologists:** Avoid mixing in too many low-skilled staff (often from low-cost vendors) for "simple coding tasks." (Chapter 11)

22. **Reinforce the discipline to keep the technical debt low:** Most important, give teams the time to do it. Foster a collaborative relationship between business and IT such that a good balance between features delivered and internal quality can be maintained. (Chapter 11)

23. **Assess your current level of digital talent:** Take a long, hard look at your real capabilities. Do you have top-class teams capable of delivering modern solutions? (Chapter 12)

24. **Create a strategic plan to insource critical areas:** But be aware that the technical landscape is now incredibly broad—you will likely need to find

partners for specialist areas because it's almost impossible to cover everything within one organization. (Chapter 12)

25. **Start measuring the "four key metrics":** Measure lead time, deployment frequency, mean time to restore, and change failure. Rate your IT teams and see whether you observe a correlation between the metrics and good delivery performance. (Chapter 13)

26. **Begin using CD's principles:** Use the principles as a litmus test for your IT organization—can the business deploy changes at will to production with high reliability and no bottlenecks? (Chapter 13)

27. **Review your organization's platform strategy:** Is there a clear difference between an infrastructure platform, an internal business platform, and a "platform business" that creates value through a connected ecosystem of participants? Is it clear how your underlying platform strategy supports the wider business strategy? (Chapter 14)

28. **Make it clear who the platform customer is:** For each of the platforms (of all types) within your organization is it clear who the customer is for that platform? What is the platform team doing to keep their customers happy? Does the customer have other options if they are unhappy with the service? (Chapter 14)

29. **Identify your products:** Look through your organization for things that you can identify as successful products. What makes them a success? Is it clarity of purpose, branding, a great product owner, a great team, or other factors? (Chapter 15)

30. **Form a product team:** Select one or two internal capabilities or services and form a product team to steward the development of that product. (Chapter 16)

31. **Start merging business and IT:** Add an item to business strategy that reflects the desired future state of your IT department. (Chapter 16)

32. **Take technology to the board room:** Ensure that key members of IT are present at key business meetings. Invite them to provide technology narratives linked to the business strategy. (Chapter 16)

33. **Create the impetus for change:** As a leadership team, regularly discuss and practice delivering the message that describes the need for change

and what your expectation is of the way work is done. (Final Reflection: The Importance of Leadership)

34. **Create your leadership development program:** Help leaders build new capabilities around the new traits and expectations of digital leaders. (Final Reflection: The Importance of Leadership)

Index

A

Accelerate (Forsgren, Humble, and Kim), 243

acquisition, activation, revenue, retention, referral (or AARRR), 49

acting small, 23

actions to take
  in aligning work to measurements, 79
  in allowing data to make decisions, 164
  in changing organizational constraints, 121
  in continuous delivery and DevOps, 245
  in digital platforms, 269
  in future shape of IT departments, 305
  in growing and empowering talent, 232
  in implementing a thin slice, 43
  in leadership, 324
  in measurements and decision making, 60
  in mitigating functional constraints, 152
  in product thinking, 285
  in promoting visibility and transparency, 96
  in pushing for technology excellence, 211
  in simplifying the business model, 10
  in technology concepts executives should know, 190
  in understanding customer value, 28

Agile, 54, 57, 297
  adopting engineering practices, beyond just management, 207-210
  card walls and cards in Kanban style, 87

continuous delivery (CD) concept, 180
  roles and Agile teams, 299
  software delivery and continuous delivery methodologies, 58
  stopping point for work, creating, 132

airline industry, digital technologies serving customers, 18

Amazon, 6
  Marketplace, 182

Amazon Web Services (AWS), 233

ambiguity, 29
  courage from leaders in face of, 7
  inherent in the Digital Age, 119
  leadership development and, 144
  living with, 43, 46
  releasing talent in a time of, 112

American Customer Satisfaction Index, 24

annual cycles in finance, 128-131

architecture
  attitudes toward changing, 114
  comparison of system architecture, 2005 to 2019, 289

architecture, capacity, stability, and scalability (IT capabilities), 136

artificial intelligence (AI), 161

augmentation (legacy systems), 264

automation
  key part of continuous delivery and DevOps, 233
  of deployment tasks, 239

autonomy, 120, 143

availability, 267

metrics lagging far behind immediate actions to deliver customer value, 48
profitability as result of delivering customer value, 6
purpose versus profit, 117
risks
exploring risk/opportunity in agile poker, 75
high- versus low-risk attitude, 118
roles, 124, 299
obsession with, 108-112, 139
abstracting titles, roles, and skills from one another, 111
building desirable roles environment for change, 111
redefining roles by what they should/shouldn't be, 110

S

safe environment, creating, 82, 84
(see also spaces)
for providing feedback, 175, 217
where it's safe to fail, 175, 218
sales leads and efficiency, 56
Sankey diagram of work alignment (or lack of), 62
scalability, 178, 226, 267
scalable storage of data, 155
scenario planning, 26
Schwab, Klaus, v
scientific management theory, 120
Scrum, 235
security, 267
legacy systems and, 261
security theater antipattern, 90
Seddon, John, 61
segments, 26
self-service data, 183, 256
sense of belonging, 221
service-oriented architecture (SOA), 252
shareholder value
versus customer value, 3
downside of, 4
shareholder-value-maximization theory, 47
skills
abstracting from titles and roles, 111

high level of technical skill in entire engineering team, 173
skills and competencies development leadership, 105
small wins, creating quickly, 38
Smith, Adam, 296, 298
Smith, Fred, 18, 192
social media
customer data generated by, 17
merging of platforms into the workforce, 145
software design and technical debt, 172
software development
developer productivity, 45
Waterfall versus Agile approach, 57
software reusability, 249
spaces, 84-90
Obeya room, 84-86
program space, 86-88
team space, 88-90
specialized expertise, 300
Spotify model, 32
stable teams, 106
staffing view, 93
standards, 148
start-up metrics, 49
Stitch Fix, using machine learning to create personalized styling, 21
stopping point for work, creating through Agile process, 132
strangler pattern, 194
strategic assets versus utility assets, IT systems, 192-198
strategic assets, 193
systems of record can be highly strategic, 193-195
utility assets, 192
strategic assets,why internal quality matters for
strategies
attitudes toward changing, 114
shareholder value as outcome, not strategy, 4
simplifying business strategy to center around customer value, 10
squeezing work into the strategy buckets, 61

About the Authors

Gary O'Brien has over 20 years of experience in helping executives, teams, and individuals adopt and improve techniques to build humanistic organizations more capable of responding to the increasing pace of change. His passion lies in assisting senior leaders to increase business agility and the alignment of strategy to the delivery of value to customers.

Guo Xiao serves ThoughtWorks Inc. as the Chief Executive Officer. Thought-Works is a global technology consultancy and a community of passionate, purpose-led individuals. Guo Xiao joined ThoughtWorks in 1999 as a software developer and has been providing advisory and delivery services to organizations to leverage digital technology as key competitive advantage and the driver for business transformation. Since 2013, Guo Xiao has been serving as the President and Chief Executive Officer, based in Chicago.

Mike Mason is the global head of technology at ThoughtWorks and is passionate about bridging the tech–business divide and helping others understand what applied technology can do for their business. He focuses on technology strategy, leadership, and execution for both ThoughtWorks and its clients, bringing industry and technology trends to life in the context of real business. Mike contributes to the ThoughtWorks Technology Radar, regularly publishes articles, and is the author of three previous technology books.

Colophon

The cover illustration is by Randy Comer. The cover fonts are Benton Sans, Helvetica Neu, and Impact. The text font is Scala Pro; the heading font is Benton Sans; and the code font is Dalton Maag's Ubuntu Mono.

CPSIA information can be obtained
at www.ICGtesting.com
Printed in the USA
BVHW080746271019
562150BV00001B/1/P

9 781492 054399